ESSAY AND DISCOURSES

D1871242

Owing to the antiquity and rarity of this book, certain pages are regrettably absent, and readability is compromised due to the blurring of the original text. If you possess any insights regarding the availability of these missing sections, kindly inform us. Your assistance is crucial in ensuring the completion of this significant work for the benefit of future generations.

ESSAY AND DISCOURSES

PRAFULLA CHANDRA RAY

GYAN

Published by

Gyan Publishing House
5, Ansari Road
Daryaganj, New Delhi-110002
Phone: 011-47034999, 9811692060
E-mail: books@gyanbooks.com

Distribution Network
gyanbooks.com
India, USA, Canada, UK, Australia

© Publisher

All rights reserved. No part of this work may be reproduced, stored, adapted, or transmitted in any form or by any means, electronic, mechanical, photocopying, micro-filming, recording or otherwise, or translated in any language, without the prior written permission of the copyright owner and the publisher.

ISBN: 978-93-6920-451-9 (PB)

First Published, 1918

2nd Impression 2025

Printed at: Gyan Press, Delhi.

The book is sold subject to the condition that it shall not, by way of trade or otherwise, be lent, resold, hired out, or otherwise circulated without the prior publisher's written consent.

ESSAY AND DISCOURSES
Author : PRAFULLA CHANDRA RAY

ESSAYS AND DISCOURSES

BY

DR. PRAFULLA CHANDRA RAY

WITH A BIOGRAPHICAL
SKETCH & A PORTRAIT

FIRST EDITION

PRICE RS. THREE
G. A. NATESAN & CO.
MADRAS

PREFACE

THIS is the first attempt to present to the public a comprehensive collection of the Essays and Discourses of Dr. P. C. Ray, the well known Indian chemist. Dr. Ray's discourses on Scientific topics and his researches in the field of Hindu Chemistry would by themselves form no negligible material for a volume of this kind. But his interests have by no means been confined to Hindu Chemistry alone. Education, social reform, industry, politics, indeed every aspect of India's material and moral progress has claimed his earnest attention and the papers collected in this volume testify to his manysided interests. Thus his statements before the Public Services and the Industrial Commissions, are full of practical suggestions for the advancement of Indian education and industries. His paper on "the Bengali Brain and and its misuse" and his address to the Indian National Social Conference at Calcutta which contain some trenchant criticisms of the Hindu Social polity evince his deep interest in subjects relating to social reform. His handsome tributes to the services of eminent patriots like Ananda Mohan Bose and Dadabhai Naoroji and his generous appreciation of the life and life work of Sir William Wedderburn testify to the silent interest he has all along been taking in he political advancement of this country. The last two papers in the book contain valuable criticisms on the history of India both Ancient and modern.

The addition of a biographical sketch and the list of original contributions by Dr. Ray and his pupils of the Indian School of Chemistry will, it is hoped, enhance the value of this publication.

The publishers desire to add a word of thanks to Dr. Ray for his kindness in selecting and revising these papers at their request.

DEC. 1918
MADRAS.

The Publishers.

CONTENTS

If I could for a moment command the organ voice of Milton I would exclaim that we are of a Nation not slow and dull, but of a quick, ingenious and piercing spirit, acute to invent, subtle and sinewy to discourse, not beneath the reach of any point the highest the human capacity can soar to. Therefore, the students of learning in her deepest science have been so ancient and so eminent among us that writers of a blest judgment have been persuaded that even the School of Pythagoras took the cue from the old Philosophy of this land. (See p. 88)

I confess, as a Hindu, the subject of Hindu Chemistry has always had a fascination for me. But there is another valid reason as to why I threw myself heart and soul into the task of recovering the precious gems bequeathed by our chemical ancestors. It is to an illustrious roll of European scholars beginning with Sir Wm. Jones, Colebrooke, Prinsep, Lassen, Burnouff and Csoma de Koros that we are mainly indebted for bringing to light and giving prominence to the priceless treasures embedded in Sanskrit, Pali and Tibetan literature. Hindu Chemistry, however, waited long and patiently for an interpreter. I thought I owed a debt to the great nation to which I am proud to belong. Hence it is that I felt it incumbent upon me to dedicate some of the best years of my life to this self-imposed task with what success it is not for me to say. (See p. 101)

India must wake up, shake off her degradation, put life and heart into every class of her people, elevate her women and depressed classes and remove the galling restrictions of caste and all social inequalities. When this is done she will enter into a new era of her life and then, like Prometheus unbound, she will be recognised as a great power in the world and will have an unique place in the comity of nations. (See p. 235)

The ultimate moral justification of England's rule over India is not Pax Britannica, not even the economic prosperity of the country, but the preparation of the Indian people for self-government. If that end is lost sight of in the pursuit of any subsidiary advantage or improvement, British policy in India will miss its true goal; its history will be the record of a huge failure, a record of immense preparations without fruition. (See p. 300)

A LIFE-SKETCH *

BIRTH AND PARENTAGE

Dr. Prafulla Chandra Ray was born in 1861 at Raruli-Katipara, a small village now in the District of Khulna, of a family well-known for generations in that part of Bengal. The village is situated on the bank of the river Kapotaksha, immortalised by the great Bengali poet, Michael Madhusudan,† in a sonnet written at Versailles. His father, the late Harish Chandra Ray, who died in 1894 at the age of 69—a good Persian scholar imbued with the writings of Sadi and Hafiz—was a student of the Krishnagur College in the early forties of the last century, when the celebrated Captain D. L. Richardson was its Principal. He was a well-read man who held enlightened views on many social questions and was a pioneer in introducing English education in his own district. Harish Chandra was a member of the British Indian Association in the early sixties of the last century, and was well acquainted with, among others, the late Raja Digambar Mitra, Kristo Das Pal, Sishir Kumar Ghosh and Pandit Iswar Chandra Vidyasagar. The local Model Vernacular School, which was founded and maintained mainly at the expense of the late Harish

---

*** The writer of this sketch has made free use of sketches of Dr. Ray's life which appeared in the pages of the "Indian World," the "Calcutta University Magazine" and the "Century Review," and also of appreciations written by some of Dr. Ray's pupils, notably Mr. F. V. Fernandez.**

† ***Michael Madhusudan Dutt*: *A sketch of his life and career*,** **Price As. 4. (G. A. Natesan & Co., Madras.)**

Chandra Ray, has now grown into a Model English High School, and is located in the very ancestral house of Dr. Ray, for the up-keep of which he spends annually a handsome amount. This ancestral home of Dr. Ray is more than a century old and is partly in a dilapidated condition, but is still considered to be one of the finest buildings in the whole district.

EDUCATION

Dr. Ray received his early training at his father's school; but his father, anxious that his sons should receive the best possible education, settled down at Calcutta towards the end of 1870. Young Prafulla Chandra was admitted as a pupil of the Hare School immediately and was there for four years. In 1874, he got a severe attack of dysentery and suffered from it for nearly two years and, consequently, was absent from school for a long period; but he utilised this time in devouring the contents of a splendid library got together by his father and his eldest brother. Being of very regular habits and disentangled from the trammels of ordinary school lessons—he kept up his studies without let or hindrance, in spite of his malady, and got passionately attached to the works of Goldsmith, Addison and some other classical English authors. When sufficiently recovered from his malady, he took his admission into the Albert School of Calcutta, then in the heyday of its glory under the rectorship of the late Krishna Vihari Sen, and here he at once made his mark as a brilliant student. From Krishna Vihari young Prafulla Chandra also imbibed a deep and abiding love of English literature. At this time, he was a constant listener to the lectures and sermons of Keshub Chandra Sen, and was slowly attracted to the Brahmo Samaj of which he has been a member since 1882. At this period of his life (about 1875-77), he also caught the enthusiasm inspired by the eloquence of the late Ananda Mohan Bose and Mr. Surendranath Banerjea and felt the impulses of a higher patriotic life.

From 1879 to 1882, he was a student of the Metropolitan Institution. He has often said that the one fascination he had for joining Vidyasagar's College was that he should be able to sit at the feet of Mr. Surendranath Banerjea. Indeed, the exposition of Morley's *Burke* and Burke's *Reflections on the French Revolution* from the lips of the great Bengalee orator made a life-long impression on Dr. Ray. All this time young Ray was also a student of the Presidency College (in the scientific department) where he attended the lectures of Sir John Eliot in physics and of Sir Alexander Pedler in chemistry. Dr. Ray's father, having lost in the meantime a considerable portion of his ancestral fortunes, was precluded from giving his brilliant son the benefit of an education in England. Young Ray, however, slowly and quietly prepared himself for the Gilchrist Scholarship Examination, and it is singular that his father and other relations were kept entirely in the dark about his intentions, his eldest brother alone having been taken into his confidence. In 1882, Ray proceeded to England as a Gilchrist Scholar and studied at Edinburgh for six years. Although his taste and inclination lay towards English literature and history, he realised that the future progress of India was bound up with the pursuit of science, and thus he gradually allowed himself to be weaned away from his former studies. At Edinburgh, he was the pupil of the celebrated Peter Guthrie Tait and of Alexander Crum Brown—two mighty intellects in the departments of physical science and chemistry—and through their teachings he shortly came to be devotedly attached to the study of chemistry. It will be interesting to note here that amongst his fellow-students were Prof. James Walker, F.R.S., now occupying the Chair of Chemistry at Edinburgh and the late Prof. Hugh Marshall, F.R.S., Professor of Chemistry, University College, Dundee. Writing from the University of Edinburgh, under date 5th April, 1888, Prof. Crum Brown states :—

I have known Dr. P. C. Ray since he came to this University in 1882, and have watched his career with much interest. Having laid a sound foundation of general scientific knowledge, he devoted himself especially to Chemistry. He took the degree of B. Sc. in 1885, and that of D. Sc. in 1887. He held the Hope Prize Scholarship in Chemistry during the year 1887-88. He worked in the Chemical Laboratories during the Summer and Winter Sessions, from May 1883 till March 1888, latterly assisting Dr. Gibson and myself in the work of the Laboratory. As much of his work was done under my own observation, I can speak with confidence as to his ability and knowledge. He has an extensive and sound acquaintance with all branches of theoretic Chemistry and is a careful and accurate analyst. He has shown that he has the capacity for original investigation —his thesis for the degree of D. Sc. being a piece of excellent analytical work, well arranged, and thoroughly and conscientiously carried out.

"INDIA BEFORE THE MUTINY"

Although Chemistry literally claimed him as her own, Dr. Ray still continued to be a close student of English politics and of Indian Economics. His *Essay on India before and after the Mutiny*, written on the eve of his appearance for the B. Sc. Examination at Edinburgh, bears impress of mature study of Indian problems. The essay was warmly appreciated at the time, and principal Sir William Muir pronounced it as "bearing marks of rare ability." The leading newspaper of the Scottish capital, the *Scotsman*, observed : "It is a most interesting little volume, and we do not profess to wonder in the least that it has earned a considerable amount of popularity. It contains information in reference to India which will not be found elsewhere, and it is of the utmost notice."

John Bright, in acknowledging a copy of the booklet, wrote a long letter to the author in which he said :—

I regret with you and condemn the course of Lord Dufferin in Burma. It is a renewal of the old system of crime and guilt; which we had hoped had been for ever abandoned. There is an ignorance on the part of the public in this country and great selfishness here and in India as to our true interests in India. These departures from morality and true statesmanship will bring about calamity and perhaps ruin, which your children may witness and deplore.

PROFESSOR

On his return to India he joined the Presidency College of Calcutta as a professor, and since that year (1889) he has practically confined all his attention to his chemical researches. The results of his devotion at the Chemical Laboratory of this College, particularly in the years between 1896-1898, were embodied in his first scientific publication under the title of "Chemical Research at the Presidency College." This little brochure was "affectionately inscribed" to "my friend, Prithwis Chandra Ray, author of the *Poverty Problem in India*," and at once established his reputation as a great Indian scientist. In 1904, he was deputed by the Government of Bengal to visit the principal chemical laboratories of Europe and was everywhere received with open arms by chemists and savants. At a meeting of the French Academy of Sciences, Mr. Troost welcomed Dr. Ray in words of generous appreciation on behalf of that august body.

" Presence of a Foreign Savant ":—

"The President announces that Mr. Rây, Professor of Chemistry at Calcutta and author of important works on the nitrites as also of History of Hindu Chemistry, is present at our meeting to-day and offers him welcome." *La Nature*, March 11, 1905.

A CAPTAIN OF INDUSTRY

The story of the foundation and growth of the Bengal Chemical and Pharmaceutical Works reads like a romance. It has proved to the world abroad that the Bengalees possess a marvellous brain, that in spite of unfavourable circumstances they can build up a vast industry only by the virtue of perseverance and tenacity. The Bengal Chemical and Pharmaceutical Works is a standing monument to the industry and intellectual capacity of Dr. Ray. He had to fight against enormous odds in laying deep the foundation of this business. "The Bengal Chemical and Pharmaceutical Works had its birth," observed its founder, "and early struggles in the dark and dingy rooms of a house in Upper Circular Road, and it started with the modest sum of Rs. 800." It was about twenty-six years ago that Dr. Ray launched this new industry. Though he was then a Professor of the Presidency College, his income only amounted to Rs. 250 a month. He had in those days to pay off some ancestral debts, besides his charity was never restricted to one or two students. With this meagre income, he worked wonders in the field of industry. Many young men complain of the lack of sufficient capital to carry on a business, but here is a concrete example of one of the greatest sons of Bengal who managed to establish a good business even without sufficient funds. One of the many causes which go to work out the failure of many an indigenous industry in India is the lack of purpose and firm determination. When the wave of Swadeshi enthusiasm passed over the country, there came to light many new industries, but how many of them are found now in a prosperous condition? How many have survived in the struggle for existence? Their number can be counted on one's finger's ends. The industry set up by Dr. Ray many years before the Swadeshi awakening, however, is still as full of hope and promise as ever.

That "dark and dingy" room saw the birth of this new industry. There could be found in those days various utensils strewn about containing sulphuric acid here and nitric acid there, all in the process of distillation. The young workers were busy in making thousand and one things and in carrying out experiments.

Fortunately for Dr. Ray, he received the co-operation and assistance of a few able workers, who were ready to do their "bit" for the benefit of chemical industry in India. First came his old friend, Dr. Amulya Charan Bose. He was a sincere worker in this field. He assisted Dr. Ray with all his heart and never looked for gain. Actuated by the love of country, his aim was always free from gross personal motives. Another young worker, Satish Chandra Sinha, joined them soon after passing the M. A. examination. He was really a martyr in the cause of science, for shortly after he died of prussic acid poisoning. Another silent worker was Prof. Chandra Bhusan Bhaduri, who never advertised himself. It has been maintained that when the story of the development of the chemical industry in Bengal comes to be written, his name is sure to obtain a high rank as one of the early promoters and pioneers.

Thus the Company, originally started as a small private concern for the manufacture of medicines and other chemical preparations, has now rapidly increased its many-sided activities. Year after year the Company made large strides and now it stands as one of the most successful industries in India. "With the recent expansions which have already been taken in hand, it will soon cover an area of 24 bighas (8 acres) and its present capital of 5 lacs will have to be doubled with a view to the installation of new plant." As we have said before, the Company was at first a private concern, but as the field of its activity began to expand rapidly, Dr. Ray did not think it proper to keep the whole income to himself. His patriotism prompted him to make it a limited company, throwing open its shares to all.

"It has always been a fixed principle with the Directors of this business," said Dr. Ray, the founder-Director, "not to take in any one as a chemist whose knowledge is not up to the M. Sc. standard of our University." Be it mentioned here that the Company has now five expert chemists working. They are all former students of Dr. Ray. Time and again it has been complained that the Bengali does not possess any organising capacity. Here is an industry which has been conceived, initiated, and managed solely by Bengali brains, energy and pluck, and it has never been necessary to call in the aid of any foreign "experts." This clearly demonstrates that the successful application of science to industry is by no means incompatible with Bengali genius.

As Dr. Travers of the Indian Scientific Institute said the Bengal Chemical Works is a piece of research work of which Professor Ray and Mr. C. Bhaduri ought to be proud. In the words of the same authority, "the construction and management of the works is the work of the past students from the chemistry department of the Presidency College, acting under the advice of these gentlemen. The design and construction of the sulphuric acid plant and of the plant required for the preparation of drugs and other products involved a large amoun t of research work of the kind which is likely to be o the greatest service to this country, and does the greatest credit to those concerned." (*Century Review*).

LITERARY INTERESTS

Dr. Ray is a man of many interests. He has not been content with only building up an industrial concern but takes a keen interest in Bengali literature and is himself a careful student of it. Ten years ago he was called upon to preside over the Provincial Literary Conference in which he read a remarkable paper on the "Place of Science in Literature," an English version of which appears in this book. He has contributed many articles to several Bengali periodicals, besides writing occasionally to the *Indian World*.

Of Shakespeare, Dr. Ray is immoderately fond and is never tired of reading and re-reading the great English Classic. Emerson, Carlyle, Epictetus and Marcus Aurelius have deeply tinged his life. His favourite novels are those of Thackeray, George Eliot and Dickens,—he cannot tolerate any present-day novelists—not even Hall Caine or Marie Correli.

DR. RAY'S RESEARCHES AND DISCOVERIES

It was in December, 1895, that Dr. Ray rose to fame and became known to the scientific world by his celebrated discovery of mercurous nitrite. In his presidential address delivered before the Asiatic Society in 1896, Mr. (now Sir Alexander) Pedler said:—"Dr. P. C. Ray, by his discovery of the method of preparation of this compound, has filled up a blank in our knowledge of the mercury series."

The reactions of nitric acid with mercury have been a favourite subject with the chemists and their predecessors, the iatro-chemists, since the 15th century A. D., if not earlier. Dr. Ray, however, was the first not only to point out distinctly but to isolate the initial product, namely "mercurous nitrite." This remarkable discovery is now almost a matter of ancient history, but how it was welcomed and received at the time will be evident from the extracts given from two scientific journals quoted below.

Nature, 28th May, 1896, thus reviewed Dr. Ray's discovery of Mercurous Nitrite:—

> The "Journal of the Asiatic Society of Bengal" can scarcely be said to have a place in our Chemical Libraries; the current number, however, contains a paper by Dr. P. C. Ray of the Presidency College, Calcutta, on mercurous nitrite, that is worthy of note. During a preparation of mercurous nitrate by the action of dilute nitric acid in the cold on mercury, yellow crystals were deposited which, upon examination, proved to be mercurous nitrite. The analysis proved somewhat difficult.........The fact, that the nitrite is stable in strongly acid solutions, is an additional proof of the views held by Dr. Divers as to the "nitronic" constitution of the nitrites of copper, mercury and bismuth. The stability of silver nitrite towards nitric acid has already been noticed by Acworth and Armstrong, and by Russell, and the behaviour of mercurous nitrite is closely analogous. Dr. Ray proposes in a subsequent communication to give the results of an attempt to prepare fatty nitro-derivatives from this compound.

The Chemist and Druggist of London, 25th July, 1896, observed:—

> It has been left to a Bengali chemist, Dr. P. C. Ray, to demonstrate that the not unfamiliar yellow crystalline deposit that is obtained by contact of dilute nitric acid with mercury in the cold is mercurous nitrite. This substance is not so much as mentioned in "Roscoe" and "Schorlemmer," nor is there any reference to it in "Watt's Dictionary of Chemistry." Dr. Ray's discovery has been well received in Chemical circles.

Among the famous chemists of Europe, Sir Henry Roscoe and M. Berthelot were the first to congratulate Dr. Ray and welcome his discovery.

Mercurous nitrite has proved to be the fruitful parent of an interesting series of compounds, and during the last 22 years Dr. Ray singly or in co-operation with his pupils has been incessantly busy in working them up. To an average lay reader the details of these discoveries may not prove intelligible, and we shall therefore content ourselves with presenting the outstanding features of some of them. One very striking outcome of the earlier researches in this field has been the establishment of an identity in the properties of "monad" mercury and silver. It was at a meeting of the Asiatic Society of Bengal in 1907 that Dr. Ray read a short paper entitled "silver mercuroso-mercuric oxynitrate," and a more elaborate account of the subject based upon further investigations appeared in the *Journal of the Chemical Society of London.*

Dr. Ray's researches have all along shown that univalent mercury should be placed side by side with silver and his latest paper adduces most convincing proof in this direction. He has at last succeeded in preparing a compound of univalent mercury in which a portion of this metal is isomorphously replaced by its analogue, silver. This isomorphous is to adopt the happy language of the greatest living authority on the subject, Groth—'vicarious' substitution of mercury by silver, will no doubt be welcomed by the scientific world. Why should one and the same metal play this sort of double role? We are at the dawn of a new chemistry. Sir W. Ramsay has shown that radium is slowly transformed into helium. Possibly the 20th century is destined to throw a flood of light on the duality as also on the transmutation of metals.—*The "Empire."*

It was no mean compliment which the late Professor Divers, F. R. S., paid to Dr. Ray's researches when, in a paper read before the Society of Chemical Industry in 1904 on the dissolution of metals in nitric acid, he made the following introductory remark:—

The occasion for presenting the theory in a more developed form to the Society has been given by the reading last month to the Chemical Society of an important paper on mercurous nitrite by Prof. Ray of the Presidency College, Calcutta.—*Journ. Soc. Chem. Ind.*

The limited space at our disposal forbids our following in detail the substance of some 80 memoirs on the subject of the 'nitrites' and 'hyponitrites.' The important discovery of the 'amine' nitrites by

Dr. Ray and his co-worker, Mr. Jitendranath Rakshit, deserves, however, more than a passing notice, and we cannot do better than quote the brief but graphic notice of it which appeared in the columns of a Calcutta print at the time :—

> The very preliminary note on methylammonium nitrite by Dr. Ray and Mr. Jitendranath Rakshit which was read at the last December meeting of the Asiatic Society has not, we are afraid, attracted the attention it deserves. The authors with commendable unobstrusiveness announce in this communication the preparation of a new compound which is destined to be hailed in the chemical world as a startling discovery. Sir William Ramsay, if our memory serves us right, has somewhere aptly said that a chemical process involves a marriage of elements (and of compounds as well). Now, the chemical union of methylamine and nitrous acid has been the despair of successive generations of chemists; all the attempts to bring them together under the matrimonial yoke have hitherto failed, as these two compounds are mutually destructive of each other and their inter-action almost instantaneously results in the formation of methyl alcohol and liberation of nitrogen. Indeed, this very reaction, as every tyro in organic chemistry knows, is made use of for diagnosis of primary amines. The authors have evidently proved to be efficient chemical match-makers, as in their hands methylamine and nitrous acid have not forgotten their antagonistic properties but have agreed to be united in chemical wedlock, giving rise to a beautiful crystalline yellowish compound. We understand that Dr. Ray has already been the recipient of warm congratulations from eminent English chemists, and it would seem almost impertinent to add our own. It is believed that since the discovery of mercurous nitrite by Dr. Ray in 1895, a preliminary account of which was also communicated to the Asiatic Society at the time and which at once made the name of its discoverer known to the scientific world, the laborious researches in the Chemical Laboratory of the Presidency College have not been rewarded with so rich a find.

Another most important discovery was the preparation and volatilisation of ammonium nitrite. "The Annual Report on the Progress of Chemistry," issued by the Chemical Society, which embodies the most important contributions on the subject by the chemists throughout the world, thus noticed the significance of the Bengalee Chemist's discoveries.

"Ray has obtained mercuric nitrite by the interaction of mercuric chloride and silver nitrite.

"Ray has continued his researches on the nitrites discussing the conditions influencing the formation of ten different products of the action of nitric acid on mercury. This author has also prepared the nitrites of alkali and alkaline earth metals which are formed by the interaction of the chlorides on silver nitrite. The solutions of these nitrites may be evaporated in contact with the air without undergoing oxidation. These nitrites have a yellow colour, the depth of which increases with the atomic weight of the metal. Magnesium nitrite is the least stable of those of the alkaline earths forming as magnesium does in many other cases, a link between the nitrites of zinc and cadmium and those of calcium, strontium, and barium. Ray and Ganguli have recently described two varieties of silver nitrite."—*Annual Report, 1905.* And so on in successive issues of the "Report."

"HISTORY OF HINDU CHEMISTRY"

We have not space here to notice more in detail the contributions of Dr. Ray to the chemical world. But no review of his life and work can be complete without a reference to his monumental work, "*The History of Hindu Chemistry,*" in which he has completely proved to the world at large, by reference to old Sanskrit texts, the antiquity of the knowledge of chemistry in this country. The first volume of the "History" appeared in 1902 as a result of the persistent study and toil of fifteen years, and was so favourably received that it was necessary to publish a second edition in 1905. The second volume came out about five years after the first. M. Berthelot, the illustrious French Chemist, reviewed the first volume of the work at considerable length in the columns of the "Journal des Savants." We quote the concluding lines:

A new and interesting chapter has been added to the history of sciences and of human thought.

The Vice-Chancellor of the Durham University in conferring on him the honorary degree of D. Sc. said in 1912:—

"A keen and successful investigator, he has long made his mark by contributions to scientific periodicals, both English and German, but his fame chiefly rests on his monumental 'History of Hindu Chemistry'—a work of which both the scientific and linguistic attainments are equally remarkable, and of which, if of any book, we may pronounce that it is definitive."

And that great German author, Hermann Schelenz, one of the greatest of the living authorities on Pharmaceutical Chemistry, and author of the *History of Pharmacy* ("Geschichte der Pharmazie") went into ecstacy over Dr. P. C. Ray's *History of Hindu Chemistry*, and authoritatively declared as his deliberate opinion that the mastery of chemical processes, as elaborately described in the Hindu work, *Rasaratnasamuchchaya*, upon which Dr. Ray has copiously drawn in his *History*, shows that the Hindu chemists were far ahead of their European contemporaries of the 13th and 14th centuries A.D. In order to introduce our readers to the subject matter of this book, we can do no better than quote a few sentences from a translation of the review of the work which appeared in the *Journal Asiatique* over the signature of that eminent scholar and orientalist, Mons. Sylvain Levi of Paris. He writes:—

In his first volume, Mr. Ray has given a picture of the chemical knowledge of ancient India, which he divides into four periods: the Ayurvedic period, from the pre-Buddhist era to about 800 A.D.; the Transitional period, from 800 to 1100 A.D.

the Tantric period, from 1100 to 1300 A.D.; the iatro-chemical period from 1300 to 1550 A.D. In the first period he places Charaka, Susruta, the Bower Mss. and Vaghbhatta; in the second, Vrinda and Chakrapani; in the third, *Rasarnava*; in the fourth *Rasaratnasamuchchaya*. To this list have been added a few monographs and a collection of Sanskrit texts. The second volume may be regarded as the continuation of the first. The author has during this interval discovered or secured new materials, which has enabled him to throw further light upon the questions previously taken up for solution. In particular the *Rasaratnakara* of Siddha Nagarjuna has floated before his vision as the figure of the great Buddhist philosopher who has acted so powerfully upon Indian thoughts. In this treatise on alchemy, Nagarjuna comes in as a friend of king Salivahana—a connection which has the support of an old tradition, as also his disciple, Ratnaghosa, whose name, though as yet unknown, has the probability of being a real personage. Alchemy was introduced into the sphere of Buddhism by Nagarjuna, which was almost neglected up till his time. Mr. Ray has undeniably proved, not without surprise, the grand role played by Buddhist monks in alchemy and the preponderating part of Buddhism in the Tantric literature. Even in the thirteenth century, a Hindu Chemist, named Gobindacharya, author of *Rasasara*, declares to have composed his work "after having derived his information from Buddhist sources," as also "from the Buddhists of Tibet." Mr. Ray also notices a good many Hindu chemical Tantras and gives a summary of them and continues the list to about the seventeenth century. The conclusion at which Mr. Ray arrives is that Indian alchemy is of indigenous origin.

The concluding words of his "History" will be ever memorable as the sombre but ennobling reflections of one of the choicest of those who "searched truth with many a sigh:"

"It is with mingled feelings that I mark the hour of my final deliverance from a self-imposed task which has occupied all my spare time during the last 15 years and more, feelings not unlike those which overpowered the Historian of the Roman Empire. The reader, I hope, will forgive me if I venture to give expression to them in the words of Edward Gibbon himself: 'I will not dissemble the first emotions of joy on the recovery of my freedom * * * * But my pride was soon humbled and a sober melancholy was spread over my mind, by the idea that I had taken an everlasting leave of an old and agreeable companion." The Hindu nation with its glorious past and vast latent potentialities may yet look forward to a still more glorious future, and if the perusal of these lines will have the effect of stimulating my countrymen to strive for regaining their old position in the *intellectual hierarchy* of nations, I shall not have laboured in vain."

AS A TEACHER AND FOUNDER OF A SCHOOL OF CHEMISTRY

As a teacher of young men for over a quarter of a century and having intimate association and close familiarity with a large number of students, Dr. Ray holds that the Bengali intellect is second to none in richness and fertility, though unfortunately it ripens rather too early and decays very prematurely. It is stated that the Bengali youth lacks the characteristic go, pluck, determination and the close application of the youths of Europe and Japan. The Bengali, according to Dr. Ray, seldom brings to bear upon anything sustained and life-long devotion and tenacity of purpose—his enthusiasm is short-lived and is of a flashy and dashing nature.

Dr. Ray has been loved and adored by his students very much in the ancient Indian spirit. On the eve of his retirement from the Presidency College, his students presented him with an address of farewell in which they said:—

> Your place in the college, sir, we are afraid can never be filled. Men will come and men will go but where else can we possibly expect to find again that sweetness of disposition, that vigour of simplicity, that unwearied spirit of service, that broad-based culture, that wisdom in deliberation and debate which for the space of thirty years or more endeared you so much to your pupils?
>
> Yours was, sir, indeed no small achievement. Your way of life, with its distinct Indian traits recalled us to the sweet and

simple and manly days of Indian attainment. You have been to us all through a guide, philosopher and friend. Easy of access, ever-pleasant, ever willing to help the poor and needy student with your counsel and your purse, living a life of sturdy, celibate simplicity, with a genuine patriotism, not loud but deep, you have been to us an ancient Guru reborn, a light and an inspiration from the treasure-house of old Indian spirituality.

Dr. Ray has always reciprocated the love of his students, and it has been his practice for some years past to invite some of his advanced pupils to take part in his research work. As the fascination grows, these young aspirants become devoted to the cause of original investigation and stick to the work. Year after year, their number has been increasing till practically a school of chemists has now been established in Calcutta without any fuss or ado. We can measure the success of Dr. Ray's school when we see that the journals of chemistry now-a-days contain rather frequent contributions of genuine merit either from him or his pupils whom he has literally trained and inspired. The May and August numbers for 1911, of the *Transactions of the Chemical Society*, London, contain simultaneously five contributions from him and his pupils. Scarcely a month elapses without some additional discoveries of his or his pupils. His own contributions up-to-date have been close upon eighty, and his work has thrown a flood of light on the chemical constitution of many of the more important compounds of nitrites. Truly, like Chevreul and Faraday, this great oriental savant has chosen research work in preference to money-making, and well has Professor Sylvain Levi of Paris remarked in the course of his review of the "*History of Hindu Chemistry*," "*that his laboratory is the nursery from which issue forth the chemists of new India.*"

HIS STUDENTS AND THEIR RESEARCHES

Among those who have taken part in carrying on

researches with Dr. Ray either as scholars, advanced students or voluntary workers, may be mentioned the names of Jatindranath Sen, Premchand Roychand Scholar in Chemistry (now Professor at the Pusa Agricultural Institute); Atul Chandra Ganguli (now Professor of Chemistry, Ravenshaw College); Panchanan Neogi, Premchand Roychand Scholar in Chemistry (now Professor of Chemistry, Rajshahi College); the late Atul Chandra Ghose, M.A., who was appointed Professor of Chemistry in the Dyal Singh College, Lahore; Hemendra Kumar Sen, who has also won the blue ribbon of the Calcutta University in Chemistry on the strength of thesis alone under the new regulations; Jitendranath Raskshit, collaborator of Dr. Ray in the researches on the amine nitrites, etc., Rasiklal Datta, Nilratan Dhar, Manik Lal Dey and J. C. Ghosh.

The work of Rasiklal Datta makes a record in the history of chemical science in new India. While yet a junior 5th year student, the discriminating eye of his Professor singled him out to work in co-operation with him on the subject of the benzyl and allylammonium nitrites. Within an incredibly short time, he succeeded in preparing several compounds of this series, but he found time also to make independent discoveries of his own some of which are of surpassing interest. The discovery of a very large number of new compounds can be put to his credit.

No less brilliant have been the achievements of Nilratan Dhar in the domain of Physical Chemistry. Dr. Ray was seriously handicapped in his investigations on the nitrites for not being able to measure their electric conductivities and other physical properties. This young student almost in his teens, who had just won laurels in the B.Sc. examination, at once came forward for the relief of his teacher.

Dhar's investigations on the conductivities of the nitrites as also the determination of their other physical constants are calculated to throw much light on their constitution. The brunt of the tedious work on the determination of the vapour density of ammonium nitrite devolved on him. Dhar has also published an elaborate investigation on the constitution of complex salts, based on Werner's Theory, for publication in the *Zitchrift fur Unorganische Chemie.* In reply to an address presented to Dr. Ray by the inhabitants of his native District—Jessore-Khulna—he thus bore testimony to the quality of the contributions of young Datta and Dhar :—

"As regards the numerous double of copper, silver, mercury, cadmium, etc., discovered by Datta, it is enough to say that I myself would have been proud to be their discoverer, but I am prouder still when I reflect that the discovery has been made by a pupil of mine. . . . . I look upon it as a manifestation of Divine Grace that a Rasiklal Datta or a Nilratan Dhar has at last been produced in the soil of Bengal." Dr. Ray has been heard to assert with some degree of confidence that Rasiklal Datta and Nilratan Dhar are fairly on the way to earning for themselves a European reputation as chemists.

The following extract from Dr. Ray's recent address on the progress of chemistry in Bengal in 1916-17 contains an account of the work done by the latest recruits of his school :—

Last year has been altogether an eventful one. It may be a little more than a year. Three Doctorates have been conferred on our students. Dr. Rasiklal Datta is the first Doctor of Science in the Calcutta University in Chemistry. It is no breach of confidence and I am divulging no official secret when I say that in presence of our worthy Registrar (Dr. Bruhl)—I am afraid that is adding to the enormity of the crime—(laughter) one of the Referees to whom Dr. Datta's paper was submitted, said that his work marked a record in Chemical researches in India. But I am placing myself under the purview of the official Secrets Act. Gentlemen, those who know Dr. Datta need not be told of the intrinsic value of his work. He has contributed some two dozen valuable papers and perhaps more. Then the Degree of PH. D. has been conferred on Professor Panchanan Neogi. Again the Degree D. Sc. of the London University has been conferred on Mr. Nilratan Dhar, and Dr. Bruhl had an opportunity of knowing him.

. . . .

One of the most remarkable papers is that of Mr. Jnanendra Chandra Ghose. It will soon appear in the London Chemical Society's Journal. He is following it up with another paper. I may be allowed to say that it is a contribution which marks a new era in the subject, namely the Abnormality of strong Electrolytes. It is a remarkable paper. This is the subject in which Van'thoff, Arrhenius, Ostwald and many mighty workers have racked their brain. But it was left to Mr. Ghose to work out the Law which gives full explanation of the phenomenon. His first paper covers about 9 pages but it has been followed by another of 18 pages and a third communication has also been made. These papers will throw a flood of light on one of the most interesting subjects in the domain of Physical Chemistry. To Dr. Nilratan Dhar also belongs the credit of being the pioneer in the field of Physical Chemistry in our land and of pointing out to our young enthusiastic friends the way to this fruitful line of research. Mr. Jnanendranath Mukerjee has published suggestive papers on Colloid Chemistry. Mr. Manik Lal Dey has just read a paper with experiments on a new phototropic salt. Its potentialities in the field of photography are obvious. These young scientists—the future hopes of our land—have kept up the fire and we expect many interesting contributions from them. I am not going to tire your patience by going into details of their researches. It is not my custom to take notice of any paper unless it has been accepted for publication in the leading Journals of Europe and America. We cannot afford to pass judgment on the work done by our own students unless it has received the stamp of the learned societies abroad.

Dr. Ray has attained fame and has rendered services to the cause of knowledge of which he and his countrymen may well be proud. But he values no part of his work more than the training of the disciples who have been attracted to him by his magnetic personality. As we have seen, some of them have very early in life, and with limitations so numerous, won for themselves an international reputation. Like the true guru that he is, Prof. Ray deems these young workers in the cause of Science the richest legacy to bequeath to his country and the world. He observed in a recent speech at Madras that, talking of his disciples, he was reminded of the Great Mother of those immortal Romans who said that her children, the two Gracchi, were her richest glory. He quotes too with an exalted humility the ancient saying of our scriptures:

"Men should desire victory everywhere; but they should covet defeat at the hands of their pupils."

Mr. F. V. Fernandez, a pupil of Dr. Ray, who is also joint author with him of an important research, has written an account of the "Indian School of Chemistry" from which we quote only the introductory and the concluding portions:—

"La chimie est une science francaise. Elle fut constituèe par Lavoisier, d'immortelle mèmoire"; thus began Wurtz in his famous "Dictionary of Chemistry," and at the time when this dogmatic assertion was made it seemed to require no word of apology from the author, so universally was the debt owed to the great master recognised by the scientific world. Yet we find that, within a few years, dissentient voices rose and darkened the halo that was surrounding the name of Lavoisier. When men were loyal to the memory of their benefactors, Lavoisier was the creator of the science of Chemistry, the reformer who taught chemists new paths of inquiry, the founder of a school of mathematical exactitude. But the searching spirit of Germany has proved to its satisfaction that the Frenchman was only a recogniser of chemical doctrine whose "great achievement consisted in abolishing old prejudices and in the masterly application of scientific principles to the explanation of chemical processes." This is about all the credit which Lavoisier gets at the present time in some of the German schools.

If such is the fate of one of the greatest master minds of the world, what judgment can we expect from the future on the work of the Hindu savant, who has revived the scientific traditions of his country? He is not a Lavoisier, and yet through his efforts the land of Nagarjuna has renewed activities which lay dormant for centuries. It was that savant himself who bitterly deplored the "intellectual torpor and stagnation" of his country; and there was left to him the noble task of regenerating Indian Chemistry. It is he who, to the nation of metaphysicians and visionaries, has added the lustre of a school of experimental and inductive scientists. The man who has accomplished these things cannot be ignored by his countrymen. India offers the tribute of respect to her illustrious son, the founder of the Indian School of Chemistry, Professor Prafulla Chandra Ray.

Such is the history of a great scientific movement in this country. The leader has carried out his life's mission. He has founded the School. He has trained a host of chemists. And now he may rest fully assured that the work he has started will be carried on in all its details. The development of the School he has created he may now safely trust in the hands of his pupils. They will prize it as their most valuable legacy, and loyally hand it down to posterity.

What an awakening for India! After centuries of scientific stagnation she has now recovered her former position in the chemical world. May the man who has effected this change be long preserved to us! May he long inspire his disciples to greater deeds! All we can do now is to pay a sincere tribute of affection, of admiration, of respect to the great benefactor and disinterested philosopher, Prafulla Chandra Ray.—*The Presidency College Magazine.*

DR. RAY ON SOCIAL REFORM

In admiring Dr. Ray as one of the greatest scientists of the present age we ought not to forget that his life has not been lived altogether within the recess of his laboratory. Dr. Ray is a patriot, and his patriotism has the ring of sincerity which is only natural in one whose life has been a dedication to the service of knowledge and the search for truth. His contributions to Science, while enlarging the bounds of knowledge, have conferred honour on his race. His work on the history of Hindu Chemistry is an undying monument to his patriotism as, through it, he has raised his country in the estimation of the world. Besides a scholar and patriot, Dr. Ray has also been a warm social reformer. His countrymen marked their appreciation of him by voting him to preside over the Indian National Social Conference of 1917 held at Calcutta. Dr. Ray, all unconscious of how he would be misrepresented by interested political factions and only alive to the great social malady in the body politic, asked in the course of his much-discussed address:—

> While the echo of *Swaraj* or Home Rule is reverberating from one end of the country to the other,—while ambitious schemes of political re-construction are being propounded by every section of the people—while gorgeous visions of a United India are capturing our imagination—loud protests of indignation are raised by classes and communities amongst us which we can no longer ignore. Why is there this note of discord where there should be only peace and harmony ? Why is this rift in the lute ?
>
> The answer lies in a nut-shell. It is our failure to recognise that the question which presses for solution at the present moment is as much a political as a sociological one. By the nature of things it must be so. For, however much we may try to divide and isolate the various parts of the national problem, they cling to one another as fast as ever and mock our attempts at self-deception. We cannot, with impunity, give undue preference to one over others. The law of *Karma* or causation is inexorable, and our past neglect in the work of social reform is bearing its evil fruit at the present hour. It has begun to clog the wheels of political progress. . . . .

Talking of "touchability and untouchability," he could not but speak in strong language :—

> What was possible in Japan in 1871 is found to be impossible in India even towards the close of the second decade of the 20th century. Even now we find that, as the saying goes, 12 Rajputs must have 13 cooking pots and 500 Congress delegates require as many kitchen arrangements. This at any rate is applicable to our friends of the Southern Presidency, who have worked out the problem to metaphysical nicety inasmuch as they have added a new category or contamination by sight of the cooked food of a Brahman when seen by a member of the Panchama class even from a distance, say by means of a telescope.
>
> * * * * * *
>
> The problem of "touchableness" has assumed a scientific aspect in these days. If a Pariah crosses your threshold you

throw away your jar of drinking water as polluted, but ice and lemonade manufactured by the untouchables pass current! A distinction conferred on a member of our society becomes the occasion for giving a dinner in the Town-Hall catered by Peliti and the recognised leaders of the Hindu society take part in the function and their names are published in the morning papers, but when on the occasion of a marriage or *Sradh* you are guilty of sitting to a feast with a Christian or Moslem or even a Hindu of the *lower* castes you are threatened with excommunication. Reason, logic and common sense are thus scattered to the four winds.

DR. RAY'S POLITICS

These views created some sensation at the time and his friends and foes thought him to be a bit reactionary in politics. His address at the Social Conference was a frank expression of the indignation which every Indian must feel at the iniquities of our social system. But it is not fair to conclude, therefore, that Dr. Ray is inimical to the political interests now dominating the country's mind. He has himself admitted the need of some far-reaching measure of reform. If in his address at the Social Conference he desired to create a body of public opinion to bring about at least a mitigation of the prevalent social evils, he did not certainly mean to be a derisive influence. On the contrary, he is passionately opposed to doing anything which would impair national solidarity and has strongly deprecated the tendencies, wherever ound, in the conduct of whatever party it may be, of weakening such solidarity. His remarks on Sir William Wedderburn, made at a memorial meeting held at Calcutta, are sure to be of interest in this connection:—

The ultimate moral justification of England's rule over India is not *Pax-Britannica*, not even the economic prosperity of the country, but the preparation of Indian people for Self-Government. If that end is lost sight of in the pursuit of any subsidiary advantage or improvement, the British policy in India will miss its true goal. Its history will be a record of huge failure, a record of immense preparations without the fruition. Sir William knew it, and, therefore, he kept his gaze steadily fixed on the true end and aim of England's mission in India, however distant that end might appear to his contemporaries, and he was only one of the noble band of Englishmen who have devoted their lives to the same cause. He was "ain brither" to Henry Lawrence and Evans Bell, Henry Cotton and Allan Hume. Such lives may seem to the short-sighted materialist, to the all-wise practical politician and experienced bureaucrat on the spot as futile. But only such lives can build a bridge between East and West—only such Englishmen can make India's inclusion in the British Empire possible. When centuries have rolled away from now, when the divine purpose has wrought itself in India and the final history of our land comes to be written, the names of Wedderburn and Hume will shine in that record as a silver thread shot through the crimson web of the British conquest of India.

UNIVERSITY LECTURES

In February 1918 the Madras University invited him to deliver a course of lectures on Ancient Hindu Chemistry. Dr. Ray's addresses, it need hardly be said, were very much appreciated by his audience. It is characteristic of the selflessness of the man that, with the honorarium which the University paid to him, he endowed a prize in memory of the late Sir William Wedderburn to be awarded to the student who showed the highest capacity of scholarship or research in chemistry. The lectures of so great and original a savant must have the salutary result of stimulating research in a University which has done so little in this very necessary direction. Dr. Ray explains the difference between the Universities of Madras and Calcutta in the matter of research in these words in an interview published in the *Hindu*:

RESEARCH IN MADRAS

In view of these high attainments of Dr. Ray, I asked him why Bengal was more advanced in research work than Madras and in what ways we could bring about development in research in this Presidency. "In the first place," said Dr. Ray, "we had in Bengal the Hindu College, latterly known as the Presidency College, staffed by Europeans and Indians, interested in research and invested with full control over well-equipped laboratory. In the second place, we have, mainly through the munificence of Sir Taraknath Palit and Dr. Sir Rash Behari Ghose, a University College of Science to which the Government of India is expected to make a handsome grant. The fact that Sir Sankaran Nair is the Education Member of the Government of India and that Sir. S. P. Sinha is in charge of the Education Portfolio in Bengal leads us to feel hopeful of that measure of Government support which are warranted under the circumstances. In the third place, we Indians in Bengal have—our researchers included, who are growing in number,—a larger measure of control over education than you have here and the scope for free and unfettered development is consequently greater. Above all, public opinion, able to make itself felt, is solidly behind researchers who are growing alike in number and in importance." "As for Madras," Dr. Ray continued, "you must first of all create an atmosphere of research and this cannot be done unless you have a dozen or so of men who have secured European reputation by solid contributions to the advancement of science. If you produce more men like Mr. Ramanujam and appoint them professors of your colleges, then they will perforce be allowed to have free scope for development along lines which they themselves choose. As a first step, you might send your students to England. As regards chemistry students, you might in the first instance send them to Calcutta. Then, as in the case of the Palit Professorships and Lectureships, you must lay down a rule that none but Indians should be appointed to high posts such as these, so that you may be sure that Indians of note, who are growing in number, shall be encouraged in their efforts to make researches with advantage to the country. Granted these conditions, strong, effective public opinion and support, and well-equipped laboratories, there is bound to be steady development." Dr. Ray spoke with feeling when he referred to qualified Indians being kept out of higher posts. He regretted that the Tatas sometime ago gave room for complaints that they did not fully encourage the appointment in their Institute of qualified Indians, but added that he believed that the mistake had been found out and matters would be improved. Our aim should be, he said, to create a set of qualified, self-reliant scientists and this could not be done unless we give opportunities of training for our promising youths.

HIS METHOD OF STUDY AND WORK

The question may arise: how a confirmed invalid or valetudinarian for the last 44 years has been able to do so much in so many different spheres of activity.

The answer lies in a nutshell—Dr. Ray believes in doing one thing at a time and doing that well—he has been heard to say that it is concentration of mind that pays and not the number of hours devoted to study—he cannot read more than one hour at a stretch and that in the morning as his brain gets easily fatigued—but he is an embodiment of order, method and punctuality. Dr. Ray's latest pronouncement is that his appetite for chemical researches simply grows by what it feeds upon: he is author or joint-author with his pupils of some four scores contributions chiefly on the nitrites and it was in the fitness of things that Prof. Armstrong should style him "Master of Nitrites." Since joining the College of Science, *i.e.*, within a space of a year and a half, he has communicated to the Chemical Society of London half a dozen papers and the "Annual Report on the Progress of Chemistry" to hand gives a summary of three of his latest researches. Work at the Laboratory is his delight and so long as he is inside his *sanctum* he forgets all about the outside world—if he passes a single day without learning something new or adding something to the stock of knowledge he grieves like Titus, "Oh Friend, to-day I have lost a day."

HIS CHARITY

Mr. Padmini Mohan Neogi, writing of him in the *Indian World*, speaks of his philanthropy in these feeling words :—

> We who have had occasions to know the influences that are working upon young Bengal, can make bold to anticipate that his goodness, his charity and inspiration if nothing else, will ever be a household topic from the centre of the metropolis to the distant corners of Bengal where the benign torch of education has been carried. Uneventful as his life has been, free from the bustle of the pompous follies of society, single in his life, his is

yet an eventful life—events not like the passing of a bill in a legislature, or the foundation of a memorial institute, or a bountiful donation for a Rai Bahadurship, but simple tears of orphans, of aspirant but indigent youngmen, of the high or the low or the warfare of an acid with a metal or the friendship of an acid with a base. How often have we seen wretched youngmen, wretched on account of poverty, going up into his laboratory room where they laid bare their heavy bosoms, and he the father of them all, fondling with all the affection as though they were his own. We have heard him say many a time and oft that poverty is a rigid school and the sessions are long and bitter; but the men and women who graduate therein come forth with physical frames capable of enduring fatigues, with hearts habituated to disappointments, and fortified against the rebuffs of fortune, with intellects trained by patient, laborious and unbending application. What an intolerable chain it binds around aspirant souls! And yet the world's greatest thinkers have felt this iron in their flesh and bursting the galling bonds, have carved their way to eminence and immortality. Though himself a prodigious man of charity (for which his friends have sometimes taken him to task), his opinion regarding money-saving has been but simple. Of all charities, he often says, mere-money-giving is the least; sympathy, kind words, gentle judgments, a friendly pressure of weary hands, an encouraging smile will frequently outweigh a mint of coin. Bear this in mind, we have often heard him say, selfishness is the real root of all the evil in the world; people are too isolated, too much wrapped up in their individual rights, interests and enjoyments. The first person singular is the God of the Age.

CHARACTERISTICS

Severely simple and ascetic in disposition, Dr. Ray has given the best part of his life to build up character among his students and inspire them with the love of knowledge for its own sake. He may have had his disappointments, but he has done more to inculcate the wisdom of plain living and high thinking than perhaps any other man now living in Bengal. A few racks of books, a miserable-looking and antiquated bedstead, an eighteenth-century table, with a few old-fashioned chairs form all his earthly belongings; and though he has been to England thrice, he has acquired none of the arts of grace and fashion of modern life. His dress is simple and his personal appearance seems so neglected. It has been often embarrassing to his visitors to recognise the man whose greatness had induced them to catch a glimpse of him. The striking sketch of him by Mukul Chandra Dey is a marvellous pictorial reproduction of the unpretentious scientist with eyes seeing deep into truth through all the veils of illusion and concealment.

Dr. Ray, having been single all his life, has not had many charges on his purse and no serious financial obligations to discharge. Almost all that he earns as a professor or as profits from the Bengal Chemical and Pharmaceutical Works, he spends on poor boys, deserving institutions and charities. It is difficult to spot out many poor boys in the Calcutta colleges who do not receive some help or other from this philanthropic professor, and there are very few deserving charities in Bengal that do not count him as their patron. Indeed, behind an unpretentious and attenuated figure—Dr. Ray has been a confirmed dyspeptic for over 44 years—he carries a heart as warm as the climate of his native land.

Absolutely oriental in habits and tastes, there are very few men in Bengal who have drunk so deep of Western knowledge and who have been so strong and steadfast champions of right thinking and right doing. A devoted and careful student of Mill and Spencer, Dr. Ray is a rationalist to the very core of his heart. He seldom allows his emotions or the prejudices of his environment to get the better of his judgment. He does not believe in caste or communal ideas and, though a member of the Brahmo Samaj, is far from thinking that that church can claim any monopoly of any moral and spiritual wisdom. He hits as hard in private life against Hindu practices as against Brahmo pretensions. About eight years ago he contributed to a vernacular periodical of Bengal an article in which he boldly came out with chapter and verse to prove how the Bengali intellect, or, for the matter of that, Indian intellect, had suffered through foolish customs and absurd religious prejudices.

Prafulla Chandra Ray is not only one of Bengal's greatest sons but is also one of Nature's truest gentlemen—every inch of him. Though a man of very strong convictions, he has hardly made an enemy in his life. He has held aloft the banner in Bengal of Mathew Arnold's culture and sweet reasonableness. He cherishes no jealousy, entertains no malice. Even when he differs from anybody, he imputes no motives nor attempts to throw any mud at his opponents. He is frankness and cordiality almost to everybody, and never plays with any cards in his sleeves. When he fights, he fights with gloves off. In all his private and public dealings, he is most scrupulously honest and above board. He believes in a clean and pure life and has himself lived up to this ideal. Sparing as an eater, a talker and correspondent, he has not allowed many distractions to disturb the even tenour and equanimity of his life. The work in the laboratory is certainly the most fascinating and engrossing work of Dr. Ray's life, but, besides a scholar and savant, he has also many social attractions. He has a warm corner in his heart for many friends to whose homes he pays regular visits and with whom he always keeps himself in intimate touch. Not very infrequently, he goes about begging from the house of one such friend or other for either half a piece of a cake or some home-made sweets or some other delicacies, and the ladies of these houses take a special delight in providing him with "good grub." Among others, with whom he has maintained life-long friendship and in whose homes he is always received with open arms, may be mentioned the names of Sir J. C. Bose, Hon. Dr. Nilratan Sircar and Messrs. Satyananda Bose and Prithwis Chandra Ray. There is another set of friends with whom he makes a point of passing about three hours every evening in the spacious maidan flanking Chowhringhee Road (Calcutta). Being almost a lifelong victim of dyspepsia and a bad nervous system and being troubled with insomnia now and then, Dr. Ray has found life and health and recreation in the religious observance of this evening programme. Every evening, in cold and heat, in rain and summer, Dr. Ray is found squatted on the grass of a quiet corner in the maidan with a number of friends agreeably occupied in the pleasant pastime of "chronicling small beer." Some of these friends are Principal Giris Chandra Bose, Kaviraj Upendranath Sen, Mr. Satyananda Bose and several of his own students and fellow-workers in the laboratory.

CONCLUSION

Dr. Ray will rank in our history as one of the greatest of those who have helped in building up the edifice of modern India. His name stands along with that of Sir J. C. Bose as evidence of the genius of the Indian mind for scientific research. It is the most hopeful sign of our renaissance that it is not confined to one or two aspects of life only but is universal and all-embracing. The wave of new life has pervaded every nerve, vein and muscle of the national being. On the side of Science and Research, the achievements of P. C. Ray and J. C. Bose represent the high water-mark of the national genius. Others have achieved eminence in other fields. But to these belong, in a special measure, the honour of living up in a materialistic age to the grand ideal expressed in the words of one of them :—

Not in matter, but in thought, not in possessions or even in attainments but in ideals are to be found the seed of immortality. Not through material acquisition but in generous diffusion of ideas and ideals can the true empire of humanity be established.

DR. RAY'S ESSAYS AND DISCOURSES

SCIENTIFIC EDUCATION IN INDIA

[*The article, though written in 1899, is of special importance still in view of the adverse criticism which the Indian Institute of Science, Bangalore, has evoked from every province in India. The opinion of Dr. Ray and other experts was sought at the time when only the provisional scheme had been submitted. The princely gift of 30 lakhs of rupees coupled with the annual grants by the Government of India and the State of Mysore, would represent a capital of nearly a crore of rupees. The mountain has been in labour and a mouse begot. Dr. Ray in his evidence before the Industrial Commission incidentally refers to the huge—we had almost said scandalous—waste of public money in the management of the Institute. The conditions favourable for the growth of the spirit of research in India are discussed in the lecture on "Higher Science in the Universities." This article is reprinted from the "Calcutta Review" Vol. cviii.*]

The Research Institute,* as foreshadowed in Mr. J. N. Tata's scheme, if it could be successfully launched upon its career of utility, might be expected to open a new era in the history of the intellectual and industrial development of India. The scheme,

* **Research Institute in India (A Provisional scheme).**

alike colossal and magnificent in its conception, is worthy of the great Parsi philanthropist, whose patriotism is only equalled by his princely munificence.

It is characteristic of the originator of the scheme that he has not suddenly sprung it upon the the Indian public for the sake of sensation making. Mr. Tata, ably seconded by his energetic and indefatigable Secretary, Mr. Padshah, has diligently studied the subject; approached the representatives of the Government, from the Viceroy downwards, and sought counsel of some of the most eminent educationists.

The present seems to be an opportune moment to take a rapid survey of all that has hitherto been done or attempted in the direction of imparting scientific education in this country, specially keeping in view the particular branch of science with which I have the honour to be connected—Chemistry. Before proceeding further, it may be better, by way of preface, to glance for a moment at the origin and development of Synthetic Chemistry.

When, some four years ago, Mr. Berthelot drew a picture of the happy millennium to dawn about the year 2000 A.D. when all the necessary articles of food would be artificially prepared by the chemist from the very elements, when foreign lands would not be worth fighting for, when wars and annexations would be things of the past as rich harvests would be gathered in the laboratory, his utterances were regarded by many as those of a visionary. But the perpetual Secretary of the Great Academy of Sciences, himself a mighty and untiring worker for nearly half a century in the field of Synthetic Chemistry, is not to be ranked as a day-dreamer. In order fully to realise what Synthetic Chemistry has already done and may be expected to achieve in the future, it is only necessary to direct our attention for a moment to Germany as it was at the beginning of this century. It was in the year 1828 that Wohler startled the scientific world by the artificial preparation of urea. "No single chemical discovery of this century," writes Professor Thorpe, "has exercised so great an influence on the development of scientific thought..............With it was opened out a new domain of investigation, upon which the chemist instantly seized. The present generation, which is constantly gathering such rich harvests from the territory won for it by Wohler, can only with difficulty transport itself back to that remote period in which the creation of an organic compound within the body of a plant or an animal appeared to be conditioned in some mysterious way by the vital force, and they can hardly realize the impression which the building up of urea from its elements then made upon men's minds."

At about this period Liebig, a countryman of Wohler's, immortalised his name by a series of equally brilliant syntheses of organic compounds. It is not a little remarkable that both these great German founders of Synthetic Chemistry had to travel to foreign lands to catch their inspiration at the fountain head. Wohler had, in 1823, journeyed to Stockholm, to sit at the feet of his master, Berzelius, and Liebig had repaired to Paris, to be associated with Gay-Lussac in his epoch-making researches on the explosive compounds commonly known as the "fulminates."

The history of the modern supremacy of Germans in the industrial world is the history of the triumphs achieved by successive generations of silent and patient workers in the laboratory, the bare enumeration of which would occupy some pages. It may suffice to allude to the synthesis of conine, the poisonous principle of hemlock, the first artificial formation of an alkaloid by Ladenberg; of alizarine from coal tar derivatives by Graebe and Liebermann; of indigo by Baeyer, and of the sugars by Emil Fischer.

In order to illustrate the economical disturbances brought about by a single chemical discovery, it is only necessary to bring into prominence that of alizarine. "The synthetic formation of alizarine created nothing less than a revolution in one of our leading industries, and completely destroyed a staple trade of France, Holland, Italy and Turkey: Alizarine is one of the main products of the madder plant, the roots of which have been used from time immemorial for the sake of the dyes which they contain. Pliny tells us that in his time madder was well known to the sordid and avaricious, and this because of the large profits obtained from it owing to its employment in dyeing wool and leather. Originally it was grown almost exclusively in India, Persia and the Levant. The Moors introduced it into Spain whence it found its way into the Netherlands. Alsace and Avignon were long celebrated for their madder. Twenty years ago, it was the most important of the natural dyestuff used by the calico printer and Turkey red dyer ; and the annual import of this country was valued at £1,250,000 sterling, the South Lancashire district alone consuming upwards of 150 tons weekly. The chemist has changed all these, and the cultivation of the various species of the Rubiaceæ. for the purposes of the dyer which has continued for thousands of years down to our own time, is now practically at an end" (Thorpe). And India, the home of the madder plant, has been reduced to the condition of having to import 31 lakhs of rupees worth alizarine annually. The fate of the indigo industry of Bengal is already trembling in the balance and although the planters have taken to improving and cheapening the process of manufacture they can at best postpone the disaster for a time; avert it they cannot. Artificial indigo will sooner or later supplant the natural dyestuff.

Sometime ago I wrote to a friend and fellow student of mine at Edinburgh, who is now engaged as a chemist in one of the big dye works (Farbewerke) in Germany to furnish me with some idea as to the working capacity of a dye work. No apology is needed for quoting some portion of the letter I received. "I merely mention that we have 22 Kms. of rails in the works for the ten little engines which carry materials from any part of the works to any other. We have gasometers, lots of electric light and electric transmission of energy. In the laboratories we have turbines and steam-engines. . . electric driven stirring apparatus, vacuum pipes, compressed air, etc. In some laboratories there is electricity. Professor Le Blanc, the celebrated electrical chemist, is head of our electro-technical laboratory. We manufacture sodium by electrolysis. There are now 100 chemists, 3,500 workmen and a staff of about 150 clerks and officials. . . . . . I am engaged almost entirely in new investigations. The work is interesting and well paid. My work has been for years almost entirely confined to Organic Chemistry."

The most notable feature in these dyeworks is the stimulus and encouragement given to original research, so that, while new discoveries are cropping up from time to time, bringing in handsome returns to the capital employed, the bounds of science are at the same time enlarged.

I trust enough has been said above to justify the commanding position assigned to chemical science in Mr. Tata's scheme at the very outset, however, we are confronted with a serious difficulty as to how to give it a practical shape; its weak point seems to be its failure to take full advantage of some of the existing institutions.

The founding of something like a Davy-Faraday Institute, where only scientists of acknowledged position would carry on their investigation, would be wide of the mark and out of place in a country like India. The conditions favourable for the growth and development of original research seem to be that a student should work under the direction and supervision of, or in conjunction with, a professor who is himself engaged in original investigations, and who is thus capable of infusing his own spirit and enthusiasm into his pupil. It is in this humble and modest way that a foundation has been laid in England, Germany, etc., for the creation of a race of original workers and thinkers. The initiative in this direction has already been taken.

Let me more fully illustrate what has been said just now by reference to the state of things which obtains at the Presidency College. Here we have already a well organised staff of professors, demonstrators, assistants, etc., and fairly well equipped laboratories to carry on the major part of the work formulated in Mr. Tata's scheme,* the electric engineering and agricultural chemistry, of which there

* Scientific and Technical Department :—The subjects in which instruction is to be given and researches conducted should include the following :—(*a*) Physics—Advanced courses in all departments, including Mathematical Physics and Electric Engineering; (*b*) Chemistry —(1) Advanced Inorganic Chemistry, (2) Organic Chemistry, (3) Analytical Chemistry, (4) Agricultural Chemistry; (*c*) Technological Chemistry applied to different Arts and Industries. For the above courses the following professional staff will be necessary :—(*a*) One Professor, one Assistant Professor; (*b*) Two Senior Professors for (2) and (3). Two Junior Professors for (1) and (4) ; (*c*) One Professor.

are no chairs in this college, are however fully represented elsewhere.

On a rough calculation, it is found that the upkeep of the scientific department of the Presidency College alone costs about Rs. 60,000, a year which, if capitalised at 3 per cent, would amount to 20 lakhs of rupees. To this must now be added the outlay incurred for the two laboratories, with fittings and apparatus as accumulated by the slow and gradual additions during the last quarter of a century—an outlay not falling short of 4 lakhs of rupees. It will thus be evident that the scientific teaching and work going on at the Presidency College represent a capital of about 24 lakhs.

In the proposed scheme we find that a sum of Rs. 1,00,000 (one lakh) has been set apart as the initial outlay for the Chemical Laboratory (apart from building). Now in the new Chemical Laboratory of this college, the fittings alone cost Rs. 65,000 and the total valuation of it, including building, apparatus and appliances, may be put down at somewhere near 2½ lakhs. This splendid Laboratory has the merit of being planned and worked out by one who combines in himself an experience of 25 years' educational labours in India and a knowledge of the best laboratories of Europe, and whose position in the world of Science stands pre-eminent—one in fact who is unquestionably the ablest expert on the subject in India. Such being the case, it is scarcely to be expected that the proposed laboratory will at all come up to the standard of the existing one, in spite of the fact that the entire gift of Mr. Tata is likely to be swallowed up by it. What has been said above applies, *mutatis mutandis* to some other laboratories as well, *e.g.*, the Physical Laboratory of this college and the Chemical, Physiological and Pathological Laboratories under course of construction in connection with the Calcutta Medical College.

In my humble opinion, it would be waste of money and a diversion, and misapplication of energies, to aim at creating a separate institute. It would be more conducive to the cause of science in India if the existing institutions in the different parts of India, the colleges for physics, science, medicine, engineering and agriculture, were utilised to the fullest extent and, whenever found necessary, widened in scope and improved upon. For instance, a wing might be added here and a chair endowed there.

A misapprehension seems to prevail, I am afraid, as regards the scope and capacity of some of the existing institutions. This misapprehension seems to arise from the circumstance that we had hitherto had to be contented with simply preparing students for a prescribed course of study in sciences as required for the University examinations, and that we have not as yet been able to produce original workers. This deplorable state of things is due to causes over which those who are responsible for teaching sciences have absolutely no control. There is, practically, no career open to those who would devote themselves to science. The flower of the graduates and undergraduates are necessarily attracted to the professions of the law, medicine and engineering, which, though they are becoming over-crowded day by day, still hold some of the highest prizes in life. A good few are also annually absorbed in the provincial executive service, now filled up by open competitive examinations. As it is, only second or third-rate students are found to take up Chemistry for the M. A. Degree, and they choose the subject, not because they have any particular liking for it, but because they want to have a diploma of the mastership attached to their names. In Europe and America the cultivation of science and its application in the arts go hand in hand. Some of the German dye-works, as has been seen above, each give employment to 100 chemists or more.

What is, however, badly needed is encouragement in the shape of handsome post-graduate fellowships, for the creation of which the fund which is proposed to be raised with Mr. Tata's donation as the nucleus, should be set apart, and these to be distributed to the several provinces of India, giving the holders thereof full option to carry on their research at any well-recognised place or institution. For instance, a graduate who has taken honours in M. A. in Botany, might be encouraged to continue his work under the Superintendent of the Royal Botanic Gardens, Sibpur, who is always a specialist.

A graduate in medicine, again, who has, in the opinion of his professors and examiners, shown aptitude for pathology and physiology should be associated with Dr. Haffkine or Mr. Hankin to study Bacteriology. Then, again, the physical and chemical Laboratories of the Presidency College might each accommodate half a dozen students engaged in original research. In this way a kind of healthy inter-provincial emulation would also be set up. For instance, if Madras found that her own graduates had to travel all the way to Calcutta and there reside for some three years to be trained in original investigations in one particular branch, she would certainly look about and take steps to wipe off what she could not help regarding as a reproach.

When, by the slow and gradual evolution of the plan sketched above, a trained band of original workers had been secured, they might further be encouraged to proceed to Europe to round off their education under veteran specialists.

Taking the scheme as it is, there seems to be some confusion of ideas. A chair of analytical chemistry is vague and unmeaning everywhere, except, perhaps, in one or two places in Germany, where the highest degree of specialisation is aimed at, and the Analytical Laboratory is under the direct control and supervision of the professors themselves, though the work is mainly conducted by efficient demonstrators. Then it is found that too much is expected of a professor of "Technological Chemistry applied to different Arts and Industries," with his staff of a demonstrator and glass-blower, etc. The industries under this head, which ought to receive earnest attention are glass, soap, matches and candle-making, earthenware and pottery, tanning, dyeing, vulcanisation of caoutchouc, pharmaceutical preparations, including the extraction of the alkaloids of the cinchona bark, nuxvomica, opium and the thousand and one other indigenous drugs. It is found that in the year ending 31st March, 1897, India had to import about 26 lakhs of rupees worth of tanned leather and articles made thereof, 11 lakhs worth of candles, 70 lakhs worth of glass articles; earthenware and porcelain valued at 21 lakhs in round numbers; matches 29 lakhs; soap at 12 lakhs; dyeing and tanning materials at 73 lakhs and so on.*

Two match factories and a glass factory were started near Calcutta only a few years ago, and they have all come to grief for lack of technical knowledge and experience. The projectors made the serious blunder of putting the cart before the horse. They discovered, when it was too late, that unless they could engage experts in England or Germany at a heavy premium—a premium which would swallow up all the profits and something more—it would be hopeless to carry on the business. It would be nothing short of a miracle if a single Professor of Technological Chemistry were to achieve for us the desired end. In these days of high specialisation in the arts, the slightest improve-

* Vide "Annual statement of the Trade and Navigation of British India with foreign countries."

ment in one direction and the cheapening of prices arising therefrom, would be enough to give a particular industry a decided advantage over its rivals. Some ten years ago "Bryant and May's safety matches" had undisputed command over the Indian market; now-a-days matches made in Sweden and Japan have almost completely ousted the former. It is of no use turning out a set of smatterers and jacks-of-all-trades, for this is what we are driving at in the proposed schemes. It is to be doubted if a dozen chairs on technological chemistry would fulfil the object. What appears to be the proper course to adopt is that a chosen and picked number of students be sent annually to Europe and America and there be apprenticed for a number of years, if necessary under payment of premium, to learn the technical arts and acquire expert knowledge. These, when they return home after the expiry of their indentures, will always be in request, and it is through the agency of such men that we hope to start the chemical industry by and bye.

One important branch of Science appears to have been overlooked—Geology and Mining. The mineral resources of our country have been only imperfectly developed, and a curriculum in science would be rather one-sided which did not take into account the vast dimensions which the mining industry is likely to acquire in the future.

India being essentially an agricultural country,

the science relating to agriculture should also demand the fullest consideration, and, instead of a single chair of agricultural chemistry representing it, ample provision should be made for the study of zoology, with special reference to entomology and sericulture, veterinary medicine, botany, forestry, etc. It will probably be objected that, by attempting too many things at a time, the scheme will become cumbrous and expensive and therefore unworkable. We have fortunately, even in the direction of agricultural education, ample materials to work upon.

The School of Forestry at Dehra Dun, Agricultural Farm at Saidapet, Madras, the newly created lectureship on agriculture at the Sibpore Engineering College, and that on Geology at the Presidency College, Calcutta, the Puna College of Science,* and the School of Veterinary Surgery and Medicine at Sodepur near Calcutta, fulfilled much of what is expected of a College of Agriculture such as they have got attached to the Imperial University of Tokyo. Surely we cannot expect a more qualified person than Dr. Leather, who was appointed on the strong recommendation of Dr. Voelcker.

---

* Staff of the Puna College of Science for scientific subjects.

1	Professor	of	Geology and Chemistry
1	"	"	Engineering
1	"	"	Forestry
1	"	"	Civil Engineering
1	Lecturer	of	Agriculture and Botany
1	"	"	Optics and Astronomy
1	"	"	Veterinary subjects

Let us now take a hasty glance at medicine. There are some ten chairs attached to the Calcutta Medical College. Bombay, Madras and Lahore each has a Medical College of the same status. There cannot be less than 30 Professorships, all told, in these four Medical Colleges. Taking the average pay of Professor at Rs. 1,500, we have the respectable sum of over Rs. 50,000 per month given away in salary alone. These medical institutions, the premier one having been founded more than sixty years ago, during the beneficent administration of Lord William Bentinck, have done excellent service in their days; but they have been allowed to outgrow the requirements of the time. The system in vogue under which recruitment for these posts is confined to the covenanted Indian Medical Service, is open to grave objections. An arrangement which tolerates that the civil surgeon, say of Sultanpur, should awake one morning and with infinite surprise, find himself appointed by telegram a Professor of Physiology, through no qualifications of his own but solely by virtue of his seniority in the graded service, must be pronounced a glaring anachronism, which is seriously hampering the progress of science in this country. None but specialists should hold these posts and the remuneration attached to them is by no means inadequate for the purpose.

There are already some sixty or more professorships and lectureships in science,* including medicine,

* I am taking into consideration only first-rate institutions. The mofussil colleges are left out of calculation.

chemistry, physics, agriculture, geology and engineering, scattered in the different parts of India. Let these all be co-ordinated to one general purpose; let these be utilised to the fullest extent, and their efficiency be increased; let a laboratory be associated with each of them. If, on an average, we can secure two post-graduate scholarships in connection with these chairs, we can thus hope to attract 120 students to carry on original investigations. A noble beginning will thus have been made. India is not a compact homogeneous country like Japan. A central Research Institute with an "Imperial University," like that of Tokyo, does not seem to commend itself. The Calcutta University is going to give a stimulus to original research by creating the degree of Doctor of Science. A separate university is not needed.

If I have been led to indulge in a good deal of destructive criticism, it is because I am sincerely convinced that the modified plan I am submitting is likely to secure a maximum of work and efficiency.

PROGRESS OF CHEMISTRY IN BENGAL

The following is the text of Prof. Ray's address at the annual meeting of the Calcutta Chemical Club, delivered on the 24th September, 1913:—

The year under review has been an eventful one for more reasons than one. There has been a growing and steady increase in the number of advanced students who are anxious to take part in original investigations. For evoking this new spirit we are in no small measure indebted to the recent University Regulations, which allow a thesis based upon some piece of research work to be substituted for mere book-learning. Since we met last year, some 40 papers have been communicated to the Chemical Societies of London and New York, the Asiatic Society of Bengal, the *Zeitschrift fur Anorganische Chemie, Zeitschrift fur Electrochemie and Zeitschrift fur Physikalische Chemie.* It is a matter for sincere congratulation that the contributions of several pupils in the Chemical Laboratory of the Presidency College are meeting with welcome and hospitable reception in the columns of the above journals. Our hearty thanks are due to the Publication Committee of the Chemical Society and to Professors Noyes, Richard Lorenz, Paul Askenasy, Ostwald and Drucker for their ready and ungrudging help in the matter of the publication of our papers.

I have all along held and am never tired of reiterating my views that those who pursue chemistry in India at the present state of its progress must not expect to reap immediate benefit in the shape of rich pecuniary rewards. To a sincere and devoted student, the pursuit of knowledge for its own sake always carries its reward. A man of science is a member of a privileged class—to him has been committed the sacred task of unravelling the mysteries and secrets of nature. Attracted by the glamour of a material civilisation we hope we shall not forget our noble heritage of plain living and high thinking.

I may, however, be permitted to point out that those who, after taking the highest degree of our University in Science, have spent two or three years in original investigations at the Laboratory of the Presidency College, have never had any serious cause of complaint even from the worldly point of view. As you may be aware, Professors Jatindra Nath Sen and Panchanan Neogi during their career as Research Scholars competed for and won the Premchand Roychand scholarship, which is justly regarded as the Blue-ribbon of the Calcutta University. Another Premchand scholar, Mr. Hemendra Kumar Sen, who was associated with me in carrying on researches, is now pursuing his higher studies in chemistry at the London Imperial College of Science and I feel confident he will be able to give a good account of himself.

I may also add that the Bengal Chemical and

Pharmaceutical Works has already absorbed as many as five chemists—all of them graduates in science and alumni of the Presidency College. I hope in due time many more chemical industries will spring up and find employment for scores of chemists.

A notable feature in connection with the recent contributions from our Laboratory is that they mostly include researches carried out by the students while preparing for the M. SC. degree and not by those who are known as "Research Scholars." I am afraid, the offer of attractive scholarships sometimes has a demoralizing effect inasmuch as it induces half-hearted workers to join the rank. Indeed, Sir William Ramsay has gone so far as to characterise tempting scholarships as partaking of the nature of briberies.

It is my pleasant duty to give special prominence to the researches of Messrs. Rasik Lal Datta, Nilratan Dhar and Jitendra Nath Rakshit. Messrs. Datta and Dhar have also won high University distinctions and I hope they will, in due time, be able to add one or more feathers to their cap. Mr. Rakshit, however, stands by himself. He is a "plucked" B. Sc., and, having failed to secure the University hall-mark, would naturally be looked down upon as an unclean pariah. By a singular piece of good fortune I happened to "discover" him, and, as you may be aware, his association with me in the investigation of the "Amine Nitrites" has been productive of happy results. He also found ample time to carry on work on his own account and we are looking forward with eagerness to the publication of his fairly elaborate paper on potassium and sodium acetamides in the next issue of the Chemical Society's journal.

I remember, some three or four years ago, the *Indian Daily News* mooted the question of granting degrees in special cases to those who have failed to satisfy the orthodox University requirements but have at the same time distinguished themselves by original researches. My humble opinion was invited at the time. I confess I have hitherto had to maintain discreet silence but waited till a specific case turned up. Recently, Dr. Rash Behary Ghosh has expressed the opinion that higher academic degrees should be conferred only on those who have done some original research work. He would abolish examinations for these degrees and make research work the only qualifying test for all higher academic distinctions. I think that a man like Mr. Rakshit is entitled to have a degree conferred on him.

I should also add that under the fostering care of Professor Watson some of the students of the Dacca College, notably Messrs. Anukul Chandra Sarkar and Jatindra Mohan Dutta, have shown marked ability in carrying on original researches. During the year under review, some 4 or 5 papers have been contributed from the Dacca Chemial Laboratory by Professor Watson and his pupils. Professor B. K. Singh's paper on the Resolution of Azonium compounds is also an important contribution.

Then, again, the Tata Institute of Science at

Bangalore, the Professoriate of which is composed of eminent experts, has started its career of utility and several of our own students are pursuing their post-graduate studies there.

We offer our hearty welcome to Dr. P. C. Mitter, who has lately returned after a successful academic career at Berlin. Mr. D. N. Chakravarti, another pupil of ours, has also just taken a Doctorate in Chemistry of the Berlin University, with distinction. Mr. P. K. Dutt, in whom Professor Cohen of Leeds has all along taken a sincere interest, has, I believe, by this time, taken the M. Sc. degree on the strength of an important thesis. Messrs. H. K. Sen and B. B. Dey, both of whom have shown aptitude for original researches, are now students at the London Imperial College of Science. It is thus highly gratifying to note that our favourite science is by no means lacking in votaries.

But the most remarkable event of the year is the princely gift of Sir T. Palit followed by the equally munificent donation of Dr. Rash Behary Ghosh for the foundation of a University College of Science, which I have always looked upon as the realisation of a dream of my life.

Gentlemen, it is impossible for me adequately to give expression to my feelings on this occasion. As contemporaries we cannot be expected to judge accurately the far-reaching character of the scheme which is about to take a tangible shape. Generations unborn will bless the pious memory of the benefactors of their country. I need scarcely add that the name of our eminent Vice-Chancellor, whose tenure of office has been signalised by such splendid gifts and whose administration of the affairs of our University at a critical period of its history has inspired so much confidence, will also be inseparably associated with the College of Science. I hope that a substantial grant will also be forthcoming from the Government. I have hitherto felt it as a national humiliation that Bengal, which has always taken the lead in India in intellectual movements, should not have a College of Science located in her midst. Thanks to the patriotism of Sir T. Palit and Dr. Ghosh that reproach is now going to be wiped out.

And now a word or two as to the supreme necessity for a College of Science. The Presidency College, it is true, has got fairly and in some cases splendidly equipped laboratories in connection with the several branches of Science and Government has not been wanting in generosity in responding to the calls of its Departments. But it should be remembered that the Presidency College is after all one of the several Colleges affiliated to the University and, as such, it has to justify its existence by the number of "passes" secured at the University Examinations. A good deal of the time of a Professor is, therefore, taken up in attending to the dull routine and mechanical duties and the requirements of "departmentalism." At best, he can make room for, or attend to the needs of, one or two post-graduate scholars. As I told you at the outset, a few students—not Research Scholars—are carrying on splendid work in our Laboratory; but they have no *locus standi* and have, in fact, no business to be there. That they are at all allowed to continue their work even after taking the M. Sc. degree is due, in no small measure, to the courtesy and encouragement of Principal James, who though not himself a man of science, has the appreciative instincts of a true scholar.

The accommodation at the Presidency College for advanced post-graduate studies in science has been very limited as I have indicated. At present, a student of science who wishes to devote himself to original investigations finds himself hopelessly at sea. He must either go abroad or find his career, full of promise, abruptly brought to a close. The College of Science is thus going to be started at the very psychological moment.

Last year, it was my privilege as a delegate to the "Congress of the Universities of the Empire" to urge the claims of our advanced students who are taking part in research work. I pleaded before my *confreres* that they should be entitled to something like preferential treatment when they proceed to an English University to further complete their studies. Much will, however, depend upon the quality of the work turned out in our laboratories. Recognition will not be slow in coming in.

I hope I shall be pardoned if I take you into my confidence and assure you that several eminent chemists warmly complimented me upon the humble measure of success achieved by some of our students in the field of research.

One word more and I have done. In my "History of Hindu Chemistry" I have devoted a chapter to the discussion of some of the causes which brought about the decline of scientific spirit in India, and how, during the period of intellectual stagnation which set in, our unhappy land was rendered morally unfit for the birth of a Boyle, a Descartes or a Newton. We hope we have slept off the torpor of ages and that it will be ours once more to extend the bounds of knowledge.

FORTY YEARS OF PROGRESS OF CHEMISTRY AT THE PRESIDENCY COLLEGE

The following contribution appeared in the " Presidency College Magazine," Calcutta, Vol. 1, 1915 :—

In his ever-memorable letter addressed to Lord Amherst in 1823 by Raja Ram Mohan Ray, the latter pointed out that the establishment of a Sanskrit College " would perpetuate ignorance " and keep India on a level with the Middle Ages of Europe with its scholastic philosophy. The great Indian Reformer pleaded for the " employing of European gentlemen of talent and education to instruct the natives of India in Mathematics, Natural Philosophy, Chemistry, Anatomy and other useful sciences which the natives of Europe have carried to a degree of perfection that has raised them above the inhabitants of other parts of the world."

Ram Mohan was far ahead of his age. The time was not yet ripe for the cultivation of Physical Sciences by natives of India. It was necessary that Western literature and culture should first strike root in the Indian soil and that at least the life-time of two generations must intervene before the craving for science would begin, especially when we bear in mind that the Hindu is steeped to the marrow in metaphysics and speculative sciences. Thus we find that among the alumni of the old Hindu College, there were thoughtful writers, speakers, social reformers like Krishnamohan Banerji, Ramgopal Ghose, Rajnarain Bose and Ramtanu Lahiri. Some of the creators of modern Bengali literature also belonged to this period, e.g., Madhusudhan Dutt and Peary Chand Mitra.

A space of two generations is but a short spell in the lifetime of a nation. The old Hindu College was founded in 1817. If we take 56 years to represent two generations in Bengal we come upon the year 1873—an *annus mirabilis* in Bengal at any rate. Sir George Campbell was a remarkable man in more ways than one. We are not called upon here to pass a verdict upon his administration of Bengal (1871—1874). Suffice it to say that he was a man of striking originality. Long before an Indian leader like Mr. Gokhale had made the cause of mass education his own, Sir George Campbell had taken care to scatter broadcast primary village schools under the grant-in-aid system. In fact, the "Campbell Pathshalas" as they are called in this province, have kept fragrant the memory of her sixth Lieutenant Governor. He had also the foresight to realize that in order to place within the easy reach of the people at large the benefits of Western medical science, instruction in it should be imparted through the medium of the vernacular. The "Campbell Medical School" of Calcutta, which is the precursor of several similar institutions in Bengal and other provinces, equally bears eloquent testimony to his wisdom. Sir George also in a way prepared the ground for the pursuit of science in Bengal. The alumni of the Presidency College in the early seventies of the last century will remember that Mr. H. F. Blandford was "Professor of Natural Science." He taught, we believe, the outlines of Physics, Chemistry, Geology, Meteorology, Physical Geography, etc. Such an arrangement at the present day may cause amusement. The student who is well up in the laws of evolution knows, however, that heterogeneity is an essential condition in the rudimentary stage of progress. Sir George Campbell realized that the time had come for each of the several branches of science to claim undivided attention. He asked for two specialists—one in Chemistry and the other in Botany. The then Secretary of State was fortunate in securing the services of Alexander (now Sir Alexander) Pedler and George (now Sir George) Watt as Professors of Chemistry and Botany respectively. Both of them proved to be efficient teachers, and successive generations of pupils speak highly of the attractive manner in which they taught their subjects. Mr. Pedler was posted at the Presidency and Mr. Watt at the Hugli College, and latterly at the Krishnagar College. When Mr. Pedler joined his duties in 1874, the premises occupied by the present Presidency College were under construction and the old Presidency College classes were held partly in the buildings now occupied by the Hindu School and the Sanskrit College, and partly in the rented rooms of the upper storey of the Albert Hall.

On the removal of the Presidency College to the new buildings in 1874, the one-storeyed house on the north of the compound in which had been located the old Hare School (then just entered into possession of its present building) was made over to the Chemical Department. Here the Chemical Laboratory slowly and silently grew up to meet the requirements of the time. The teaching in Chemistry even for the B. A. course was comparatively elementary, and no training in practical work was necessary; this luxury was confined only to the students preparing for the M.A. degree in science, who in addition to Chemistry had also to take up some branches of Physics. Thanks to the presistent pressure brought to bear upon the Senate by Sir A. Pedler, Sir John Eliot and others, the claims of Science began to obtain fuller recognition. For the B.A. degree in science attendance in practical classes in Chemistry and Physics was made compulsory.

The Chemical Department was housed in the old one-storeyed building for close upon twenty years, but the growing demand for increased accommodation due to the popularity of the subject and to the opening of the practical classes began to be keenly felt. Thanks to the devoted efforts of Sir A. Pedler, backed by Sir. A. Croft, the construction of a new wing of buildings was sanctioned by Sir Charles Elliott at a cost of about 1,60,000 rupees. The Chemical Department was removed to the existing premises in 1894. It should be remembered, however, that some of the valuable researches of Sir A. Pedler, *e.g.*, those on "Cobra Poison," "Action of Light on Phosphorus," etc., which won for him the distinction of Fellowship, of the Royal Society were carried on in this earlier, humble, unpretending laboratory. The more complete differentiation of the Science Course and the institution of the B. Sc. degree in 1907 gave a fresh impetus to the study of Science. A candidate for a Science degree was now relieved of the heavy handicap of taking up English literature as one of his subjects, and he was thus in a position to devote more time and attention to Science. He had on the other hand to go through a systematic training on the practical side. The wisdom and foresight of Sir A. Pedler have now been more than justified. Practical teaching in Science is now recognized in Europe as a *sine qua non* for a student of science, and laboratory experience constitutes the most essential part of his knowledge.* There is now no room for a mere smattering in Science. The requirements on the practical side of the new University Regulations

* Even in England practical instruction in chemisty is of comparatively recent date, as the following extracts will prove:—

"At the time (70 years ago) public laboratories for the systematic teaching of chemistry did not exist in London. The number of real students of chemistry in this country was very small. They were looked upon by their friends as being eccentric young men, who probably would never do any good for themselves, and these few students found practical instruction in the private laboratories of some of the London teachers * * . . . . . . It was not till several years later, till 1850 and 1851, that the Medical Schools in London established classes of practical chemistry.—*The Jubilee of the Chemical Society of London*, pp. 6-7."

after 1906 became so heavy and pressing that by 1908 the laboratory blocks of 1894, though spacious, proved to be quite inadequate to accommodate all the classes. It was a fortunate circumstance that the late lamented Mr. J. A. Cunningham was in charge of the Chemical Department from 1906—1909. His zeal and enthusiasm for the spread of scientific education in Bengal was unbounded. Not only at the Presidency College but often in his capacity as a University Inspector under the New Regulations he was indefatigable in his efforts to improve the quality of science teaching in the colleges of Bengal, Government and private. The accommodation for the I. Sc., practical classes, as also many necessary appliances for teaching, proved insufficient, so much so that the premier college in Bengal was in imminent risk of being disaffiliated. At the instance of Mr. Cunningham, Mr. (now Sir) Archdale Earle, the then Director of Public Instruction, made a special grant of Rs. 23,000 for the purchase of indispensable apparatus and chemicals and sanctioned the erection of a temporary structure with corrugated iron roofing in the quadrangle of the college buildings, and this was fitted up for the purpose. A similar arrangement was made for the I. Sc. Practical Physics. The removal of the Physical, Physiological and Geological Departments to the new Baker Laboratory Buildings considerably lightened the congestion on the "Arts" and Chemical side as the rooms vacated by the former were equally distributed between the latter. The one-storeyed building on the northern side in which, as we have already seen, the entire Chemical Department was accommodated from 1874—1894, and which has since the present time been an adjunct of the Physical Department, has now reverted to the Chemical Department, and is being specially fitted up to meet the requirements of Physical Chemistry; whilst the entire wing on the ground floor, which was so long in the possession of Dr. Bose, has been fitted up at a cost of Rs. 40,000 to relieve the congestion in the M. Sc. classes, and also to afford better facilities for research work. The corrugated iron shed is not only an unseemly structure but in the summer months the heat is unbearable; and moreover the quadrangle being thus blocked up, the ventilation of the ground floor has been seriously affected. The real solution of the difficulty lies in pulling down the old one-storeyed building and raising in its place a three-storeyed one. A scheme to this effect has already been submitted to Government.

It will thus be seen that the Chemical Department has made large strides, although judged by the standard of the most progressive countries in Europe, it may still be found to be wanting in some directions.

An illustrious Chemist thus eloquently advocates the claims of science on the attention of Government:—

"Englightened countries at last comprehend that all scientific research is a battle to be won, and that every victory increases national power. Intelligent nations no longer deny to scientific men, worthy the name of Captain, either arms for the conquest, soldiers devoted to their cause. or subsidies for their maintenance. Science is no longer an unrecognised power, of which, nevertheless, much is expected; to-day, every government which does nothing for it must expect to be vanquished by rivals, and to receive the censure of posterity for its want of forethought"—J. B. DUMAS, "Faraday Lecture."

Thirty years ago, while a student at Edinburgh, I began to notice that original contributions by Japanese students of Science had become a prominent feature in the Journals of the London and Berlin Chemical Societies. Here was an Asiatic people, who could scarcely look back to a glorious past, adding to the world's stock of knowledge; while India, the land of Buddha, which through the medium of China had contributed in no small degree to the civilization of Japan, was sleeping the sleep of ages. This thought had often filled me alternately with pangs of despair as also with emulation. It is a matter for sincere congratulation that contributions from our advanced post-graduate students now bulk largely in the pages of the Chemical Journals of England, Germany and America, and are beginning to shed lustre to the chemical laboratory of the Presidency College. It is not necessary to recount the names of the many past students who have worked here during the last twelve years, and some of whom are now holding chairs of Chemistry in Government Colleges of Bengal. I hope I shall be pardoned, however, if I give special prominence to the brilliant contributions of two of our latest toilers in the field—Messrs. Rasik Lal Datta and

Nilratan Dhar—both of whom have shown conspicuous talents and marked originality ; nor should I omit the name of Mr. Jitendranath Rakshit, who has recently been awarded a research grant by the London Chemical Society for his investigations on sodium di-acetamide, etc.* When the history of the progress of chemical research in India comes to be written the names of these three zealous investigators will naturally occupy a conspicuous place.

I cannot conclude this article without recording my sincere gratitude and obligations to Principal James for the warm and abiding interest he has always taken in the affairs of the Chemical Department. The difficulties which beset the path of a research student in science in India are many and often prove to be well nigh insurmountable. Mr. James has always done his best to smooth the path of the young workers and offer facilities to them. The progress of recent chemical research at the Presidency College is thus destined to be closely associated with his name.

---

* How highly some of these researches are esteemed will be evident from the following extract:—

"J. N. Rakshit (J. Amer. Chem. Soc., 1914, 36, 1221-1222) failed in his attempt to prepare tetra-amino-methane by the reduction of tetra-nitro-methane with nikel coated zinc and hydrochloric acid and also by tin and the latter acid, ammonia and guanidine being formed in each case. Two evidently appear to be the limit of the attachment of amino-groups to a single carbon atom, the additional nitrogen being usually present as a cyano or imino-group."—*Vide* "Notes on Recent Theory and Practice," by Herbert H. Hodgson, M.A., B.Sc., Ph. D.—*The Chemical World*, November 1914.

PURSUIT OF CHEMISTRY IN BENGAL

The following is the text of Dr. Ray's University Extension Lecture, delivered on the 10th January, 1916, at Calcutta:—

Modern Chemistry, by which I mean Scientific Chemistry, is only of yesterday's origin. It may be said to date from the time of Lavoisier, who, as you all know, was one of the earliest victims of the fanatical outburst which followed in the wake of the French Revolution. In England, just a century ago, Dalton and Davy were in the zenith of their fame. Germany, such as we now understand by the term, did not exist at all at this time as a political entity. It was composed of Prussia and a number of petty states warring against each other and all crushed in turn under the heels of Napoleon. The two great chemists, Liebig and Wohler, who were destined in after life to be the makers of modern German chemical greatness, were then mere lads. But, in France, the state of things was altogether different. The impetus given by Lavoisier's doctrine had spread far and wide, and a brilliant galaxy of experimenters including-Gay Lussac, Dulong, Thenard, Ampere, Arago and Chevreul were almost every day opening out new spheres of investigation; but their inestimable acquisitions found no soil, and could bear no fruit in unhappy Germany, where, to quote Liebig's own words, "it was a wretched time for chemistry." But, in the course of two decades, Liebig and Wohler by their epoch-making discoveries almost revolutionised the views of chemists on Organic Chemistry; in fact, one may go so far as to say that they *created* organic chemistry. Neither of these great apostles could catch inspiration in their native land. The former went to Paris to learn at the feet of Gay-Lussac, and the latter preferred to repair to Stockholm in 1823, to be initiated by the great Swedish chemist Berzelius. The fire which these great pioneer chemists borrowed from Paris and Stockholm was rekindled with vigour on their return to Germany and has been ever since burning with increased and dazzling brilliancy.

England, though she could boast of a Boyle, a Priestley, a Cavendish, a Dalton and a Davy, was, however, slow to follow in the wake of the chemical renaissance in France and Germany. Up till the forties of the last century she was found lagging behind in the race. Liebig who visited England in 1837, writing to Berzelius naively says: "England is not the land of science; her chemists were ashamed to call themselves chemists because the apothecaries had appropriated the name." According to Sir Edward Thorpe there were not in 1837 more than a couple of dozen persons in the British Isles altogether receiving systematic instruction in practical chemistry, and even that supply was probably fully equal to the demand. There was in fact little to tempt men to take up chemistry as a means of livelihood. Teacherships were few in number, analytical chemistry as a profession hardly existed, and chemical manufacturing was done by rule of thumb, and for the most part very badly done.

Such was the state of things in the forties in England in the last century, and such is the state of things in the India of to-day, so far as chemistry can offer attractions to young men as a means of livelihood. It is scarcely too much to say that 99% of our University students who take up chemistry do so simply because it happens to be a branch of the Science curriculum, and they have to give it up and forget all about it as soon as they have secured a degree. Yet in the midst of such discouraging and depressing circumstances we must cultivate our favourite science.

If we read carefully the history of the different branches of science we invariably find that they have attracted votaries in the early stages of their progress in the midst of almost insuperable difficulties. You all know that Copernicus held back the publication of his great book "On the Revolutions of the Heavenly Bodies" for 36 years for fear of giving offence to the all-powerful Church; that Bruno was burned at the stake for teaching the plurality of worlds, and Galileo visited with the terrors of the Inquisition for his vindication of the Copernican doctrine. Nay, Roger Bacon, one of the precursors of our own science, was thrown into prison and had to rot in a dingy cell of a cloister at Oxford for practising the Black Art, as chemistry was then called. Browning in his "Paracelsus" has delineated the wrestlings and inward longings of an ideal alchemist, who is only an honest seeker after truth, who pursues knowledge for its own sake irrespective of what it brings. Voltaire tells us that at the time of Newton's death there were not 20 readers of Principia out of Britain. These great and mighty interpreters of the laws of nature cared not for name or fame, but considered themselves lucky if only they could be instrumental in giving to the world the results of their life-long labours. Kepler had imposed upon himself years of incessant toil including midnight vigils in observing and recording the motions of heavenly bodies; and after embodying the results of his labours he exclaims, "I may well wait a hundred years for a reader, since God Almighty has waited six thousand years for an observer like myself."

If Europe is what she is to-day—if she is in the van of scientific progress—it is in no small measure due to the self-denying ordinances of these great heroes in science and their worthy successors.

I have been led to indulge in this digression because without a brief historical retrospect of the development of sciences in Europe much of what I am going to say will not be properly understood.

Those who intend to pursue chemistry in India must not expect to reap a rich harvest in the immediate or near future. India has been a *tabula rasa* so far as the cultivation of physical sciences is concerned for the last 1,000 years or perhaps more. In Germany or in England for the last 300 years—*i.e.*, from the time of Paracelsus and Basil Valentine and Newton and Boyle the lamp has been burning dimly in the early stages, but more and more brilliantly in the 18th and 19th centuries. We in the East, on the other hand, have been living in silent and ecstatic meditation. To the Hindu the material world is but an illusion and Sankara as an exponent of the Vedanta Philosophy is unsparing in his criticism and denunciation of the atomic theory as propounded in the Vaiseshika philosophy, ridiculing the author of the system itself as 'Kanada' or atom eater. No wonder M. Cousin in his "History of Philosophy" in giving an analysis of the Yoga philosophy and the Bhagavat-Gita, which he calls a monument of the greatest price, quotes such passages as these: "Science is superior to practice, and contemplation is superior to Science; prefer contemplation to Science, inaction to action, faith to work, etc.," and concludes by observing that as man despising himself has not been able to take any thought for recalling the memory of his actions there is no history of man, and no chronology in India. No wonder Mill should write: "The Hindu boys display marvellous precocity in appreciating a metaphysical proposition which would hopelessly puzzle an English lad."

Remember, gentlemen, what the transplantation of Western sciences in such a land and amidst such environments means. Those who are pioneers in this field have no traditions to go by or follow up; they have to chalk out their own path and formulate their own schemes and carry them out as best as they may. Difficulties arise at every turn but with faltering steps the weary pilgrim must keep marching on towards the goal; happy if he reaches it but equally happy if he perishes in the attempt.

This is the dawn of the year 1916—a memorable year—the centenary of the foundation of the old Hindu College, of which our own Presidency College is the direct and lineal descendant. I need not enter here into the merits of the bitter controversy between the Orientalists and the Anglicists, which ended in the triumph of the latter. The whirligig of time had brought on its own revenge. Rajah Ram Mohan Ray, the maker of modern India, who was the first to resusciate the Upanishads in Bengal and to translate some of them into English, and himself deeply imbued with the *Vedanta* doctrines, characterized Sanskrit learning as calculated to cause "a lamentable check to the diffusion of knowledge." "Nor will youths be fitted," cried this great Reformer, "to be better members of society by the Vedantic doctrines which teach them to believe that all visible things have no real existence, that as father, brother, etc., have no real entity, they consequently deserve no real affection, and therefore the sooner we escape from them and leave the world, the better." He, therefore, appealed to the then Governor-General, Lord Amherst, to discourage "such imaginary learning and employ European gentlemen of talent and education to instruct the natives of India in Mathematics, Natural Philosophy, Chemistry, Anatomy, and other useful Sciences, which the natives of Europe have carried to a degree of perfection that has raised them above the inhabitants of other parts of the world." These memorable words were uttered close upon a century ago; but they bear repetition even to-day.

In my article on the "Forty years of Chemistry at the Presidency College," published in the *Presidency College Magazine*, I have described the successive steps in the development of chemical teaching in Bengal and I need not take up your time by their useless recapitulation. Suffice it to say that for the first 60 years or more the intellectual *pabulum* of the Bengali youths was furnished by Shakespeare and Milton, Bacon and Locke and Hume and Gibbon. It is barely two decades since Bengal has seriously taken to original investigations in the fruitful field of chemistry. At my request, Mr. Rasik Lal Datta, one of the most devoted, assiduous and successful of our workers, has drawn up a fairly exhaustive list of contributions by Bengali chemists. It is found on reference to it that within this time as many as 130 communications have been sent from the chemical laboratory of the Presidency College alone. The laboratory of my friend, Professor Watson, is also responsible for two dozens or more papers.

Indeed, on opening the latest numbers of the Journals of the Chemical Societies of London and America one's eyes are regaled with the sight of an increasing number of papers by our own students and pupils, working in Bengal as also at the laboratories of the Imperial College of Science and Technology and the University College, London.

Gentlemen, I cannot here resist the temptation of alluding to an incident, the more so as my friend the Vice-Chancellor himself is mixed up with it, and I hope he will pardon me for what I am going to divulge, and will not regard it as a breach of confidence. As you all know, my friend and myself had the honour of representing our University at the Congress of Universities held in London in 1912. On the first day of the Session the main object of discussion was introduced by Principal Peterson of McGill University, with the reading of a paper of singular merit entitled, "Inter-university arrangements for Post-Graduate and Research Students." I arranged with my brother delegate whose oratorial gifts I have always envied ever since he was my school-mate now some forty years ago, that so far as making of speeches was concerned he should take upon himself all the burden leaving me a silent spectator and participator: he was, however, the first to give a go-by to this tacit understanding. "Now is our opportunity," he exclaimed, and he modestly added that this was a subject to which a student of science was calculated to do more justice. I hesitated and pleaded hard to be let off. My friend proved to be inexorable; he cut short my vacillation by tearing off a bit of the printed programme and putting down my name and forwarding it to the chairman (Lord Roseberry). Imagine my trepidation when in response to summons from the chair I ascended the platform, the more so as I was preceded by so great a master of Physical Science as Sir J. J. Thomson. I ventured to point out that the Indian degrees, based as they are upon teaching imparted in India, are often stamped with a badge of inferiority simply because they are labelled as "Indian ware!" Speaking with some degree of confidence about my own branch I further took the liberty to lay stress upon the fact that the contributions of our students were being hospitably received in the columns of the leading chemical Journals of Europe and America and I made bold to assert that their researches, if embodied in the shape of theses, would be readily accepted for a Doctorate in a European University. A distinguished chemist, whose name I am not at liberty to disclose, on going through the published papers of Mr. Nilratan Dhar, has expressed his opinion that he would not hesitate for a moment to award him a Doctorate, so far as his own University is concerned. Two of our late pupils, Messrs. Biman Behary Dey and Hemendra Kumar Sen Gupta, who have lately returned home after winning golden opinions of their Professors at the Imperial College of Science and the coveted distinction of the London D. Sc., may also be cited as instances. Messrs. Brojendranath Ghosh and Sudhamoy Ghosh, who have also just won Doctorates of the London and Edinburgh Universities respectively, on the basis of their theses have added lustre to the Dacca Laboratory. Mr. Anukul Chandra Sarkar, the first Ph. D. of our University in Chemistry, has amply proved that travelling abroad is by no means a *sine qua non* for completing one's chemical education. Mr. Rasik Lal Datta has also preferred to be a stay-at-home worker, at least for the present; he has already had about thirty published papers to his credit.

Datta's researches on the halogenation of organic compounds constitute a brilliant record and have added materially to our knowledge of the subject. From the abstract of a paper in the *Berichte*, which has appeared in the London Chemical Society's Journal, 1915, we learn that the German chemist Kempf has been anticipated by Datta, whose work is all-embracing and covers a wider field.

Physical Chemistry is yet in its infancy, but thanks to the labours of Ostwald, Arrhenius and others it is beginning to assert itself. To Mr. Nilratan Dhar, one of the most brilliant amongst our late pupils, belongs the credit of initiating work in this branch in our country, and it is gratifying to note that a monograph on complexions recently published in England quotes him as an authority. Messrs. Jnan Chandra Ghosh and Jnanendra Nath Mukherji are also devoted labourers in this field; the former is carrying on investigations on electrolysis by alternating current and the latter has taken up the fascinating subject of colloids; their researches are being regularly published in the Journal of the American Chemical Society.

Mr. Rajendra Nath De has shown in connection with his work on the molecular volumes of the hyponitrites that he has the making of a chemist in him. Nor should I omit to mention the name of Mr. Jitendranath Rakshit. As some of you may be aware, he was associated with me in the research on the isolation of the amine nitrites. Rakshit's papers on "The sodium derivatives of acid amides" show fertility of resources and marked originality. He has been receiving a grant from the Research Fund of the Chemical Society to enable him to continue the work. Mr. P. K. Dutt, also an old pupil of ours, has taken the M. Sc. degree of the University of Leeds on the strength of his thesis, I understand, on "The Progressive Bromination of Toluene." Mr. Dutt is now engaged in research work there in connection with the manufacture of explosives. The mention of Leeds raises in my mind pleasant associations. The chief town of York has often been a place of pilgrimage for our advanced students, and Professors Cohen, Green and Smithells have always been ready there with their welcome and genial hospitality.

I need not proceed further. What has been said above will suffice to prove that Physical Science, though an exotic plant, has like the potato taken kindly to the soil of Bengal. Four centuries ago, Vasudeva Sarbabhauma and his illustrious pupil, Raghunatha Siromani, founded the famous school of *Navya Naya* (Modern Logic) at Navadwipa, whose *tols* even now attract pupils from distant parts of

India. Paradoxical as it may seem this province of ours—the land *par excellence* of scholasticism and logic-chopping—has been equally propitious for the cultivation of Physical Sciences; and to point a moral and adorn a tale I have only to refer to the brilliant record of my distinguished colleague, Professor Bose, who has been as a beacon-light in his own Department and whose researches bid fair to be epoch-making.

Gentlemen, just 13 years ago in my "History of Hindu Chemistry" in the chapter devoted to the decline of scientific spirit in India, I lamented that the spirit of inquiry had died out amongst a nation naturally prone to speculation and metaphysical subtleties. Little did I dream then that in the course of a decade or so I should have to revise the estimate I then formed of the capacities of my own countrymen and chronicle that a bright chapter is about to dawn in our life history.

It is scarcely necessary now to enter into an elaborate *apologia* for the cultivation of our own science. Even the man in the street realises that the battles which are being daily fought and the new surprises sprung upon the wondering public in connection with this the greatest war since the creation of the world have had their rehearsals in the laboratories of chemists. Nor need I allude to the part which chemistry is destined to play in the industrial development and progress of a country. You have only to read the articles, correspondences and controversies which are going on in the columns of "Nature." We in Bengal are lamentably backward in commercial and industrial pursuits and have almost become a bye-word of contempt and reproach to our more fortunate brethren in Bombay, which can boast of merchant princes and captains of industry. Perhaps it may be excusable in me to point out that we have an humble and unpretending object lesson in our infant indigenous chemical undertaking; it shows at any rate that something can be done even in Bengal when science is wedded to industry. Some of you may be aware that the Bengal Chemical and Pharmaceutical Works had its birth and early struggles in the dark and dingy rooms of a house not far from this place and that it started with the modest sum of Rs. 800/-. With the recent expansions which have already been taken in hand it will soon cover an area of 24 bighas (8 acres) and its present capital of 5 lakhs will have to be doubled with a view to the installation of new plants. It has always been a fixed principle with the Directors of this business not to take in any one as a chemist whose knowledge is not up to the M. Sc. standard of our University. There is another matter—rather of a delicate nature—which may not be passed over in silence. The works has been conceived, initiated and managed solely by Bengali brains, energy and pluck and it has never been necessary to call in the aid of any foreign "experts." Perhaps you may be interested to know that owing to the serious dislocation in chemical trade due to the war and the stoppage of supplies from

Germany it has been doing a roaring business in some lines; *e.g.*, magnesium sulphate is being turned out by tons and a consignment has been shipped to England; it has also been its privilege to be of some little help to Government in the matter of supply of acids, etc., for munition. If I have at all referred to this chemical works in my address it is only to demonstrate that the successful application of science to industry is by no means incompatible with Bengali genius.

I have always been reluctant to appeal to the sordid instincts of man in giving a stimulus to the cultivation of science. I prefer to take our stand on a higher platform. The heroes of science some of whose names have been mentioned in the earlier part of my address have always pursued their favorite branches with a singleness of purpose and without an eye to material gains and neither penury nor persecution could damp their ardour and they have left priceless legacies as the common heritage of mankind. As a new light flashes across the mind of the inquirer or as he hits upon a novel discovery which has made him lose his sleep and appetite for days and months, he is seized with ineffable joy often bordering upon delirium and unconscious of all that is around him is led to exclaim—*Eureka.* The vocation of a student of science is sacred—he is a citizen of the world—he transcends all artificial barriers of race and nationality.

In a country like India, where the ignorance

and illiteracy of the mass of the people are simply appalling and where every natural phenomenon from the eclipse of the moon to the breaking out of a plague is apt to be ascribed to providential interference or divine wrath, the cultivation of physical sciences is of special importance. Buckle somewhere aptly observes that a nation perfectly ignorant of physical laws will refer to supernatural causes all the phenomenon by which it is surrounded and that other things being equal, the superstition of a nation must always bear an exact proportion to the extent of its physical knowledge. The late Lord Salisbury, who, if I mistake not, was an amateur chemist and who used to seek solace and relaxation from his busy political life in his private laboratory, observed on a memorable occasion that "even from the social point of view chemistry has undoubtedly this claim, that it is one of the most powerful agents that has moved the world, that the application of a science of that kind to the national mind by constant familiarity with its teachings, by constant knowledge of its achievements, is of the highest human value. It teaches the mind the immortal difference between guessing and knowing. And the farther chemistry goes on and the more it asserts the superiority of its ways and canons in all departments of human thought, so far shall we drive guessing to a distance and be satisfied with nothing but what we can know."

Modern India's contribution to the world's stock

of scientific knowledge is almost *nil*, only the first sod has been turned. What little has been done represents only the feeble individual attempts of a limited number of stray workers scattered at isolated centres. There is only a hopeful indication that the spirit of research is abroad. We have unfortunately no guarantee, and, as yet no provision has been made that the continuity of the work begun will be kept up. In Science, we are almost three centuries behind the European nations and we have to make up for the lost ground. It should not be left to the chance or haphazard caprice or convenience of a solitary worker here or there, whose exit from the scene by death or retirement may spell the extinction of the spirit of research thus awakened. Moreover, the average Professor in an affiliated College is an overworked man. The head of the institution Shylock-like exacts from him the drudgery of th routine work and it is only by sacrificing the holi ıys that he can expect to do some work; and there is after all but one single properly equipped College with very limited accommodation, which is affiliated to the University up to the M. Sc. standard. Every year the gates of scientific learning are cruelly barred against scores of eager aspirants knocking for admission. Add to this that there is but a single Government Research Scholarship in Science annually available to the advanced student. When all these are taken into consideration the wonder is that so much has been done with so little help and such meagre materials. Surely, a state of things like this is not creditable to Bengal (including, of course, Behar and Orissa) with a population of eighty millions. A vast amount of potential research talent is lying unutilised and running to sheer waste. It is for these reasons that I have always looked upon the University College of Science as the materialisation of a dream of my life. Here the Professors relieved from the tedium of routine work will have ample time at their disposal to devote to post-graduate teaching, but their main function will be to undertake and teach *research*. And the several departments working in healthy emulation and co-operation will create a scientific atmosphere. The pious founders of the endowments have with commendable foresight taken care to make ample provision for fellowships and scholarships, which will be bestowed only upon such advanced students as have already given proof of their capacity for undertaking original investigation. It would be idle to disguise the unpalatable fact that unless the Palit and Ghosh endowments are adequately supplemented, the Science College will not be in a position to start fully on its active career. I hope Bengal has not seen the last of her great benefactors to our University. I trust another Palit or Ghosh will open his purse-strings in this our hour of dire need. I appeal to our Government which has done so much in the past for the progress of education to come forward with a liberal grant.

Gentlemen, I am afraid I have already exhausted your patience. One word more and I have done. I spoke of Physical Science as an exotic plant in India. Perhaps, I should modify or qualify the expression. Ancient India was the cradle of mathematical and chemical Sciences and I have narrated in my "History of Hindu Chemistry" how these filtered to Europe through the medium of the Arabs. Indeed, the first Faraday lecturer of the Chemical Society in the introductory part of his lecture observes: "What an awakening for Europe! After two thousand years, she found herself again in the position to which she had been raised by the profound intellect of India, and the genius of Greece." Remember it is to India that the place of honour has been thus assigned by the illustrious French chemist, Jean Baptiste Andre Dumas. I hope it will be hers once more to hold aloft the torch of Science and assert her true place in the comity of nations.

POSSIBILITIES OF CHEMICAL INDUSTRIES IN INDIA

The following is the full text of the address delivered by Dr. Ray at the Industrial Exhibition at Baroda, January, 1917.

The development of chemical industries is dependent on the economic utilisation of the bye-products and can only proceed *pari passu* with the general industrial development and educational advancement of the country. The simultaneous growth of a system of interdependent industries is essential so that the bye-products in one industry may be profitably utilised in another. The growth will necessarily be slow, but when the foundation will have been successfully established on a continuous chain of connection, the progress will be steady and sure. The total production of coal tar colours in Germany now comes to over £50,000,000 annually and the industry as it stands to-day is the result of over forty-years of continuous research work and of untiring manufacturing and merchandising effect and development. The coal tar colour industry has now become essentially a German industry and the success is attributable to a large extent to the growth of a chain of allied industries in which the bye-products of the great colour industry are most economically utilised.

It will be seen from the trade returns of British India that United Kingdom contributes a considerable portion of the total imports of heavy chemicals in India.

The principal heavy chemicals which constitute the bulk of the total imports from the United Kingdom are—

1913-14	Quantity (Cwts.)	Value (£)
Carbonate of Soda (Soda ash and Soda crystals)...	422,720	106,054
Bicarbonate of Soda ...	86,353	28,244
Caustic Soda ...	91,018	53,871
Other Soda Compounds	27,958	13,520
Bleaching Materials...	58,062	25,427

The soda compounds came almost exclusively from the United Kingdom.

The most important chemicals which are required in the many industries in India, and for the matter of that in every country, are alkalis and sulphuric acid. They are required by themselves in the manufacturing processes connected with many industries as well as for the manufacture of other chemicals. In fact, it has very aptly been said that sulphuric acid is the mother of all industries. The importance of the local manufacture of alkalis is still more emphasised by the fact that the bye-products, *viz.*, hydrochloric acid and chlorine, are essentially required for the preparation of a series of chemicals, the various chlorides and bleaching materials which are so important for daily consumption in the textile and paper mills and for various other industries in India.

The manufacture according to modern processes of the alkali and compounds of soda named above has not been taken up in India. Practically the whole of these compounds, the bleaching materials and various chlorides required for Indian consumption are imported. Consequently, any shortage of production in the United Kingdom leading to restricted imports into India may seriously handicap many industries.

Caustic Soda.—Caustic soda apart from feeding the chlorine Industries by its bye-products is itself essentially necessary in many industries in India, the most prominent among them being (1) manufacture of soap, (2) refining of oils, (3) dyeing, (4) manufacture of paper-pulp.

Soap.—The manufacture of soap in its various branches (toilet soap, household washing soap, laundry soap, etc.) is comparatively a new industry in India. But already there are indications of its growing expansion. With the spread of education and with the growth of ideas of sanitation this industry with its advantages in raw materials will probably expand. Up to now the work done in this direction is insignificant and up-hill.

For trade purposes the import of soap falls under three heads. The imports under these heads in 1913-14 shown below will indicate India's requirements.

		Cwts.	
(a) Household and laundry soap (in bars or tablets)	...	301,369	314,511
(b) Toilet soap	...	45,339	166,194
(c) Other sorts	...	16,152	19,695

It is remarkable that of the total imports of soap (362,860 cwts.), imports from the United Kingdom alone stood at 350,703 cwts. or, in other words, nearly 97% of the total imports came from the United Kingdom. This predominant position of the United Kingdom is due to her cheap alkali, the command over the soap-producing oils and to her capability of utilising the bye-product, namely glycerine. India is rich in oilseeds, and her export trade in oilseeds is very large. Even if the oils for soap making are produced here largely, absence of cheap alkali and our inability to utilise the waste liquors for recovery of glycerine are great obstacles to the development of soap industry.

Paper Pulp.—Pulp of wood or other materials imported for the purpose of paper making in India amounted to 247,636 cwts. valued at £115,800 in 1913-14. This quantity is consumed in the few paper mills in India which cannot even meet a small percentage of India's paper requirements. Materials for manufacture of paper-pulp are largely available in India, and high price of caustic soda, bleaching powder and other alkali products stand in the way of the manufacture of paper pulp.

There is yet another industry with considerable

possibilities which has not been undertaken in India and in which large quantities of caustic soda are required. The use of aluminium utensils for various purposes is gradually becoming popular in this country. But the aluminium metal for this purpose is wholly imported. This is anomalous for a country where the raw material for the purpose occurs in abundance. Thr first stage of the manufacture is extraction of alumina from bauxite with alkali and the second stage is the manufacture of the metal from alumina. Bauxite of good quality occurs in India near Jubbulpore.

India abounds in forests and jungles and the distillati on of wood may prove to be a profitable business—the products of distillation being acetic acid, wood-spirit (methyl alcohol) and acetone with charcoal as a bye-product.

From the foregoing observations it will be seen that local manufacture of alkali is urgently necessary to meet gradually increasing requirements for the development of other Chemical Industries. The raw materials are available or can be made available in India. The difficulty of obtaining cheap electric power is not insuperable. The Hydro-Electric Scheme for the supply of cheap electric power in the Bombay mills is an indication of advancement in this direction. The most important is that unless the manufacture is conducted on a very large scale economical production of the alkalies and of the various bye-products, so as to compete with imported articles, is believed to be impossible.

The capital already sunk in the alkali works in England is enormous and from the Indian point of view simply colossal. The profits made by one firm alone last year exceeded a million pounds sterling. Unless a captain of industry with the genius and resources of a Tata were to enter the field, I am afraid, there is very poor chance of success.

By harnessing the Cauvery the Government of Mysore has secured a supply of cheap electric power which is now utilised mainly in the Kolar Gold Fields but which may also be diverted to the manufacture of chemicals.

The subject of alkali manufacture and its bearing on the general industrial development has been briefly dealt with. It has been already said that the extent of industrial development of a country is indicated by its requirements of sulphuric acid. This is a subject on which I can speak with some personal experience.

There are two principal factors which stand out prominently as bar against the development of the sulphuric acid and consequently to the alkali and chlorine industries. One of these is due to natural causes—the absence of suitable Iron or Copper Pyrite mine which supplies the sulphur content, the chief content, of sulphuric acid. There is a move now in the right direction and the country is being searched for Pyrite mines and some day one may find workable Pyrite in the Central Provinces or in the Santhal Pergannas, those hitherto sealed treasuries of India's mineral wealth. Pyrite has to be imported and one may look forward to a near future, to the introduction of Pyrite sulphuric acid. We are making all throughout in India and Burma small quantities of sulphuric acid from sulphur, technically called crude sulphur but which is practically a pure product containing 98 per cent. sulphur. The price of sulphuric acid made therefrom is necessarily very high. But even if we find Pyrite locally or import conveniently yet there is that other bar, that of transport difficulty, and heavy railway freights; that appears to be insurmountable. If sulphuric acid were made at Calcutta or Bombay as cheap as at London, yet for you at Baroda it will make little difference in cost whether you import from Bombay or from London, taking into consideration the heavy railway freights common to both and the high charge of acid proof vessels.

Fertilisers and Superphosphates.—One of the uses of cheap sulphuric acid is for the manufacture of fertilisers; notably the manufacture of superphosphates from bones the use of which, however, has not yet become popular in India on account of absence of education of the agricultural population in the matter of "intensive cultivation." Yet India has recently purchased 2,000 tons of superphosphates half of which is coming from Osaka. India exports large quantities of bones annually. Her total exports during 1913-14 amounted to 105,413 *tons* valued at £ 522,233. This enormous quantity of bones is going out of the country for conversion into fertiliser elsewhere. This is an indirect loss to the soil of India and the condition is alarming. This loss is, however, unavoidable till the agricultural population realises the utility of the fertiliser. Meanwhile the country should be able to manufacture superphosphates and export them instead of the raw bones and importing bone superphosphates. Here again, absence of cheap supply of sulphuric acid is a handicap.

Ammonium Sulphate—This is being manufactured at present to a limited extent in certain places in connection with gasworks and bye-product recovery in coke-ovens. Ammonium sulphate manufactured in India is being used locally in sugar cane plantations and some amount is also being exported to Ceylon and Strait Settlements. With a large number of coke-ovens, and cheap supply of sulphuric acid there is prospect of the industry going ahead.

Oil Products.—There is a large export trade in oil cakes from India. They are castor, cocoanut, groundnut, linseed, cotton cake and other sorts of cakes. The total export in 1913-14 amounted to the large quantity of 3,506,272 cwts. valued at £ 920,249. This is no doubt a valuable trade for India, but this large figure shows that the use of oil cakes as fertiliser has not become popular in India. This is due to ignorance of the agricultural population. Total export of oils of castor, cocoanut, groundnut, linseed and cotton amounted to the figure of 2,491,535 gallons. A great part of this amount could be converted into various oil products and exported as such instead of in the condition of raw oil. It is remarkable that India is a large producer of cotton seed, but she exports most of the seeds instead of building up a large industry of cotton oil and cotton oil products. The export of cotton seed from India in 1913-14 amounted to 5,686,533 cwts. valued at £1,416,743, whereas she exported only 2,507 gallons of oil valued at £347. The cotton oil industry is in its infant stage in India. The oil is valuable for soap making. The oil itself by proper refining process can be made a valuable edible oil. The main difficulty is that as long as the cotton cake does not find a ready market in India the manufacture of the oil locally is not likely to prove profitable.

We may learn a good deal from the history of the cotton oil industry in the United States of America which produces a large amount of cotton seeds. As far back as 1834 the settlers in the United States utilised most of the seeds as manures and only a meagre portion was expressed for oil, which was used for burning and painting. During the period of the American civil war attention was turned to the expression of the seeds and since then its trade is continually increasing.

The oil contains certain volatile principles which caused a disagreeable odour when the oil was used for cooking and created natural prejudices. The oil was made edible by removing the volatile principles and by improving its flavour and consequently the industry made a rapid stride. This was the chemist's service and we find that in 1913 nearly 76 per cent. of the entire crop was expressed for oil which fetched about 49 crores of rupees. The chemist was not satisfied with his triumph and has now converted the liquid oil, an unsaturated body, by hydrogenization into a saturated substance which is a solid fat and has proved to be a better substitute for animal fat used in cooking.

The oil cake obtained in that country has been found to be a good cattle food, having the food value of low-grade hay. The price of the cake varies according to its quality but generally it is a rupee per maund.

It will thus be seen that a vast amount of profit is derived from the cotton seeds and it has been calculated that the chemist has added from Rs. 30 to Rs. 35 to the value of the crop for every bale of cotton grown. Considering the fact that India grows about 5 million bales of cotton we are only left to shudder at the immensity of loss that we are suffering on account of our ignorance and incapacity.

Elementary Education of the agricultural population is essential for the improvement of agricultural conditions in general in India and it is a matter for sincere congratulation that the enlightened state of Baroda is forging ahead in this direction. One acre of land in Java produces cane which gives 3.44 tons of sugar whereas in India one acre yields cane capable of producing only about 1.3 tons of sugar.

Tanning Industry—India is one of the largest suppliers of raw hides to the world. The export of total hides and skins (raw) from India in 1913-14 amounted to 1,602,310 cwts. valued at £7,990,882. There is some export trade in leather, tanned or dressed, mainly from Madras and Bombay. This leather is only half tanned by bark and is subjected to further tanning on arrival in foreign countries. The industry of chrome tanning is of recent growth in India. There is great scope for its development.

Tannin Extract—India abounds in tannin materials. The most prominent are myrobalans, babal bark, wattle bark, avaram bark, mangrove bark, etc. Tannin extracts can be made in India and exported to other countries.

Starch—Import of starch into India under head 'starch and farina,' in 1913-14, amounted to 101,967 cwts. valued at £65,606. Starch is required mostly in cotton and paper mills for sizing. Starch generally used is obtained from wheat, potato, rice or maize. Some starch derivatives, such as dextrine, are also used considerably, especially for soft dressing.

India is *par excellence* the country for cereals and starch ought to be manufactured in extensive quantity for export.

Some of the other chemicals required for various industrial purposes are—

Potassium Compounds.—Cyanide of potassium imported from United Kingdom during 1913-14 amounted to 5,239 cwts. valued at £22,657. Other potassium compounds imported amounted to 8,733 cwts. valued at £15,812. Of this, United Kingdom contributed 3,318 cwts., Germany 3,225 cwts. and Italy 1,320 cwts. The rest came from other countries. Potassium compounds are used in the manufacture of soft soap, potash glass, in textile and dyeing processes and as manures. Stassfurt in Germany is the chief source of world's potash supply. Potash deposits occur in the salt range of the Punjab, but they are of very poor quality.

Ammonia and Ammonium Salts.—Of the total imports to the amount of 13,340 cwts. in 1913-14, United Kingdom alone contributed 12,985 cwts. valued at £28,428. The manufacture of ammonium sulphate in India has already been referred to.

Carbide of Calcium.—Total import in 1913-14 amounted to 19,998 cwts. valued at £14,474 of which 2,783 cwts. came from United Kingdom and 10,901 cwts. from Germany. Its manufacture does not appear to present special difficulties provided a cheap supply of electric power is available.

Disinfectants.—Total import in 1913-14 amounted to 25,395 cwts. valued at £26,394, of which 23,815 cwts. valued at £24,599 came from United Kingdom alone. Germany contributed only 623 cwts. valued at £1,045. The source of practically all disinfectants is coal tar distillation products. Coal tar is made in very small quantities in India and no attempt has hitherto been made to distil what little tar is produced in this country.

Industrial Alcohol.—There is a very large import trade from Java in this article. Java makes huge quantities of alcohol from molasses which it gets as a bye-product in its sugar factories. There are hardly any sugar factories here working on a large scale and almost all the alcohol that is made here is used as liquor. The price of molasses is high and would not warrant manufacture of cheap alcohol. But we need not look to molasses for alcohol having an abundant supply of mohua. The sugar content of mohua is identical to that of molasses whereas its price is only half. There is no reason why mohua should be permitted to be exported as food for cattle and pigs and not utilised in the manufacture of spirits. Representing one of the Pharmaceutical Works I have had to feel keenly the want of rectified spirit cheap enough to be utilised for manufacture of tinctures and other medicinal preparations. It only needs an enterprising organiser to establish this industry.

There has been a dearth of organic dye-stuff employed in our textile and leather industries and also of other chemicals used in medicine, while there has been a constant demand of chemicals made in India from outside, owing to the present war. It is chiefly this cause, aided by our Swadeshi awakening, that has made us feel the necessity of developing our chemical industry. In this respect, however, we must be guided by prudence and also by the experiences of other countries. Let me be more clear.

An undertaking for starting a factory for the production of dyestuff and fine chemicals would be futile and is foredoomed to failure and disappointment. Even in England and America, where there are already such industries in existence and where the people are feeling still more keenly the scarcity of these, there is still some hesitation among a section of the people for further attempt towards the advancement of the industry, because of the competition of Germany. Let me quote from the presidential address delivered by Professor Perkin, perhaps the highest authority in England on Organic Chemistry and the worthy son of the first discoverer of the aniline dyes, at the Annual Meeting of the Chemical Society of London, held in 1915, to illustrate this. He says, "I am inclined to think that we must be prepared to face the certainty that some years must elapse before we can compete successfully against organisations which have taken years to develop and bring to perfection. Many of us hold the view that in order to prevent underselling and other methods of competition, the Government ought to protect the new venture for ten years at least by placing an import duty of not less than 25 per cent. on all German dyes and other organic products."

Let me also give you an idea of the enormous German organisation by giving a few figures, regarding the Badische Anilin and Soda Fabrik, one of the big German companies. For transportation within the plant the company utilises 42 miles of rail road.

Its water works supply 10 billions gallons yearly and its ice factory 12,000 tons of ice. It has four hundred steam engines and five hundred electric motors, nearly as many telephone stations, and 25 steam fire engines. It has a frontage on the Rhine of one and a half miles and handles sulphuric acids in tank steamers. In about the year 1908, it employed 217 chemists, 142 civil engineers, 8,000 workmen and a commercial staff of 918.

Another dye industry, the Farbwerke, vormals Meister, Lucius & Bruning, in Hochst, employs 350 chemists, 150 engineers and technical experts, 600 clerks and about 10,000 workmen.

There are such four great and eighteen smaller companies in Germany involved in dyestuff industry, and in addition to these there are Kahlbaum, Merck, Schering, de Haen and a host of others engaged in producing fine chemicals. So that the number of research chemists alone in all the factories, we believe, would come up to several thousands.

Under these circumstances, we can only profitably direct our energies in other channels where we have already found some indications of success. India exports annually from 12 to 14 crores of rupees worth of practically raw hides and skins. Bark tanning of a crude sort is done in Madras by *chamars* but experts are of opinion that the unscientific process adopted by them only deteriorates the quality of the skin. India again exports considerable amount of dyeing and tanning materials.

Here we have to open the first dismal chapter in the economic condition of our country. We have an abundant supply of raw materials both in] hides and tannin yielding barks and fruits and yet we remain contented with talking things aloud. It is an act of national folly and crime to allow a single raw hide or skin to leave our shores, which has not been properly turned into the finished leather. If we take the average price of a raw skin at Rs. 1-12 and that of a properly tanned leather at Rs. 7, a very moderate price, a simple calculation will show that we in our helplessness and ignorance allow about 50 crores of rupees per annum to slip out of our hands.

Patience and perseverance should be our watch words. Rome was not built in a day. More than two centuries and a half ago, England produced a Newton and a Boyle and in the nineteenth century a Faraday and a Kelvin. In Germany, again, Agricola who has been called the Father of Mineralogy was born in 1494 being the contemporary of Paracelsus the Great. The celebrated Glauber who was born in 1604 wrote his encyclopædic work—" The Prosperity of Germany "—in six volumes, in which he pointed out that the application of science to industry would be the means of bringing forth untold wealth to his Fatherland. The self-sacrifice and assiduity of Bernard Palissy, the founder of modern art pottery, are known to all of you. The services rendered to ceramics by Pott who died in 1692, are no less invaluable. " The mode of preparation of the Meissen porcelain being naturally kept secret, the King of Prussia instructed the celebrated chemist Pott to determine the nature of materials used, and he, being unable to obtain any satisfactory explanation, was obliged to investigate the properties of those substances which might possibly be used in the manufacture, mixed in varied proportions; for this purpose Pott is said to have made no less than thirty thousand experiments. To these we are mainly indebted for the establishment of the reactions which occur when various minerals are heated, and much valuable information applicable to the manufacture of porcelain was thus obtained."

Very few of us realize the training that is necessary and the research that has to be done before success can be achieved. The Badische Company spent seventeen years completing the indigo work after the first synthesis, and expended about a crore and half rupees before a pound was put on the market.

Like the other advanced nations we must pass through a probationary and evolutionary period and should not be in a hurry to reap the fruit before we sowed the seed.

Local conditions and the genius of the people should determine which particular industry should be chosen. Jute mills flourish on the banks of the Hooghly; for cotton mills, Bombay and Central Provinces offer greater facilities. For tobacco manuacture, Rungpore, Cooch Behar. Tirhut and the adjoining districts are favourable. For the metallurgy of aluminium, not only proximity to the ore, bauxite, but also to water powers should be looked for as already pointed out. In this respect, the location of the Tata Iron Works has been almost an ideal one. Not only is there limitless supply of superior quality of hæmatite, but coal and limestone are within very easy reach. Local circumstances will often secure a monopoly for peculiar industries, provided, of course, the people are advanced in scientific attainments. In Germany, the Stassfurt mines contain an almost inexhaustible deposit of potash and magnesium salts. The blockade of Germany has resulted in the cutting off of this supply of these two chemicals. The entire world, including America, is now suffering from what has been called a "potash famine." Potash is not only a basis for many important chemicals, *e.g.*, bichromate of potash, permanganate of potash, but in a crude form is an essential constituent for manures. Magnesium sulphate is largely consumed in the textile industries. Before the war broke out this chemical used to sell at Rs. 3-8 per cwt. The post-war price has fluctuated between Rs. 9 to Rs. 15, and only a day or two before I left Calcutta, my firm (The Bengal Chemical and Pharmaceutical Works, Ltd.,) entered into a contract with the manager of one of the leading mills on your side for a few consignments at about Rs. 9 per cwt. The abnormally high price which now rules in the market for many fine chemicals, notably the aniline dyes, has no doubt given a stimulus to the starting of chemical industries in England. But in this respect it is necessary to exercise the utmost self-restraint and caution, otherwise the promoters of any hastily-got up scheme are sure to be landed into dangerous quagmires. As soon as peace is concluded, Germany will make a frantic effort to recapture her lost market and India along with other countries will be the unhappy dumping soil for the output of her factories. Such Industries alone should be taken in hand, which have a fair and reasonable chance of outliving foreign competition.

I need not tire your patience farther. I shall conclude with the pregnant words of His Highness the Gaekwar uttered at the Calcutta Industrial Conference 10 years ago,—words which are still ringing in my ears. "The industrial prosperity of a country may be said roughly to vary directly with its exports of manufactures and imports of raw materials; and inversely with the exports of raw produce and imports of manufactured goods. This is a safe and reliable canon of industrial economics. One most sad and prominent feature of the foreign trade of India is the constant excess of exports over imports which is not conducive to the prosperity of the people.

"Famine, increasing poverty, widespread disease —all these bring home to us the fact that there is some radical weakness in our system and that something must be done to remedy it. But there is another aspect of the matter and that is that this economic problem is our last ordeal as people. *It is our last chance.*

"Fail there, and what can the future bring us? We only grow poorer and weaker—more dependent on foreign help. We must watch our industrial freedom, fall into extinction and drag out a miserable existence as hewers of wood and drawers of water to any foreign power which happens to be our master.

"Solve that problem and you have a great future before you, the future of a great people worthy of your ancestors and of your old position among nations."

Ancient India was famous for her metallurgical skill: the wrought iron pillar close to the Kutub near Delhi, the iron beams in the temples of Puri and Kanarak and the iron pillar at Dhar excite the wonder and admiration of even modern experts. In my History of Hindu Chemistry, in the chapter devoted to the "Knowledge of Technical Arts, and Decline of the Scientific Spirit," I have discussed some of the causes which brought about our present abject condition. I shall quote one para:

"The arts being relegated to the low castes and the professions made hereditary, a certain degree of fineness, delicacy and deftness in manipulation was no doubt secured but this was done at a terrible cost. The intellectual portion of the community being then withdrawn from the active participation in the arts, the *how* and *why* of phenomena—the co-ordinaion of cause and effect—were lost sight of; the spirit of enquiry gradually died out among a nation naturally prone to speculation and metaphysical subtleties and India for once bade adieu to experimental and inductive sciences. Her soil was rendered morally unfit for the birth of a Boyle, a Descartes, or a Newton and her very name was all but expunged from the map of the scientific world."

In bringing my brief survey of the Chemical Industries to a close, I cannot but think of the many passages in which I have made mention of the difficulties in our way and the keen competition of industrial countries backed by superior scientific and technical skill. But this instead of damping our spirit should make us all the more resolute and cautious in our industrial undertakings. Already a beginning has been made. The youth of India will no longer tolerate to be told that he lacks this and lacks that. I see—I feel the fire of life burning in him. It requires a guiding impulse and a helping hand to lead him on the right path of industiral progress. That impulse and that help are being supplied by the enlightened states of Baroda and Mysore. And in the great honour you have done me by inviting me to be before you I read the throbbing impulse of that industrial progress that is animating you. You have already the nucleus of a chemical works here and I hope the name of your state will stand high in connection with the future industrial development of our land.

CHEMISTRY IN ANCIENT INDIA

The following is the full text of the address delivered by Dr. Ray before the Madras University in February, 1918.

I shall endeavour to unfold before you to-day a forgotten chapter in the history of the intellectual development of the Indian people, namely the cultivation of the Experimental Sciences. It is generally taken for granted that the Hindus were a dreamy, mystical people given to metaphysical speculation and spiritual contemplation. Due credit is, no doubt, assigned to them for the production of such priceless treasures as the Upanishads, the Six Systems of Philosophy, including the abstruse *Samkhya* and the *Gita*, with their transcendental teachings. But the fact that the Hindus had a very large hand in the cultivation of the exprimental sciences is hardly known in these days.

It should, however, be borne in mind that Experimental Sciences such as we now understand them are of very recent origin and growth, even in Europe.

The controversies of the Schoolmen in the Middle Ages lend colour to the theory that in approaching the discussion of the most evident truths of nature the learned men of Europe always avoided the test of appealing to experiments. As some of you are aware, a solemn discussion arose among the foundation members of the Royal Society as to whether a dead fish weighed more than a live one, though it never occurred to them that the solution of the problem lay in directly weighing a fish—live and dead. When the Royal Society was founded in 1662 by Boyle, Hooke, Christopher Wren and other students of Nature, Hobbes sneered at them as "experimentarians." If such was the respect for accurate knowledge even in England in the 17th century, we should not be justified in applying a rigid test to the knowledge of India in the past ages.

Experiments and observations constitute the fundamental bases of Sciences. It is naturally a relief to come across such dicta as laid down by two standard works on Hindu Chemistry, namely *Rasendrachintamani* by Ramchandra, and *Rasaprakasa Sudhakara* by Yasodhara, both belonging to the 13th or 14th century A.D.

Says the former :—"That which I have heard of learned men and have read in the Sastras but have not been able to verify by experiment I have discarded. On the other hand those operations which I have, according to the directions of my sage teachers, been able to perform with my own hands—those alone I am committing to writing.

"Those are to be regarded as real teachers who can verify by experiments what they teach—those are to be regarded as laudable disciples who can perform what they have learned—teachers and pupils, other than these are mere actors on the stage."

Yasodhara, the author of the latter, observes :— " All the chemical operations described in my book have been performed with my own hands—I am not writing from mere hearsay. Everything related is based upon my own conviction and observations."

The progress of chemical knowledge among the ancient nations has always had a fascination for me. The classical works of Thomson, Hoefer and Kopp have been my favourite companions ever since I was a student at Edinburgh now 35 years ago. In the course of my studies in this field I was naturally led to an inquiry into the exact position which India occupied therein, and with this view I undertook a systematic examination, from the chemical standpoint, of the Charaka, the Susruta, and such other standard works of the Ayurvedic and Iatro-Chemical periods as had escaped the ravages of time.

My investigations in this direction naturally brought me into communication with M. Berthelot some twenty-one years ago—a circumstance which proved to be a turning point, if I may say so, in my career as a student of the history of Chemistry. The illustrious French savant who was then the recognised leader of the chemical world, who has done more than any other person to clear up the sources and trace the progress of Chemical Science in the West, expressed a strong desire to know all about the contributions of the Hindus, and even went the length of making a personal appeal to me to help him with information on the subject. In response to his sacred call, I submitted to him, in 1898, a short monograph on Indian alchemy based chiefly on *Rasendrasara-samgraha,* a work which I have since then found to be of minor importance and not calculated to throw much light on the vexed question as to the origin of Hindu Chemistry. M. Berthelot not only did me the honour of reviewing it at length but very kindly presented me with a complete set of his monumental work, in three volumes, on the Chemistry of the Middle Ages, dealing chiefly with the Arabic and Syrian contributions on the subject, the very existence of which I was not till then aware of. On perusing the contents of these works I was filled with the ambition of supplementing them with one on Hindu Chemistry.

I confess, when I first entered into the self-imposed task, I was filled with misgivings for I apprehended that the materials were meagre and fragmentary. I set vigorously to the task. As I proceeded with my labour of love I was simply appalled by the number of old, worm-eaten Chemical Manuscripts which began to pour in from every quarter of India—from Madras, Tanjore, Ulwar, Kashmir, Benares, Katmundu (Nepal) and last but not least from Tibet—the Tanjur or the Encylopædia comprising the wisdom of India—being now accessible to us since the temporary occupation of Lhassa in 1904-05. I was filled with the ecstasy which a prospector feels when he suddenly comes across a vein of precious metal after years of fruitless efforts. The discovery of such unexpected and forgotten mine of wealth amply sustained me during the 12 years of the best period of my life although much difficulty was felt in apportioning my time between the demands of the library and the laboratory. I will now take you over to some of the results of my inquiry. In the various seats of learning in ancient India, along with other branches of literature and science, medicine also formed an important subject of study. Some 2500 years ago the University of Taxila, of Jivaka Komarvachcha, was studying medicine under the sage Atreya. Now, there is a world of meaning hid under the term "Komarvachcha," which is a Pali corruption of the Sanskrit "Kaumarabhritya." A student of Ayurveda is well aware that the science of Indian medicine is divided into eight sections of which "kaumarabhritya" or treatment of children's diseases is one. Jivaka afterwards became the celebrated Court Physician to King Bimbisara of Magadh, a contemporary of Buddha. We have thus historical evidence of the cultivation of Ayurveda in India several centuries before the birth of Christ. Now the branch of science which I have the honour to represent, namely *Rasayana*, cannot, however, be traced to such an early date. Strictly speaking, Rasayana does not mean Chemistry. Its radical meaning is a medicine which promotes longivity, retentive memory, health, virility, etc. (Charaka, ch. 1,

2·6); in other words, it is the *Elixir Vitæ* of the alchemists of the Middle Ages. Later on, in the Tantric ages, Rasayana was almost exclusively applied to the employment of mercury and other metals in medicine and at present it means *alchemy* or *chemistry*. In an alchemical treatise of the 13th or 14th century A.D., the author speaks of his subject as "*Rasayanividya*," *i.e.*, the science of mercury and metals. In the celebrated work called *Rasaratna-samuchchaya* (or a collection of gems of mercury and metals), to which I shall have occasion to refer more than once subsequently, the author begins by offering salutation to 27 adepts or "*Rasasiddhipradyaka*." The term *Rasasiddhipradayaka* is derived from *rasa*, mercury, *siddhi*, accomplishment, and *pradayaka*, giver or bestower; it therefore means giver of accomplishment in mercurial preparation, *i.e.*, an expert on alchemy. It is necessary to bear in mind that in the standard Ayurvedic works, *e.g.*, *Charaka*, *Susruta* and *Vagbhata*, there is scarcely any mention of mercury or its preparations.

Here it is necessary to make a slight digression in order to realise the impetus which the study of Chemistry received in ancient India. In Europe, in the middle ages, chemistry—call it alchemy if you like—made considerable progress chiefly as a handmaid of medicine. In our country, though the pursuit of this science was made an auxiliary to the healing arts, it made rapid strides by entering into an alliance with the Yoga philosophy. According to this system, as you all know, knowledge has to go through seven stages before it is perfect and eight means are prescribed by which this perfect knowledge can be obtained; of these *Dharana* (steadfastness), *Dhyana* (contemplation) and *Samadhi* (meditation) are the essential constituents. When these last three are united, *samayama* follows and results in the acquisition of occult powers (or *siddhi*). In later times, the philosophy of the Yoga was pressed into the service of science and degenerated into Tantrika rites, especially in Bengal.

What is it that made these Tantras the repositories of chemical knowledge? The answer is given in the words of *Rasarnava* (lit. sea of mercury) itself, a most authoritative Tantric work on chemistry, which has been edited in the *Bibliotheca Indica Series* by myself in collaboration with Pandit Harischandra Kaviratna. This work extols the virtues of mercury and its various preparations. Thus,

"As it is used by the best devotees for the highest end, it is called *parada* (quick-silver)."

"Begotten of my limbs, it is, O Goddess, equal to me. It is called *rasa* because it is exudation of my body."

"It may be urged that the literal interpretation of these words is incorrect, the liberation in this life being explicable in another manner. This objection is not allowable, liberation being set out in the six systems as subsequent to the death of the body, and upon this there can be no reliance and consequently no activity to attain to it free from misgivings. This is also laid down in the same treatise."

"Liberation is declared in the six systems to follow the death of the body."

"Such liberation is not cognised in perception like an emblic myrobalan fruit in hand."

"Therefore a man should preserve that body by means of mercury and of medicaments."

A few more typical extracts are given below which will throw further light on the subject:—

"The body, some one may say, is seen to be perishable, how can then its permanency be effected? Think not so, it is replied, for though the body, as a complexus of six sheaths or wrappers of the soul, is dissoluble, yet the body as created by Hara and Gauri under the names of mercury and mica may be perdurable. Thus it is said in the *Rasahridaya.*

"Those who without quitting their bodies have attained to new ones through the influence of Hara and Gauri (mercury and mica), are to be praised as *Rasasiddha* (alchemists). All mantras are at their services."

"The ascetic, therefore, who aspires to liberation in this life, should first make to himself a glorified body. And inasmuch as mercury is produced by the creative conjunction of Hara and Gauri (and mica is produced from Gauri), mercury and mica are severally identified with Hara and Gauri in the verse:—

"Mica is thy seed, and mercury is my seed. The

combination of the two, O Goddess, is destructive of death and poverty."

"There is very little to say about the matter. In the *Rasesvarasiddhanta*, many among the gods, the Daityas, the Munis and mankind, are declared to have attained to liberation in this life by acquiring a divine body through the efficacy of quicksilver."

"Certain gods, Mahesa and others, certain Daityas, Kavya (Sukracharyya, and others); certain sages (Balakhilyas and others); certain kings (Somesvara and others); Govinda-Bhagabata, Gavindanayaka, Charpati, Kapila, Vyali, and others—these alchemists having attained to mercurial bodies and therewith identified are liberated though alive."

Now this alliance between alchemy and the Yoga Philosophy had already become cemented in the 11th century A.D. Thus, Alberuni, the celebrated Moslem contemporary of Mahmud of Gazni, who was as much at home in Arabic and Greek as in Sanskrit literature, says:

"The adepts in this art try to keep it concealed, and shrink back from intercourse with those who do not belong to them. Therefore, I have not been able to learn from the Hindus which methods they follow in this science and what element they principally use, whether a mineral or an animal or a vegetable one. I only heard them speaking of the process of sublimation, of calcination, of analysis, and of the waxing of talc, which they call in their language *talaka*, and so

I guess that the incline towards the mineralogical method of alchemy.

"They have a science similar to alchemy which is quite peculiar to them. They call it *Rasayana.* It means an art which is restricted to certain operations, drugs and compound medicines, most of which are taken from plants. Its principles restore the health of those who were ill beyond hope, and give back youth to fading old age, so that people become again what they were in the age near puberty; white hair becomes black again, the keenness of the senses is restored as well as the capacity for juvenile agility and the life of the people in this world is even extended to a long period. And why not? Have we not already mentioned on the authority of Patanjali that one of the methods leading to liberation is *Rasayana.*"

The number of works on alchemy which are connected with the practices of the Tantric cult is simply legion and they rose to such importance in the 11th to 14th centuries A.D., if not earlier, as to claim a place among the *Darsanas* (Philosophies) in vogue at this period. As you all know, the celebrated Madhavacharyya, Prime Minister of King Bukka I. of Vijayanagara, in his treatise on the sixteen systems of Philosophy extant in his age—called *Sarvadarsnasamgraha,* devotes a chapter to *Raseswaradarsana* or the "Science of Mercury." In his exposition of the subject the learned Head-Abbot of the Monastery of Sringeri, not far from the city of Madras, quotes at length from the standard works on Chemistry, notably Rasarnava, Rasesvarasiddhanta and Rasahridaya of Govind-Bhagabat.

I shall now read one or two extracts from *Rasarnava* from the chapter dealing with chemical apparatus and the colour of flames and the extraction of the metals from the ores (metallurgy). It is scarcely necessary to remind you that the Tantras are in the shape of Dialogues between the God Siva and his consort Parvati.

On Apparatus and the Colour of Flames.

"Sri Bhairava said:—The rasas, the uparasas, the metals, a piece of cloth, *bidam*, a pair of bellows, iron implements, stone pestles and mortars, the apparatus known as *koshti*, mouth blow-pipe, cow-dung, substantial wood (as fuel), various kinds of earthen and iron apparatus (*e.g.* crucibles), a pair of tongs and earthen and iron vessels, weights and balances, bamboo and iron pipes, the fats, the acids, the salts and the alkalis, the poisons—all these are to be collected and chemical operations begun."

Efficacy of the Apparatus.

"For killing and colouring mercury, an apparatus is indeed a power. Without the use of herbs and drugs, mercury can be killed with the aid of an apparatus alone; hence an expert must not disparage the efficacy of the apparatus."

Crucibles.

"Earth of black, red, yellow and white colour, burnt husks of paddy, soot, earth from the ant-hill, well-burnt excrements of the goat and the horse, rust of iron " [varying proportions of the above ingredients are used for making crucibles, retorts, etc.]

Colour of Flames.

" Copper yields a blue flame............that of the tin is pigeon-coloured; that of the lead is pale-tinted ....that of the iron is tawny;.........that of the " peacock ore " (sasyaka) is red."

Tests of a Pure Metal.

" A pure metal is that which, when melted in a crucible, does not give off sparks nor bubbles, nor spurts, nor emits any sound, nor shows any lines on the surface, but is tranquil like a gem."

Copper from the Pyrites.

" Makshika, repeatedly soaked in honey, oil of *ricinus communis*, urine of the cow, clarified butter, and the extract of the bulbous root of *musa sapientum*, and heated in a crucible, yields an essence in the shape of copper."

Extraction of Zinc from Calamine.

" Rasaka, mixed with wool, lac, *T. Chebula*, and borax and roasted in a covered crucible, yields an essence of the appearance of tin; of this there is no doubt."

Let me now quote one or two extracts from *Rasaratna Samuchchaya* or a " thesaurus of gems of mercury and metals." The author gives the following description of initiation of disciples and of a Chemical Laboratory :—

Initiation into Discipleship.

" The instructor must be wise, experienced, well-versed in chemical processes, devoted to Siva and his consort Parvati, sober and patient. The pupil should be full of reverence for his teacher, well-behaved, truthful, hard-working, obedient, free from pride and conceit and strong in faith.

"Chemical operations are to be performed under the auspices of a ruler, who is God-fearing, who worships Siva and Parvati, and whose territory is free from anarchy; and the Laboratory, to be erected in the depth of a forest, should be spacious, furnished with four doors and adorned with the portraits of the Gods.

"Take of gold-leaf 3 niskas in weight and quicksilver 9 niskas and rub them with acids for 3 hours. Make the amalgam into a *phallus* (emblem of Siva, the creative principle).............the phallus to be worshipped in due form. By the mere sight of phallus of mercury, the sins accumulated by the killing of 1,000 Brahmans and 10,000 cows are redeemed.

"The science of mercury was communicated to man by Siva himself and is to be imparted by the instructor to the disciple according to the prescribed rules with closed eyes.

"The science of mercury is to be strictly kept a secret...................if it is divulged, its efficacy is gone."

On the Laboratory.

"The Laboratory is to be erected in a region, which abounds in medicinal herbs and wells........... It is to be furnished with the various apparatus. The phallus of mercury is to be placed in the east, furnaces to be arranged in south-east, instruments in the south-west..................The "koshti" apparatus for the extraction of essences of metals, the water vessels, a pair of bellows and various other instruments are also to be collected as also the threshing and pounding mortars, the pestles, sieves of various degrees of fineness, earth for the crucibles, charcoal, dried cow-dung cakes, retorts made of glass, earth and iron, and conch-shells, iron-pans, etc.

"Those who are truthful, free from temptations, given to the worship of Devas and Brahmans, self-controlled and used to live upon proper diet and regimen—such are to be engaged in performing chemical operations."

The mercurial and metallic preparations of the Tantric age began slowly to supplant if not altogether supersede the treatments by the administration of herbs and simples as prescribed in the Charaka, Susruta, and Vagbhata, *i.e.*, the genuine Ayurvedic System. Already as early as the 11th century, we find Chakrapani Datta, himself a learned commentator of Susruta and author of the well-known medical work which goes by his name, not only recommending certain mercurial preparations but taking credit for introducing them. In fact, from the 12th century onwards inorganic (or metallic) remedies rapidly gained in popularity and this circumstance in its turn reacted upon the spirit of the age in giving fresh impetus to the study of Chemistry. I can quote *ad libitum* from the Chemical Tantras of this period, as treasures of all kinds lie scattered in inexhaustible profusion in these works, but I need not tire out your patience by doing so. I hope I have indicated enough to show with what zeal and zest my favourite branch of science was once cultivated in Ancient India: I cannot conclude better than by quoting the apposite words of Bacon :—

"We see then how far the monuments of wit and learning are more durable than the monuments of power or of the hands. For have not the verses of Homer continued twenty-five hundred years and more, without the loss of a syllable or letter; during which time infinite palaces, temples, castles, cities have been decayed and demolished? It is not possible to have the true pictures or statues of Cyrus, Alexander, Cæsar, no, nor of the kings or great personages of much later years; for the originals cannot last; and the copies cannot but lose of the life and truth. But the images of men's wits and knowledges remain in books, exempted from the wrong of time and capable of perpetual renovation."

Thus it is that even after a lapse of 7, 8 or 10 centuries, Govinda, Somadeva, Nagarjuna, Ramchandra, Svachchanda Bhairava and others appeal to modern India in eloquent terms from dust-laden shelves and worm-eaten tomes and manuscripts not to give up the pursuit of the Science they so dearly professed. As I find gathered round me the flower of the youth of Madras, may I join in the appeal so eloquently given utterance to by the chemist Nagarjuna some 1,000 years ago:

"For 12 years I have worshipped in thy temple, O Goddess; if I have been able to propitiate thee, vouchsafe unto me, thy devotee, the rare knowledge of Chemistry." If twelve years was considered as the irreducible minimum of time which an ardent student ought to spend in mastering the intricacies of our science at such a distant date how many years' assiduous devotion is required to master it to-day? Chemistry is the science *par excellence* which at present determines the fate of nations and the assiduous pursuit of it has given Germany an enviable predominance in world politics. There is, however, such a thing as pursuit of science for its own sake as also misapplication and prostitution of it. A genuine student of science is filled with joy ineffable as he finds that it enables him to unravel the hidden and mysterious laws of nature. If I could for a moment command the organ voice of Milton I would exclaim that we are of a Nation not slow and dull, but of a quick, ingenious and piercing spirit, acute to invent, subtle and sinewy to discourse, not beneath the reach of any point the highest the human capacity can soar to. Therefore, the students of learning in her deepest science have been so ancient and so eminent among us that writers of a blest judgment have been persuaded that even the School of Pythagoras took the cue from the old Philosophy of this land.

It is not for nothing that this ancient land of ours

has been chosen by the all-wise Providence to be the birth-place of a Valmiki and a Vyasa, of a Kalidasa and a Bhavabhuti, of a Sankaracharyya and a Ramanuja, of a Nagarjuna and a Yasodhara, of a Varahamihira and a Bhaskara and last but not least of a Rammohan, a Keshabchandra and a Vivekananda. You, youngmen of the rising generation, will not, I trust, fail to play your part. As in the glorious palmy days of old, so in the days to come, it will depend upon you whether or not our dear Mother-land is to hold her head aloft and secure for herself a recognised place in the comity of nations.

ANTIQUITY OF HINDU CHEMISTRY

The following is the second address delivered by Dr. Ray before the Madras University in February 1918.

To-day's lecture is a natural sequence of the previous one. Very vague notions seemed to prevail even among oriental scholars of repute as regards the origin and antiquity of Hindu Chemistry—indeed many scholars openly expressed doubts as to whether there existed at all such a thing as Hindu Chemistry. Thus, Barth in his "Religions of India" incidentally observes:

"In regard to alchemy, anyhow, in which the Sittars are zealous adepts, they were disciples of the Arabians, although other Sivaites had preceded them in the pursuit of the philosopher's stone. Already, in his exposition of the different doctrines of Saivas, Sayana thought he ought to dedicate a special chapter to the *Rasesvaradarsana,* or "System of Mercury," a strange amalgamation of Vedantism and Alchemy. The object contemplated in this system is the transmutation of the body into an incorruptible substance by means of *rasapana, i.e.,* the absorption into it of elixirs compounded principally of mercury and mica, that is to say, of the very essential qualities of Siva and Gauri, with whom the subject of the operation is thus at length identified. This species of transubstantiation constitutes the *jivanmukti*, or state of deliverance commencing with this present life, the sole and indispensable condition of salvation. It is clear that the devotional formulæ of the Vedanta are here only a sort of jargon under which there lies hid a radically impious doctrine; and it is not less clear that in this doctrine, which had from the fourteenth century produced a rather considerable literature, there is an infusion of Muhammadan ideas. The Arabs of Khalifat had arrived on these shores in the character of travellers or merchants, and had established commercial relations and intercourse with these parts long before the Afgans, Turks or Mongols, their co-religionists, became conquerors."

Burnell, again, under the influence of pre-conceived notions has been led into the same error, namely, that Indian Chemistry owed its origin to the Arabs. Thus, in his notice of Sanskrit MSS. in the Tanjore Palace he draws the conclusion from the colophon at the end of the chemical Tantra, *Rasasara*, "I have composed my work after consulting the traditions and opinions of the Baudhas"—that by Baudhas (Buddhists) the author probably means the Muhammadans." Had Burnell patience to go over the body of the text of *Rasasara* he would have been disabused of his sad error, for the author candidly admits that he derived his information from the very fountain-head, namely the Buddhists of Bhot or Tibet. I shall have to say much later on about Bhot being the asylum of chemists. Now, as far as Chemistry and Arithmetic are concerned the Hindus far from learning any thing from the Arabs were their teachers. This is gratefully acknowledged by the Arabian writers themselves of the 10th and 11th century. Any one who is interested in the subject may consult my History of Hindu Chemistry in which a chapter has been devoted to the discussion of it. The outstanding feature is that in the reign of the Khalifs Mansur and Harun, Indian pandits went to Bagdad at their invitation and translated the *Charaka, Susruta* and many other medical treatises.

The preparations of mercury began to be prescribed for external administration as early as the 11th century A.D., if not earlier. Chakrapani prescribes *Rasaparpatica* (a variety of sulphide of mercury) for chronic diarrhœa, etc., and claims to be its discoverer. In Europe, on the other hand, the discovery of this black sulphide of mercury, called also *Æthiop's Mineral,* is ascribed to Turquet de Mayerne in the beginning of the 17th century. In the European Histories of Chemistry, on the other hand, the credit of being the first to press chemical knowledge into the service of medicine and to introduce the use of the internal administration of mercurial preparations is given to Paracelsus the Great (1493—1541.) But the French Parliament and the Faculty of Medicine of Paris interdicted what was regarded as the dangerous innovation of Paracelsus.

The Mussalman Hakims had also a horror of the

metallic mercurial drugs of the Hindu Pharmacopœia. Thus, Taleef Shareef says: "My advice is to have as little to do with these as possible."

All this goes to prove that the Hindus not only did not borrow from the Arabians or from the western sources but were precursors in this field.

It is, however, in the domain of metallurgy, *i.e.*, the extraction of metals from the native ores, that the Hindus made marked progress at an early age. The Indians were noted—in fact their fame had spread far into the West—for their skill in the tempering of steel. The blades of Damascus were held in high esteem and it was from India that the Persians, and through them the Arabs, learnt the secret of the art. The wrought-iron pillar close to Kutub near Delhi which is some 1,500 years old; the huge iron girders at Puri; the ornamental gates of Somnath and the 24 ft. wrought-iron gun at Narwar—are monuments of a by-gone art and bear silent but eloquent testimony to the marvellous metallurgical skill attained by the Hindus. Regarding the Kutub pillar, Fergusson says: "It has not, however, been yet correctly ascertained what its age really is. There is an inscription upon it, but without a date. From the form of its alphabet, Prinsep ascribed it to the 3rd or 4th century; Bhau Daji, on the same evidence, to the end of the 5th or beginning of 6th century. The truth probably lies between the two. Our own conviction is that it belongs to one of the Chandra Rajas of the Gupta dynasty, either subsequently to A.D. 363 or A.D. 400."

Another authority says:

"It is well-known by every manufacturer of crucible cast-steel how difficult it is sometimes to get the exact degree of hardness to suit certain purposes, especially with reference to steel for cutting the blades, etc. With the ordinary process endeavours are made to reach the required degree of hardness by selecting such raw materials as on an average have the required contents of carbon in order to correspond with the required degree of hardness as far as possible. The natives [of India] reached this degree by introducing into their cast-steel an excess of carbon, by taking this excess gradually away afterwards, by means of the slow tempering process, having it thus completely in their power to attain the exact degree by interrupting this de-carbonising process exactly at the proper time in order to cast steel of a quality exactly suitable for the purpose."

The Hindus are also entitled to the unique credit of being the first to extract zinc from its ore calamine (Sanskrit: *rasaka*). The process is so circumstantially described in *Rasaratnasamuchchaya* and is so highly scientific that it can be quoted almost *verbatim* in any treatise on modern Chemistry. I shall purposely withhold here the technical details, which are reserved for a separate lecture to *bona fide* students of Chemistry to be delivered in the next few days. But I may be permitted to point out that the skill displayed as also the marvellous powers of observation recorded therein extort our wonder and admiration.

The exact date of the discovery of the Hindu method cannot be ascertained but the description occurs in the chemical treatises of the 12th to 13th century A.D. Roscoe and Scherlemmer observe:

"Libavius was the first to investigate the properties of zinc more exactly, although he was not aware that the metal was derived from the ore known as calamine. He states that a peculiar kind of tin is found in the East Indies called Calaem. Some of this was brought to Holland and came into his hands."

The priority of the Hindus is thus also indirectly admitted. As you are aware the two leading works of our Ayurveda are the *Charaka* and the *Susruta* and both of them belong to remote antiquity. The latter describes at length the method of preparing alkalies and rendering them caustic by the addition of lime. The nice distinction shown between *mridu* (mild) and *tikshna* (caustic) alkali and the direction given for the preservation of caustic alkali in iron vessels are equally scientific and leave very little to improve upon. It is enough to add here that at the present day caustic alkali is imported in iron drums. The chapter on *Ksharpaka* (preparation of alkalies) in Susruta can well be cited as a proof of the high degree of perfection in scientific pharmacy achieved by the Hindus at an early age. Indeed, M. Berthelot was so much struck with the originality of this process that he goes so far as to suggest that this portion in the *Susruta* is evidently a recent interpolation inserted into the body of the texts sometime after the Hindus had contact with the European chemists. Now, Chakrapani, whose father was Court Physician to King Nayapala of the Pal dynasty of Gour and who thus flourished in the middle of the 11th century, *i.e.*, about the time the battle of Hastings was fought, borrows this portion almost *verbatim* from Susruta. Moreover, in the Pali ethical romance called "Milinda Panho" there is mention of the cauterisation of bad wounds by means of caustic alkali. The date of this process can thus be traced to about 140 B. C. So there is not the remotest chance of inspiration from the European chemists.

Let me now proceed with some historical evidences of the age of the chemical Tantras to which I referred in my previous lecture. Madhava in his summary of the *Rasesvaradarsana* (lit. science of mercury) quotes at length from the *Rasahridaya* of Govinda whom he speaks of as Bhagavat and an ancient teacher. Now the qualifying epithets "Bhagavat" as also "prachina" (ancient) are only applied to venerable Rishis of old. A contemporary author is never mentioned in such terms of the deepest reverence. It is therefore evident that during the life-time of Madhava a halo of antiquity had encircled round the name of Govinda, who must have lived at least four or five centuries before the time of the Prime-Minister of Bukka Rao. In other words, the latest date we can assign to Govinda is 9th or 10th century A.D. Internal evidence also corroborates the view I have taken. I was so fortunate as to be able to procure 3 MSS. of this rare work—one from the India Office, the other from the Library at Katmundu (Nepal) and another from Benares. The last is 386 years old and is of special historical importance; from its colophon we learn that it was written at the request of the King of the Kirataland, *i.e.*, the region round about modern Bhotan. Our author says, "Bikshu Govinda, well versed in chemical operations and loaded with honours by the King of Kirata, composed this *Tantra* called *Rasahridaya.* May Tathagata (Buddha) pronounce his blessings." The Buddhistic creed of the author is thus revealed. There is a belief current in some parts of the Madras Presidency that our Govinda is no other than the celebrated teacher Samkaracharyya and some verses from "Samkaradigvijaya" are cited in support of this view. Apart altogether from the question whether at so early a date the progress of chemical knowledge such as we glean from *Rasahridaya* had been attained in India, the colophon quoted above would tell against such an hypothesis. We need not seriously discuss whether Samkara, the sturdy champion of Brahminical faith, the mighty dialectician, whose activity was mainly instrumental in sounding the death-knell of Buddhism in India, ever sat at the feet of a Guru of the opposite creed. In 1839 the celebrated Hungarian scholar Csoma de Koros who had spent years in the monasteries of Tibet, created quite a sensation by publishing in the "Asiatic Researches" an analysis of *mdo* or the Sutras from the Tibetan Encyclopædia, the Tanjur. When the

Tibetans embraced the faith of Sakyamuni an intellectual craving was created among them and they were eager to remove their mental barrenness by greedily devouring the contents of the literary and scientific works available in North India. Several eminent Pandits of Bengal visited Tibet at the invitation of its king. Some of the most famous amongst them were Sant Rakshita, high priest of the monastery of Nalanda, Padma Sambhaba and the sage Dipamkara Srijnana (Atisa), who later on at the request of King Nayapala accepted the post of high priest of the monastery of Vikramasila. These scholars took a prominent part in the dissemination of Hindu learning in the Land of Snow. The Sanskrit works were rendered into Tibetan with wonderful fidelity to the original and thus many old Hindu works on literature and science, which at one time were supposed to have been lost, can now be recovered.

In the analysis of Csoma de Koros mention is made of a work on "quicksilver (mercury), the most powerful tonic for subduing every sickness and for improving the vigour of the body" and of another work "on turning base metals into gold."

Chemistry was vigorously pursued in India during the Mahayana phase of activity of Buddhism and a fragmentary work of this period on this subject has been recovered entitled *Rasaratnakara* and ascribed to Nagarjuna. From this priceless treatise we can glean much valuable information about the progress of chemistry in India before the Muhammadan invasion of

North India. I have no time to pursue here the chronological sequence of the various chemical works available now. It will suffice to state that the colleges attached to the monasteries of Nalanda, Vikramasila, Udandapur, etc., and which sometimes contained as many as 10,000 students, were recognised seats of learning and chemistry was included in the curriculam of studies. The last two monasteries were destroyed by Bakhtiyar Khilji and his hordes, and most of the monks thereof put to the sword, only a few managing to escape. The learned Sakyasri fled to Orissa and afterwards to Tibet, Ratnarakshita to Nepal and Buddhamrita and others sought asylum in South India. Many emigrants from Magadha rejoined their brethren in the South and founded colleges on a moderate scale in Vijayanagar, Kalinga and Konkan. It will thus be noted that the scholarly monks of the above monasteries, on their dispersion bore with them their learning in the same manner as the Byzantine Greeks on their expulsion from Constantinople carried with them their intellectual treasures to the Italian cities. In the kingdoms of the Deccan and in Tibet the Buddhist refugees found hospitable asylums just as the Greek scholars did in the Florentine Republic under the Medicis. We have thus a ready explanation of the apparent puzzle as to why Tibet and Vijayanagara—the two kingdoms which were cut off and isolated from the external world—should boast of works on Chemistry—as to why Madhavacharyya should be in a position to quote from these standard authors. Again, if Chemistry were the only branch of science pursued in ancient India a *prima facie* case could be made out that its origin lay outside it and that it was borrowed by the Hindus; but the capacity of a nation must be judged by what it has independently achieved in the several fields of knowledge and branches of literature, Mathematics, including Arithmetic and Algebra, Geometry and Astronomy; Phonetics, Philology, Grammar, Law, Philosophy and Theology.

Cantor, the historian of Mathematics, was so much struck with the resemblance between Greek Geometry and the Sulva Sutras that he, as is natural to a European, concluded that they were influenced by the Alexandrian School of Hero (215 B.C.) The Sulva Sutras, however, date from about the 8th century B. C. and Dr. Thibaut has shown that the Geometrical theorem of the 47th proposition, Bk. I, which tradition ascribes to Pythagoras, was solved by the Hindus at least two centuries earlier, thus confirming the conclusion of V. Schroeder that the Greek philosopher owed his inspiration to India. Nor must we forget that the most scientific grammar that the world has ever produced, with its alphabet based on thoroughly phonetic principles, was composed in India about the 7th or 8th century B. C. As Professor Macdonell remarks, "We, Europeans 2,800 years later, and in a scientific age, still employ an alphabet which is not only inadequate to represent all the sound of our language but even preserve the random order in which vowels and consonants are jumbled up as they were in the Greek adaptation of the primitive Semitic arrangement of 3,000 years ago." Nor is it necessary to point out here that the decimal notation was familiar to the Hindus when the *Vyasa Bhashya* was written, *i.e.*, centuries before the first appearance of the notation in the writings of the Arabs or their Greco-Syrian intermediaries.

I began by quoting the opinions of two orientalists, namely, Burnell and Barth, both of whom were evidently under the impression that the Chemistry of the Hindus had its origin during their intercourse with the Arabs. Before I conclude let me cite the authority of another Sanskrit scholar, who also hints as much. Thus, Aufrecht in his monumental *Catalogus Catalogorum* (Catalogue of Catalogues) while noticing the MSS. of "*Rasaratnasamuchchaya*" goes somewhat out of his way in asserting that the 27 chemists to whom invocation is made in the opening lines are mostly *apocryphal*. From what I have said above it will be abundantly clear that these chemists, far from being mythical, existed in real flesh and blood and that Govinda, Nagarjuna, Yasodhara and others included in the list have left imperishable records of their attainments in their works, some of which are fortunately extant.

Gentlemen, one word more and I have done; it is of a personal nature and I hope you will forgive me for referring to it. I confess, as a Hindu, the subject of Hindu Chemistry has always had a fascination for me. But there is another valid reason as to why I threw myself heart and soul into the task of recovering the precious gems bequeathed by our chemical ancestors. It is to an illustrious roll of European scholars beginning with Sir Wm. Jones, Colebrooke, Prinsep, Lassen, Burnouff and Csoma de Koros that we are mainly indebted for bringing to light and giving prominence to, the priceless treasures embedded in Sanskrit, Pali and Tibetan literature. Hindu Chemistry, however, waited long and patiently for an interpreter. I thought I owed a debt to the great nation to which I am proud to belong. Hence it is that I felt it incumbent upon me to dedicate some of the best years of my life to this self-imposed task with what success it is not for me to say. We have no reason to be ashamed of the contributions of the ancient Indians to the science of chemistry. On the contrary, considering the time and age in which they flourished I am justly proud of them. I implore you to take to its pursuit and I hope that you will justify by your work that you are no unworthy successors of your glorious forefathers in the world of learning.

HIGHER SCIENCE IN THE UNIVERSITIES

Under the auspices of the South Indian Teachers' Union Dr. P. C. Ray delivered the following lecture on "Higher Science in the Universities" in the Hindu High School Hall, Triplicane, before a very large audience, on February 3, 1918. Dewan Bahadur L. A. Govindaraghava Aiyar presided.

Gentlemen, An almost impossible task has been committed to me by Mr. Subramaniya Aiyar, the more so because the subject is so very vast that to deal with it adequately it requires thought and leisure which, I am afraid, I have not been able to command. I thought, when I undertook this journey to your beloved city, I should have to deliver six lectures (University lectures,) one each day, and walk about in the Marina and the beach and enjoy the cool breeze, and also the social company of many of your eminent men. But since I have been here I find to my agreeable surprise that barely ·5 per cent. of my time is devoted to University lectures and 99·5 per cent. to extraneous matters. If your Chairman claims to be very innocent of science and asked your indulgence for presiding on this occasion, I think I have been far more guilty of trespassing into the functions of politicians and lawyers, and of encroaching upon the sacred preserve of politicians, for to be worthy to unveil the portrait of our illustrious countryman Dadabhai Naoroji (cheers) one should be a politician and also a lawyer. In this country, with rare exceptions like Dadabhai Naoroji and Gokhale and one or two others, a lawyer is synonymous with a politician, and a politician is synonymous with a lawyer. So, if I could be guilty of the atrocious crime of unveiling the portrait of Dadabhai Naoroji, the greatest of the sons of India in modern times and the greatest of our patriots and statesmen, I think our Chairman has as much right to be here as I had to be there. I am no match for him in forensic ability and I am sorry I have not got the time to write out a paper and read it to you. I shall, therefore, try to do the next best thing, namely, to say something on the subject. The subject is a very complicated one, and one can scarcely be expected to do adequate justice to it. It can be looked at from so many different points.

To start with the position of science in the Universities in the glorious days of Moorish activity, they had in Spain several universities, just as we had in India of which I talked to you only a few days ago, in the days of Buddhism—universities of Nalanda, Taxilla, Vikramasila, Udandapur, in some of which there were as many as 10,000 scholars. I do not think the whole of Madras could accommodate so many in our colleges, but barely a fraction. In the glorious days of the Moors there were several Universities—the Universities of Granada, Seville, and Toledo, where astronomy, medicine, mathematics and philosophy as also my favourite subject chemistry, were taught and scholars used to flock there from England, Germany, France, and even more distant parts of Europe. That was in the 14th century and earlier. Later on, science scarcely flourished in connection with Universities. It was by the effort of individuals working in a state of isolation and detachment in various parts of Europe that science flourished. You had most notable scientific discoveries in the field of astronomy made by Copernicus of Poland, Galilio, an eminent Italian, Tych Brahe, a Dane, and Kepler of Germany who were working on their own account, irrespective of any relation with any particular seat of learning or university. It was only the celebrated Sir Isaac Newton who occupied a chair in the University of Cambridge, the chair of mathematics in the great Trinity College, which has since maintained its unique reputation as a seat of mathematical learning. The celebrated Roger Bacon, the precursor of chemistry, was credited with the discovery of gun-powder and was called a wizard. In those days chemistry or alchemy was called the black art and was forbidden. Any one who tried to discover the hidden secrets or mysteries of nature was condemned to severe punishment. Roger Bacon was imprisoned by the Pope in a solitary cell and was made to rot there for years before he was liberated. That was the encouragement given to our earliest chemical ancestors. (Applause). I find another great precursor in the field of chemistry in England, Robert Boyle. He was the earliest to dissociate chemistry from alchemy and place it on a high pedestal. He was a well-to-do man and could afford to indulge in his favourite pursuit. Joseph Priestley is another great man of England who shares with Lavoisier, the Frenchman, the glory of being the founder of modern chemistry. Priestley was a clergyman. He used to earn his livelihood as chaplain to a nobleman. He carried out many chemical experiments. To make experiments was his hobby. He was a great theologian and a political reformer. He was known in the political history of England as being one of the earliest Englishmen who openly sided with the French Revolutionists, so much so that the conservative mob of Birmingham set fire to his house with his working laboratory. He escaped through the back door and went to France and there openly showed his sympathy with the revolutionaries. He is really entitled to the credit of being the discoverer of oxygen. He also was in no way connected with a university, nor his contemporaries who may be regarded as the creators of the modern science of chemistry. In those days there was not much distinction drawn between chemistry and physics. Physical science embraced Chemistry and Physics. I find two other names. Lavoisier is really the founder of modern chemistry. He was guillotined for being immensely rich. Another man who was doing his work in an obscure corner in Stockholm was Scheele. He earned his livelihood by doing the duties of a compounder in an apothecary's shop. During his spare time he used to carry on experiments silently and slowly in a corner of his ill-fitted apothecary's shop. These two were also unconnected with any university. Coming to latter times also we find a very remarkable thing, which has been now and then given expression to, that some of the greatest discoverers in the field of science were not only not connected with but were quite innocent of any sort of university education. They owed very little to any seat of learning. James Watt, the inventor of the steam engine, was only a scientific instrument maker who had not much to do with university education. Stephenson, the inventor of the locomotive engine, was a cowherd, and Arkwright the inventor of cotton spinning started on his career as a barber and was equally innocent of university education. Coming nearer our life-time I find the immortal Darwin, the propounder of the evolution theory. Though educated in the Edinburgh and Cambridge Universities, he, too, worked in a private capacity. His father was a very successful medical man and left him a good fortune. Darwin, instead of squandering it in luxury, utilised it in the study of biology and gradually evolved the theory of evolution and natural selection. There are two other names also innocent of university education. In the field of chemistry and science, Humphrey Davy is one of the greatest names, the inventor of the Davy's lamp which has been the means of saving the lives of the workers in coal mines. He made many discoveries. He was a very poor man and was a self-made man. If you study his life, you will be surprised to find that much of what he learnt in this world was due to self exertion. One day he happened to come across a second hand book on chemistry written by the immortal Lavoisier. He bought it very cheap in a hawker's shop. When reading it he improvised his apparatus out of bottles, tobacco pipes and so on. In that way he made brilliant discoveries, one of them was that of the intoxicating properties of the gas called nitrogen monoxide. When you inhale it you are thrown into hysterical fits of laughter. When patients had to undergo surgical operations they were made to inhale the gas. It was called the laughing gas. But owing to unpleasant after-effects to the patients the use of it was practically given up. When Humphrey Davy discovered the laughing gas, he was sought after, brought to London and appointed Professor at the Royal Institution. Michael Faraday was a book-binder's boy, equally unknown to fame. He was brought into contact with Humphrey Davy and his very touch made a man of him. Any professor of physics will be able to tell you what his achievements are. All these show that epoch-making discoveries and inventions have been made in the field of science apart from and irrespective of any help given by any university. It is only latterly that science has come to be associated with universities, and that too for obvious reasons. In the early days everything was of a novel character, and any single experiment would at once bring out very important results, but latterly all the simple experiments have been practically exhausted. Now in order to bring out the hidden mysteries of nature, you require very elaborately constructed, very sensitive and delicate apparatus, and experiments with such apparatus cannot be conducted except with the aid of well equipped laboratories. It is here that science comes into close association with universities. Even in England it is only in recent times that we have got well equipped laboratories in connection with universities. Not many years ago, I mean only fifteen or twenty years ago, the laboratories of most of the colleges at Oxford and Cambridge were miserably fitted up. These colleges were chiefly famous for what is called humanistic studies, *viz.*, the study of classics, just as we had here not long ago the study of our own classical languages (Sanskrit and so forth) and various systems of scholastic philosophy. Even in England until the fifties of the last century, the chief attention of the colleges was diverted to classical learning, Latin, Greek and so forth. It was only in the early seventies or eighties of the last century that Huxley and others began to wage a crusade against humanistic studies on behalf of the study of sciences. If you open the columns of "Nature" you will see how the eyes of the English people are opened as to the comparative backwardness of science. I purposely use the word comparative. We are sometimes apt to think lightly of England as though we have been raised to the height of scientific glory.

England is by no means a backward country. England is the land of Newton, of Boyle, of Faraday, of Davy and of Kelvin. To speak of England in a rather condescending tone argues a poverty of knowledge. But England is backward compared with the gigantic strides which Germany has been able to make within the last few years. I should say, even twenty years ago as far as physical science was concerned England was ahead of Germany, though not in chemistry. You will find in the columns of "Nature" very angry and acrimonious debates going on as to the relative claims of sciences and classics in the high school classes. When this has been so even in England, you should not at all despair that we have not been able to do much. In the various colleges of Oxford the largest amount of attention was paid to the study of classics. In underground dark rooms called cellars with very poor accommodation, arrangements were made for practical experiments in chemistry and physics. It is only very recently that Oxford and Cambridge, the great seats of learning, began to construct suitable university laboratories of their own, well fitted up, where students of various colleges pursue the higher branches of science.

This brings me to the subject proper which was proposed by my inexorable friend. He said he wrote to me and saw me in Calcutta when he went there as a Congress delegate, and therefore he had the right of priority over others and to compel me to lecture on this occasion though I am ill-prepared.

But I am a captive slave. I am your property. I came here as the property of the University of Madras. Now I find I am the property of anybody and everybody. (Loud applause.) However let that pass. Till recently the various colleges were frittering away their energies; each college has rich endowments earmarked by pious donors for particular purposes. In those days theology played a very important part. Just now in our land the various temples have got rich endowments and we cannot by any means divert them to other purposes, unless public opinion is educated to that extent. One of your distinguished countrymen, Ananda Charlu, tried to introduce a Bill and Sir Rash Behari Ghose introduced another Bill called the "Religious Endowment Act." Our Chairman knows more about it. The public opinion was dead against it. The cry was raised "Religion in danger." Of course a foreign Government, alien alike in religion and in race, could not do anything in the matter. If public opinion is sufficiently educated, then we shall be able to divert a portion of those endowments to modern education *i.e.*, to sequester or secularise a percentage of their incomes for the up-to-date teaching of science. With that money colleges should spring up side by side as they did in Oxford. If colleges are established we should have various branches of learning pursued in those colleges. But it will not come within the range of practical politics for years to come. I know it will come, by and bye. Well, I shall also take my law from the learned Chairman (Laughter). The difficulty was experienced in Oxford, and the same difficulty is experienced here. Each college in Oxford (there are 17 or 18 colleges) could afford to spend very little for scientific study; everything was earmarked for humanistic studies, classics, theology and so on. Very little could be set apart for scientific purposes. There are fourteen or more colleges in Cambridge. Each college had a kind of poorly equipped laboratory. They have recently pooled their resources, mobilised their incomes and instead of frittering away their energies, instead of each college teaching every kind of subject, they thought it better they should pay a certain amount of subsidiary grant, raise subscriptions among themselves and have a common University laboratory where all advanced students may be sent up to study particular branches of science. The time has come when that kind of thing ought to be done in Madras, and more so in Calcutta. I find in Calcutta a very deplorable state of things has sprung up. We have besides the Presidency College, which accommodates about 1,000 students, some six or seven private colleges each containing as many as 1,500 or 1,700 students. Each of these colleges is self-contained. Each college teaches not only every branch prescribed in the arts curricula but also the most important subjects in the science curriculam, namely, chemistry and physics and sometimes botany. Teaching chemistry and physics to so many students becomes very inconvenient and costly. They ought also to pool their resources. One college should teach chemistry only. The colleges should combine their funds together so that a big laboratory may be constructed and well equipped. The teachers should also be well paid. The private colleges of Calcutta can afford to pay only Rs. 100 or Rs. 150 to a science professor and after years of patient work some of the professors may be so fortunate as to get Rs. 200 or 250. The teachers are very badly paid there. You cannot expect them to be contented, and the best men will not be attracted to these chairs. It would be a rather national calamity if this state of things should continue. I think that Madras has not so many colleges, but by and bye more colleges will spring up here too. I do not think the Presidency College will accommodate many students. Many have to go away disappointed. There is accommodation for a limited number. No doubt there you can have the best possible education available. But very few can gain admission there. The time has come when the University should try to have a University laboratory well equipped and spacious, where you would have many capable and experienced teachers who have given proof of their capacity for research work. Many scholarships have to be founded. If it is started in Madras, I am sure the patriotism of the citizens of Madras and of the Province will be equal to the occasion. Many rich endowments will be forthcoming. By and bye we hope to see magnificent institutions springing up. In Calcutta we have just made a beginning. The University College of Science, which I have recently joined, is the outcome of the princely endowments of Sir Taraknath Palit and Sir Rash Behari Ghose. The former gentleman gave away his entire life-earning of Rs. 15 lakhs and the latter gave us a cheque for Rs. 10 lakhs. I have always quarrelled with lawyers, because they divert with their seductive power the best intellects and induce the flower of our youths to the profession of law. (Cheers). But I have made my peace with the lawyers, because two leading lawyers of Calcutta have been the means of founding a noble institution. I hope the leading lawyers of Madras would follow in their footsteps and I shall be glad to make my peace with them on very easy terms. We owe a good deal to these two gentlemen for the bequest of Rs. 25 lakhs. We should remember also one man to whose magnetic influence these big endowments to the University College of Science are mainly due. He was present here only yesterday. I mean Sir Ashutosh Mukerjee. (Cheers.) During his Vice-Chancellorship almost every farthing which the University could lay by during the last thirty or forty years in the shape of savings from fees (close upon Rs. 4 lakhs) was given to this institution. We have thus 30 lakhs of rupees to start with. We expect a handsome grant from the Government of India. Unfortunately, owing to war, their finances have been totally upset and we have not been able to secure large grants from the Government of India. But it goes without saying that when financial equilibrium is once more established, we shall have at least as much, if not more, from the Government of India. I am sure that with Sir Sankaran Nair, another great Madrasi, as our Educational Minister, we shall have no reason to be disappointed. We have just begun our career. The University College of Science should be well equipped with laboratories in every department of science, chemistry, physics, experimental psychology, botany and zoology. It is only the chemical department which we have been able to fit up fairly well; but on account of the war the other departments have been only inadequately fitted up. This difficulty will be removed as soon as peace is concluded. We have got the money in the banks, and there will be no difficulty in the distant future as to ways and means.

I have declared on more than one occasion that students of Madras are not a whit inferior in intellectual capacity to their brethren in Bengal. In fact they are even more intelligent. We have not been ashamed to borrow our Professor of Physics from your Province. Another eminent student of Madras has earned for himself a European distinction as a mathematician at Cambridge. You have no reason to despair. What you have to do is to divert your attention to the study of science. I know that when the fertile brain of Madras is turned into this new channel, science will rise up in no time. You should remember that the study of science is fraught with many difficulties. Those who want to take up science must elect their vocation irrespective of any future consequences. You must take the chance of gain or loss. If you are daunted at the very beginning, the Goddess of Science will not appear before you, she will think you are no genuine devotee. You must choose your line. You must consult your taste. When once your choice is made after consulting your taste, you will not be disappointed.

We have another institution in Bengal which your Chairman has unfortunately failed to mention but which I believe he visited. We have in Bengal a "Chemical and Pharmaceutical Works," which is under the charge of four chemists each of whom has got the qualification of M. A. or M. Sc. in Chemistry. I have spoken about it from another platform. Each one of those gentlemen will get over and above his legitimate pay, a profit for his share of work; one of them will this year get half a lakh of rupees as royalty for the invention of a fire extinguisher; other chemists will also come in for their share of profit. Even from the point of view of earning money, taking to chemistry is not an unprofitable bargain. You have no reason to be disappointed. In fact even in Germany they speak of bread and butter sciences. There is no need to be ashamed of the profession of a practical chemist. If you pursue the subject assiduously, it will bring you some means of livelihood. In Germany eminent chemists who have made discoveries in the laboratory take patents of their discoveries, make them over to manufacturing chemists, and earn lakhs. Chemists in India are generally very ill-paid, because they have to earn their livelihood by teaching alone. In England the proprietors of some chemical firms are millionaires. If there is any branch of science which is calculated to develop the resources of our country and increase its wealth it is chemistry. There is no reason why you should fight shy of it. At the initial stages we must have a band of young men devoted to Chemistry simply for the sake of the study of science, the pursuit of truth and not for anything else. The truest pleasure of man is to be able to unravel the hidden mysteries of Nature. That should be the highest and greatest happiness imaginable.

I should like to speak to you for a longer time, but as I had to raise my voice to the highest pitch in addressing this big gathering you will bear with me if my physical strength fails. Almost for the first time in my life I have been made to stand on the platform to address an audience of this magnitude. Some of my friends dragged me out of my laboratory obscurity on to the platform and made me preside at the All-India Social Conference in the Congress pandal and there I was confronted with an audience 8,000 strong. This is the fourth or fifth time I have had to address big meetings like this. The subject is a vast one. After years and years of study one should go to the various centres of scientific activity before he will be able adequately to do justice to it. I have had one advantage over and above my long stay in England for six years during my student life. I visited England once more in 1904-05, having been deputed by the Government of Bengal to visit the Laboratories of England and Europe so that I might be up-to-date. In the year 1912 I had once more to visit England in the capacity of a delegate of the Calcutta University to the Conference of the Universities of the Empire. I travelled in company with the delegate of the Madras University, Sir John Wallis, the present Chief Justice. In that capacity I had to visit most of the British universities and come into close contact with the method and working of various scientific departments. It was because I have had a fairly good experience of the method of teaching science that I could venture to address you almost off hand. After addressing two meetings in the morning I returned home and after a few minutes I took a sheet of paper and noted down what I meant to say here. I am glad I have been able to go through the whole. I can talk to you till midnight. I have given you a fair idea of the national importance of the subject. I have not come to Madras in vain, if I have been in any way instrumental in rousing your activity, however feeble it might be, with reference to this very important question. The progress of Madras and the progress of Bengal mean the progress of India. As I have said in other places, we are Indians first, and Bengalees or Madrasees afterwards. (Cheers.) As a Bengalee I shall be proud to see a day when you have started a big laboratory of your own in connection with the great University of Madras. (Cheers).

CHEMISTRY AND MEDICINE

Dr. P. C. Ray delivered an address to the students of the Medical Colleges, Madras, in February, 1918, when Lieutenant-Colonel Miller, Principal, presided. In the course of his interesting address Dr. Ray said :—

At present the association of chemistry with medicine was brought out in a variety of ways. For the first time at the Edinburgh University, his own professor (Dr. Crum Brown) showed the relationship between chemical constitution and physiological properties. Joseph Black, graduate of the Edinburgh University, wrote his notable thesis for the degree of M.D., in the year 1756 entitled "Some Experiments on Magnesia Alba." He showed for the first time that magnesium carbonate when heated would part with an invisible air or gas and leave behind oxide of magnesium. This air which escaped was called fixed air. He also showed the quantitative relationship between mild alkali and caustic alkali; mild alkali minus imprisoned or fixed air was caustic alkali. With regard to ancient Hindu medicine it was a doctor of the East India Company—Royle—who first published a treatise on the subject. It was entitled "Antiquity of Hindu Medicine." It was after reading that book that the speaker was inspired with the idea of writing something about the history of Ancient Hindu Chemistry. "Nature" reviewing some of his (speaker's) lectures on the

Antiquity of Hindu Chemistry was surprised that many things then done in Europe were known to Hindus long, long before. They had two ancient books *Charaka* and *Susruta* which represented all the wisdom of the old ages. In *Susruta* they had many forms of surgical apparatus and even lancets for surgical operations. The preparation of caustic alkali with burnt limestone was described in *Susruta*. Only one would not find equations in the book. What was called caustic alkali was used for the cauterisation of bad wounds. Then a period of darkness set in. Owing to the teaching of Manu and others, people thought one was polluted by touching a corpse. Owing to this everything was in stagnation, and instead of going forward they went backwards. The result was that when Lord William Bentinck opened the Calcutta Medical College in 1835 he had to induce students to join the College by offering scholarship. Now the difficulty lay not in getting students in but in keeping them out. When the first Hindu student of the first modern Medical College in India, Mr. Madhusudan Gupta, performed an operation and touched a corpse the event was thought to be one of such national importance that a gun was fired from the ramparts of Fort William to announce it! Within a period of 80 years things had changed for the better, so much so that now at the Calcutta Medical College there were so many applicants every year seeking admission that accommodation could be found for scarcely one-fourth of them.

THE PLACE OF SCIENCE IN THE VERNACULAR LITERATURE

The following is a free translation of the Address delivered in Bengali as President of the Second Bengali Literary Conference. Although it is meant for Bengal, the main purport of it is equally applicable to other Provinces :—

When our respected friend, Mr. Sasadhar Ray, called upon me on your behalf and requested me to occupy the Presidential chair of the second Bengali Literary Conference, I was overwhelmed both with wonder and terror. At first I thought that he had mistaken me for somebody else. It has never been my lot to be of service to my mother-tongue. I am ashamed to have to make this confession; the more so since to aspire to occupy the chair which has been filled by the illustrious cham of literature, Rabindra Nath, would be sheer impudence and madness on my part. Moreover I have been a life-long invalid. To undertake a tedious journey and a laborious task is beyond the power of physical endurance. On these grounds I declined the honour. But when the next day Mr. Ray, along with the two main pillars of the Bengali academy of literature—Messrs. R. S. Trivedi and Byomkesh Mustaphi—spread the net to catch this tiny and fragile person, I had to surrender and now I have been brought here as a captive. You have been pleased to lay on my shoulders a heavy responsibility and I shall try to acquit myself as best as I can and enter on my duties in the spirit of the adage in the *Gita* " One can go on doing his work, leaving others to gather the fruit." According to the suggestions of the local committee I shall say a few words on the propagation of Science and scientific literature in the vernacular.

The literature of a people is a measure of its intellectual activity. If we study the literature of a country we gain an insight into its manners and customs and culture. Bengali literature from its very origin shows a bias towards religious thoughts—this is the predominant tone from the songs of Manick Chand and Govinda Chand down to the poems of Ram Prasad and Bharat Chandra. The climax has been reached in the Vaishnava literature, to which we owe the immortal sonnets of Bidyapati and Chandidas.

The current of the devotional literature which began to flow in the eleventh century A. D. has fertilised and developed our literature. It is still in full swing. The majority of the books published last year was devoted to religious subjects.

We have no time to discuss here as to when Bengali prose made its appearance. Roughly speaking, it may be said that it is a hundred years old. From the foundation of the Fort William College dates the new era of Bengali literature; the trio of Serampore Missionaries, Carey, Marshman and Ward,

Rajiba Lochan and Mritunjoy Tarkalankar, Ramram Basu, Ram Mohun Ray and others are the inaugurators of the new epoch. The historian of the Benglai literature, Dinesh Chandra Sen, having given an account of the pre-British period of Bengali literature concludes with the following notable words: "With the advent of the British, the current of thought has taken a new turn in our social and political life. The rise of the Bengali nation has followed in the wake of new ideas and new aspirations. Owing to the importation of Western ideas Bengali literature has made giant strides. It is a hopeful sign that the Bengalee has now learnt to appreciate his mother tongue. The progress which Bengali literature has made during the last half-century fills us with hope for the future." Our literature is now fairly rich. The seed which was sprouting at the time of Raja Ram Mohun Ray, developed into a full blown tree, thanks to the genius of the immortal Iswar Chandra Vidyasagar, so much so that the present era of the Bengali literature is known as the era of Vidyasagar. But modern Bengali literature has taken a new departure. His "Betal Panchavinsati" was full of stiff Sanskrit words. In the infant stage of Bengali prose, this was the established practice. When we read of "Probada Chandrika" of Mritunjaya, which was a text book in the College of Fort William, we come across a tissue of hideous terms, copiously borrowed from the Sanskrit. I shall quote here what Bankim Chandra says in his foreword to Alaler Gharer

Dulal or "the spoilt child." "The Pandits disdained to speak of clarified butter as ghee, but insisted on calling it 'Ajya.' Perched rice they would speak of as 'Laja,' and Sugar as 'Sarkara.' Fortunately, the new wave has swept away the old order of things." Bankim Chandra in his "Anandamat," in his clarion voice, inspired patriotism on one side, and inculcated in the columns of "Bangadarsan," the high class Bengali journal founded by him, self-restraint, and preached new ideas and also ushered in another epoch. The uncommon genius of Bankim Chandra added a new lustre to Bengali prose and to him we are indebted for the place of honor which our literature occupies in India. Akshya Kumar, Dinabandhu, Kaliprasanna, Romesh Chandra have fertilised this field with their genius. Again Iswar Gupta, Madhusudan, Hem Chandra, Nabin Chandra and Rabindra Nath have immortalised themselves by further enriching our literature with their poetical contributions. But in spite of all these there is a serious danger ahead. The progress of our literature is only one-sided; romance and poetry are expanding, it is true, but there is no all-round development. Physiologists are of opinion that the limbs which are called into play become hardy and muscular while those which are in disuse become atrophied.

In ancient India the *Risis* were always in search of truths and the laws of nature. But in the middle ages, the spirit of enquiry died out. There were 64 *Kalas* (branches of art and learning) and proficiency in several of them was regarded as the hall-mark of learning. The "Kamasutra" of Vatsayana is regarded as a very old work. We learn from it that chemistry and metallurgy were included among the *Kalas*. The *Charaka* enjoins the cultivation of botany in order to enable one to identify the herbs and plants; and in the *Susruta* directions are given for the dissection of dead bodies. The *Ayurveda* is divided into eight limbs (branches) of which surgery is regarded as the most essential. The chapter on the preparation of 'caustic alkali' in the Susruta may be adopted in any treatise on modern chemistry. But alas! the ancient *Risis* of India whose productions in the field of literature and philosophy excite the admiration of the civilised world have had their place filled by unworthy descendants, and the sun of progress is set. Darkness encompassed the land. The task of identifying medicinal plants has devolved upon Vedias (aboriginal tribes). The lancet was left to be handled by the barbers. It is however of no use lamenting the glory of the past.

The few books on Science which have appeared from Bengali press within the last few years belong to the category of text books. Barely one or two are meant for the general public. It is thus evident that Science has practically been divorced from our literature. The Goddess of Science has been expelled from India, and has taken shelter in Europe and the extreme East. Indeed 60 or 70 years ago our literature was better off in this respect. Science occupied its proper place in the periodicals of the day. The articles which Akshya Kumar used to write in the *Tatwabodhini Patrika* on Natural Philosophy, and those by Rajendralal Mitra in the *Vividharta Sangraha* on Geology, Geography and Physics, etc., have become a part and parcel of the Bengali literature. Before their time, Krishna Mohan Banerjea published *Vidya Kalpadrama* (Encylopædia Bengalensis) under the patronage of Lord Hardinge. It also contained articles on Western sciences. Both Rajendralal and Krishna Mohan were scholars and linguists, and though their writings will not be regarded among the classics of our literature, still they will long be remembered as among the pioneers in the field. But even before their time, the place of Science in Bengali literature was duly recognised. It is no exaggeration to say that the Serampore Missionaries are the creators of Bengali prose, and they were also the first to introduce Science into Bengali literature. It may wound our national vanity to admit it but the future historians of Bengali literature will have to offer the due meed of praise to Carey, Marshman and their co-workers. In 1825 Wm. Yates published the first book on Natural Philosophy in Bengali ; it contains also an account of fishes, insects and birds. From the Serampore press also was issued the first book on elementary chemistry.

In 1818 the Serampore Missionaries also published the first Vernacular newspaper called *Samachar*

Darpan or the "Mirror of News" and they were also the first to start the "Digdarsan"— a journal which dealt in a variety of subjects including Science. The next step was taken in 1828 when the "Society for Translating European Sciences" was founded. Professor Wilson was the President of the Society and through its efforts an Encyclopædia was started which consisted of 15 parts. The Vernacular Literary Society was founded in 1851; although its main object was the improvement and expansion of Bengali literature; it had also in view the spread of elementary education into the zenanas. Messrs. Bethune and Joy Krishna Mookerjee were its patrons and it received a monthly grant of Rs. 150 from the Government. It was under the auspices of this Society that Dr. Rajendralal Mitra conducted the *Vividhartha Sangraha*, a journal which lasted for several years and which treated scientific subjects popularly. Mr. Hodgson Pratt was also one of the energetic founders of this Society and he thus explains its aims:—"Any attempt to teach science to the people through the medium of English is doomed to failure. Efforts should be made to improve the vernacular and to adopt it as the vehicle for primary education and to create a thirst for learning. It is necessary to write elementary text books containing easy and interesting lessons. In every town and in every village these cheap books should be placed within the reach of every one. These books should contain principles of science, sanitation and physiology."

The efforts of the society for the spread of science were not very successful. After the publication of 17 books, the committee came to the conclusion that amusing story books alone appeal to the taste of the mass of readers.

It is here necessary to mention that three normal schools were established at Calcutta, Hooghly and Dacca respectively. For the use of pupils of these schools many books on Natural Philosophy, Geology, Zoology, Geometry and Geography were published in Bengali; over and above these Primers of Science, books on Botany and Chemistry were published suited to the capacity of the pupils of the primary and middle vernacular schools. Later on, text books on Anatomy, Physiology and Chemistry were written for the use of the medical schools. Bengali literature on the scientific side has been much improved by these publications.

It is now a subject for discussion as to whether much good has come out by the publication of these text books in Bengali during the last half century. Only those scientific books which have been adopted as the text books for the passing of examinations commanded a sale. It is an open question whether the present system of making lads of eleven or twelve years old to learn by rote scientific subjects is productive of benefit or harm. The fact is there is scarcely any genuine thirst for knowledge in our land. One may have the hall-mark of two or three degrees, but that is no proof that he has acquired a love of learning. You can bring the horse to the trough, but you cannot make it drink. The passing of examinations has become the be-all and end-all of the existence of our youths. And thus we cannot expect any good result from their study of sciences. Indeed, nowhere in this world is to be found such a mad craving for securing the University degree. And our graduates bid farewell to the Goddess of learning as soon as they have passed the examination. After his graduation a young man often thinks that he has nothing more to learn. Whereas in other countries, the university career is regarded as the period for apprenticeship. He begins to specialise himself after finishing his university career. As you turn the pages of university calender, and go through the list of successful candidates, you are filled with momentary delight; for instance, you come across a dozen of M.A'S. or M.S.C'S., in Botany; but you forget that the spark has been extinguished in them for ever. I give below the account of Japan as published in the journal "Sanjibani," from the pen of a Bengali student who was out there! "The thirst for knowledge of the Japanese is scarcely excelled by any other people. The rich and the poor, the great and the small, the learned and the ignorant—everyone is permeated with the ardent desire to learn something new. Even the maid-servants know so much of the affairs of the world outside, that the ladies of our households cannot come up to them."

Let us now turn our eyes to France. Shortly

before the breaking out of the French revolution, the thirst for knowledge became prevalent among every class, as the following extracts from Buckle's History of Civilisation will show : " The first great blow to this state of things was the unprecedented impulse given to the cultivation of physical science. Those vast discoveries which were being made not only stimulated the intellect of thinking men, but even roused the curiosity of the more thoughtless parts of society. The lectures of chemists, of geologists, of mineralogists, and of physiologists were attended by those who came to wonder, as well as by those who came to learn. In Paris the scientific assemblages were crowded to overflowing. The halls and amphitheatres in which the great truths of nature were expounded were no longer able to hold their audience, and in several instances it was found necessary to enlarge them. The sittings of the Academy, instead of being confined to a few solitary scholars, were frequented by everyone whose rank or influence enabled them to secure a place. Even women of fashion, forgetting their usual frivolity, hastened to hear discussions on the composition of a mineral, on the discovery of a new salt, on the structure of plants, on the organisation of animals, on the properties of electric fluid. A sudden craving after knowledge seemed to have smitten every rank. The largest and the most difficult inquiries found favour in the eyes of those whose fathers had hardly heard the names of the sciences to which they belonged. The brilliant imagination of Buffon made geology suddenly popular; the same thing was affected for chemistry by the eloquence of Fourcroy and for electricity by Nollet; while the admirable expositions of Lalande caused astronomy itself to be generally cultivated. In a word it is enough to say that during the thirty years preceding the Revolution the spread of physical science was so rapid that in its favour the old classical studies were despised; it was considered the essential basis of a good education, and some slight acquaintance with it was deemed necessary for every class, except those who were obliged to support themselves by their daily labour."

The cry has recently been raised that science cannot be taught except with the aid of costly laboratory. There are lying scattered in the hamlets, gardens, jungles, ruins, rivers, and ponds, and in the caves thousands of natural objects of the animal and vegetable kingdoms. Does anybody care to study them? If you have to learn anything about the habits and natural history of the mosquitoes, the snakes and fishes, and the birds of Bengal, you have to consult the works of the European specialists. A botanical laboratory for a private individual need not cost more than Rs. 100. A microscope, a lens, a pair of scissors, a razor, and a few chemicals will suffice for ordinary purposes. But where is the thirst for knowledge? I spoke just now about our graduates. Let us now turn our eyes to Europe, and you will find genuine students of nature. To collect materials for natural history and to study them first hand on the spot, they penetrate into the dense jungles of Africa infested with the lion, the gorilla and other dangerous animals. With them Nature study amounts to a passion. As some of you may be aware, Sir Joseph Hooker in 1845 undertook a perilous journey to the Himalayan regions to collect rare specimens. Many an explorer has lost his life in the Arctic expeditions. The indomitable energy, the insatiable thirst for knowledge of the westerners excite our admiration. When Nansen returned from his expedition the whole of Europe and America were anxious to read the account of his adventures. Our next subject for discussion is Bengali Scientific Literature—its present state and the method to be adopted for its improvement. The history of literature of three countries may be of some use. For what has been possible in Germany, Russia and Japan may be possible in our country. These three countries have won a recognised place in Science within a comparatively short period. A hundred and fifty years ago German literature was poor indeed. It is true Martin Luther popularised his mother-tongue by his version of the Bible; but Latin and Greek were taught in the schools and French was the court-language. Even Frederick the Great was ashamed to write in his mother-tongue. He used to compose poems in French and submit them to Voltaire.

But within a short time after Frederick's death, Schiller, Goethe and Kant on the one hand, and in the beginning of the 19th century men of science like Liebig, Wohler, and Humboldt enriched the German literature. As for Russia, it is enough to say that Buckle speaks of it as a semi-civilised country at the time of the Crimean War. But within a period of half a century she has produced a Tolstoy and the celebrated chemist Mendeleef and his school have published their researches in the Russian language. This is the royal method of enriching one's mother-tongue.

Let us now turn our attention for a moment to an Asiatic country. It is needless to speak of the land of the rising sun, as she was some 40 years ago. The patriotic makers of modern Japan not only sent scores of enthusiastic and hopeful youths to Europe and America to learn the western sciences but also engaged the services of Europeans of established reputation in the field of science. In the early stages these used to deliver lectures in English or French or even German. But Japan soon realised the necessity of improving and expanding her own language and made arrangements for the delivery of lectures in the Vernacular. For, at best only a handful of scholars can afford to learn through the medium of a foreign tongue.

The fact is that until we are able to take part in original researches and publish the results in our own vernacular so long it will remain poor and imperfect. For 2,000 years the Hindus have been practically as a 'dead nation' and has scarcely added anything to the stock of knowledge of the world, and we only live on our past glories. According to Lecky the spirit of free enquiry set in Europe in the 12th century, but from this time India began to be enveloped in intellectual darkness. Professor Weber has truly said that Bhaskara was the last star in the firmament of India.

True it is that we are wont to take pride in the acuteness of the Bengali intellect as evidenced in the subtleties of disputations based upon the modern school of Nyaya as also of Smriti (of Nava-dwipa). It should however be borne in mind that while the great promulgator of Smriti (Raghunandan) was ransacking the pages of Manu, Yajnavalkya, Parasara and others, and laying down the rigid rules of fasting to be observed by a child-widow of nine years of age and in default thereof holding out the terrors of hell-fire for her ancestors on the paternal and maternal side ; while Raghunatha, Gadadhara, Jagadisa and other mighty logicians were engaged in composing glosses and commentaries on the classical works of logic and were thus adding to the consternation of the pupils of the *tols* ; while our astronomers were calculating the omens and prognostications from the cawing of a crow at a particular moment in the south-west quarter ; while our pandits were disturbing the peace of the assemblies by acrimonious dispute over the controversy 'whether the sound raised by the falling of the palm-fruit accompanied it or was an after-effect' ;—I say when the intellectuals of

Nava-dwipa were thus utilising the precious gift of time, in Europe Galileo, Kepler, Newton and other philosophers were unravelling the mysteries of Nature and ushering in a new epoch and thus glorifying the intellect of man.

Fortunately a wave of new ideas and aspirations is sweeping over the land. I regard it as a kind dispensation of God that Raja Ram Mohun Ray should be born in our midst with the mission to bring about the union of the east and the West and thus to lay the foundation of new India. If we study the history of the world we find that those nations which have tenaciously clung to old customs and manners and have refused to keep pace with the surging tide of progress, have become decadent or extinct. The vast stridies which Japan has made within the last 30 years is mainly due to her assimilation of western ideas and sciences.

I shall now say a few words on scientific technical terms. The Japanese have not been as yet able to publish their original researches in their own language; but they do so in English and German and rarely in French. In order however to make the general principles of science intelligible to the masses, they publish popular expositions in the vernacular. Although there is a diversity of language among the European nations, there is uniformity in the use of technical terms. It is scarcely necessary to point out the advantages of common technical terms in the scientific world. The Japanese have fully realised this and have thus adopted the middle course. We should also follow in their footsteps.

One of the main duties of the Literary Conference is the creation of technical terms. It is a matter for congratulation that the Bengali academy of literature has taken the lead in this matter, and Messrs. R. S. Trivedi, Yoges Chandra Ray, and others have been labouring in this field. The *Nagari Pracharini Sava* (Hindi Literary Society) have collected many technical terms in geography, astronomy, political economy, chemistry, physics, etc.; it is to be hoped that our Conference will appoint a committee of experts to settle the question of technical terms.

The promoters of the conference have done well by dividing our literature into two branches, *viz.*, literature proper and scientific literature;—the sphere of activity of the latter being based upon the model of British association for the advancement of learning and science. We shall have to discuss subjects relating to anthropology, history, ethnology, geography, natural history, chemistry, botany, geology, etc., and publish treatises on these in vernacular.

We stand on the threshold of a new era. The future of our country depends upon the direction and impetus which we can give to-day. If we fail in our duties, the future generations will hold us to infamy.

INDIAN EDUCATION

The following is the written statement of Dr. P. C. Ray on the Provincial Educational Service, submitted to the Royal Commission on Public Services presided over by Lord Islington, published in Vol. XX of the Report :—

83,675. I may begin by emphasising the fact that recent experience has brought the problem of education well to the foreground as the most important problem which British statesmanship has to face and solve. Education occupies a prominent place in the gracious speech of His Imperial Majesty the King-Emperor in his reply to the address presented by the graduates of the Calcutta University. The supreme importance of education was also recognised by Lord Curzon's Government. The recent policy of Government, as embodied in the scheme of Provincial Universities and University chairs, has focussed attention on education as the problem of the day. It is also significant that the most prominent of our public men—men like Sir Gooroo Das Banerji, Kt., Sir Ashutosh Mukherji, Kt., Sir Tarak Nath Palit, Kt., Dr. Rash Behari Ghose, and the Honourable Dr. Devaprasad Sarvadhikari—have come to realise that education is the most fundamental problem to which all other problems must be subordinated. It is therefore essential that the Educational Department should be recognised as one of the most important branches of the public service. The work of education is the most responsible duty undertaken by the State. The department trains men for the various branches of the public service as well as for the several learned professions.

In view of the extreme importance and the responsible nature of the work done by the department, it is absolutely necessary that it should be staffed by men recruited from the very best materials in India and in Europe. The officers of the department should not only possess very high academic qualifications but should also be inspired by the ideals of duty. They should all feel an ardent enthusiasm for the work of education. This can be only secured by (1) enhancing the attractiveness of the service (2) enforcing the strictest conditions of admission, so as to rigidly eliminate inefficient or incompetent candidates, Indian and European. Merit and efficiency should be the sole tests of admission and preferment and all other considerations, *e.g.*, race, nationality, prestige, etc., should be completely ignored or subordinated to the supreme test of competency. Every care should be taken to secure the best men, for an incompetent man, once admitted into the service, acts like a clog in the educational wheel and impedes the rapidity and smoothness of its motion. All distinctions should be based upon real differences, and not on considerations of race or prestige which now form the dividing line between the two branches of the superior service, the so-called "Indian" and "Provincial." This unfortunate distinction—a distinction without a difference—should be abolished, and the two branches of the superior service should be merged into one service. The distinction should never have been made, for even at the time when it was made—it was made as early as 1896—there were Indian candidates available who were at least as qualified or competent as the European officers who then staffed the Indian Educational Service. These Indians—most of whom were graduates of the British Universities—were thus denied a place in the Indian Educational Service, and the anomaly, as unjust as it was inexplicable, compelled these unfortunate men to enter the Provincial Service for no other or stronger reason than their nationality. This glaringly unjust treatment meted out to them still rankles in their mind, and in the case of some of them it is almost too late to repair the consequences of this grievous mistake. I advocate therefore the amalgamation of these two branches of the superior service with all the earnestness and emphasis that I can command. The amalgamation will strike at the root of the bitter discontent which prevails among the officers of the Provincial Service. This discontent was created by the fact that though the two branches of the superior service are admitted to have the same status in theory, in practice a stigma of inferiority has come to be attached to the Provincial Service officer as such, no matter what his qualifications or length of service may be. This brand of inferiority, which is purely gratuitous and unmerited, not to say illogical, has produced in this branch of the service an intense feeling of bitterness, which it is absolutely necessary to remove in the interests of sound education and for the efficient working of the department, for we cannot get the best and the most out of a man who smarts under a sense of unjust and undeserved treatment. In the Presidency College, for instance, the most senior man in the Provincial Educational Service is treated as junior to the latest recruit to the Indian Educational Service. Thus when there are two Professors of the same subject, one in the Indian Educational Service, and the other in the Provincial Educational Service, the officer in the Indian Educational Service is invariably held to be the senior Professor, even though the Provincial Educational Service officer, besides being a teacher of acknowledged efficiency, may be a man of much greater experience and of equal or even greater academic distinctions.

After considering the matter with all earnestness and fair mindedness, I am firmly convinced that the only remedy for this most anomalous and unsatisfactory state of affairs is to effect this amalgamation which I have already advocated. The treatment now accorded to Indians by the Educational Department, whether graduates of European or Indian Universities, does not accord well with the British sense of justice and this reproach should be completely wiped out.

With these general observations, I beg now to proceed to the specific points on which the Commission has been pleased to invite opinion.

83,676. (1) The methods of recruitment.—As regards recruitment, I would widen the field of selection by employing more open methods. In the case of appointments carrying special allowances, referred to in paragraph 15, page 5, recruitment should not be made as heretofore. The post should be advertised in the Indian and English papers, and appointment made by a properly constituted Board under the Local Government, which alone knows the local requirements, from among candidates for the post, *including* those already in the service.

That the present method of recruitment, through the India Office, has not been altogether satisfactory, will appear to be obvious to any one who examines the actual facts. The appointments made, say, during the last ten years, cannot be considered, from an academic point of view, as altogether satisfactory. If better men have not been available, that only shows the desirability of adopting the more open method of recruitment as suggested above. Under the present mode of recruitment, men already in the service are excluded from the class of appointments under consideration. Further, the chairs recently created in the Calcutta University are being filled up by the mode of recruitment which takes account of academic qualifications alone. Under this system on the one hand Europeans like Professor Young, F.R.S.,

Dr. Oldenberg, Professor Sylvain Levi, Dr. Strauss, Mr. Leslie (as an Assistant Professor in Economics), on the other, Indians like Dr. B. N., Sil whose qualifications are entirely Indian but whose distinction as a scholar cannot be questioned, have accepted posts under the Universities.

As regards appointments, other than those carrying special allowances, recruitment should be made among Indian candidates possessing the highest academic qualifications. Officers of the present subordinate Educational Service possessing high academic qualifications and doing college work or belonging to the inspecting staff, should also be regarded as eligible for these appointments. I would advocate, however, that no one doing the work of a College Professor should in future be appointed to the subordinate service.

83,677. (ii) System of training and probation:—The conditions of work in the College Department require that an officer should be fully capable of entering on his work as soon as appointed. If the choice is confined to men with real academic distinctions, this object will be secured. There should, however, be a period of probation for two years. Training in the case of a College Professor is synonymous with academic qualifications, and understood in this sense the methods of recruitment should be so devised as to secure only trained men for the service. But at the same time, officers of the Department, Indian or European, who may have shown special aptitude for research, whether in Arts or Science, should be encouraged by being given facilities, on equal terms, for visiting Europe and other centres of culture. In the case of a member of a superior inspecting staff, experienced in teaching at a college or as Headmaster of a collegiate or Zilla school a knowledge of the vernacular should be considered essential.

83,678. (iii) Conditions of Service:—The officers should have ample leisure for study and research. The rule acquiring a medical certificate for physical fitness may be relaxed at the discretion of the Local Government. Free quarters should be provided for all officers, or quarters provided in consideration of a small percentage deducted from the salary as is the practice in the judicial and executive services in the more important stations. In Presidency towns where such quarters cannot be provided, or provided with a great difficulty, liberal house allowances should be paid, no distinction being made as between Europeans and Indians. At present the Presidency house allowances are given only to members of the Indian Educational Service. This is an irritating distinction which should be done away with as early as possible. Special allowances should be given to Principals of Colleges. The scale of travelling allowance in the case of an officer of the Educational Department should be the same as that of an officer in the Indian Civil Service. Travelling allowance should be determined by the nature of the work done, and not by the amount of salary drawn.

83,679.(iv). Conditions of salary :—

If the extreme importance of the work of education as explained in paragraph 83,675 be adequately realised, it will be readily admitted that the scale of salary in the Educational Department should be so fixed as not to lower the status of an educational officer, as compared with that of the offices of the other branches of the public service. The present scale was fixed more than a quarter of a century ago, and the cost of living has rapidly gone up in the meantime. It has more than doubled and this fact demands a very substantial increase in the present rate of pay.

83,680. (v). Conditions of leave :—Greater facilities should be given to all officers, Indian and European, in the Educational Department for study in Europe. In particular, officers should be permitted to combine a vacation with privilege leave, if the total period of the leave is to be spent in study and research.

83,681. (vi). Conditions of pension :—Twenty-five years' service should qualify for full pension. Twenty years' service should also qualify for full pension, if an officer is medically invalided.

83,682. (vii). Such limitations as may exist in the employment of non-Europeans and the working of the existing system of division of services into Imperial and Provincial :—

In my preliminary remarks I recommended most strongly and earnestly that the two branches of the superior service be amalgamated into one service and gave some general reasons which clearly necessitate this step. This I regard to be the crucial point at issue. I now proceed to explain the absolute necessity of adopting this measure, which alone can do away with various anomalies which have arisen in practice and radically remove the bitter and deep-seated discontent among those officers of the superior service who are now branded as "Provincial."

In the first place, I am in general agreement with the views which have been submitted through me by the entire body of officers of the Provincial service, and the main portion of which I take the liberty of reproducing for purposes of ready reference.

I should, however, strongly deprecate the proposed differentiation of posts into those carrying a full salary and those carrying a lower salary. All the posts in the superior service should, in my opinion, be on the same scale of pay; in the case of certain specified posts, however, I am prepared to admit that there should be a special system of allowances ranging from Rs. 300 to Rs. 600 and even Rs. 800, it being understood that recruitment to those posts should be according to the method already advocated by me in paragraph 5. I am opposed to any invidious distinction based on racial considerations, as such a distinction is in reality opposed to the spirit of the recommendations made by the last Public Services Commission. That competent Indian candidates were available at the time when the existing division between the two branches of the service was initiated, is abundantly evidenced by the fact that the last Public Services Commission recommended that recruitment should as a rule be locally made except for certain specific appointments.

In accordance with these recommendations, seven Principalships of Colleges, three Inspectorships and a majority of the Professorships under the Bengal Government were reserved for Indians, and the European service was reduced from 41 to 27 (including the Director of Public Instruction, Assam). Since then there has been a distinctly retrograde move. All the Divisional Inspectorships, practically all the Principalships of Colleges have now been reserved for the Indian Educational Service, which is virtually European, and the number of posts in this service has been raised from 26 to 54, the corresponding increase in the Provincial Educational Service being from 104 to 165. While thus, in all the other services, progress has been in the direction of throwing open to Indians an increased number of appointments usually held by Europeans in the Educational Department most of the more important posts formerly reserved for Indians have now been reserved for Europeans. And yet if the conditions of local recruitment were favourable at the time the last Public Services Commission made their recommendations, they are much more so now after a steady educational progress for over a quarter of a century. I have already mentioned the fact that Dr. B. N. Sil, a graduate of the

University, has recently been appointed to the King George V. Chair of Philosophy by the Calcutta University. In my subject, *viz.*, Chemistry, we have got distinguished scholars and investigators like Rasik Lall Datta and Nilratan Dhar, men who are now on a fair way towards earning for themselves a European reputation, but under the existing mode of recruitment for the Indian Educational Service, such men have absolutely no chance of entering this higher service. Finally, if graduates of Indian Universities can be appointed to be High Court Judges, members of Executive Councils and Accountants-General of Provinces, I see no reason why they should be debarred from holding the highest appointments in the Educational Departments.

Dr. P. C. Ray called and examined.

83,684. (Chairman). The witness said his main contention was that no organisation of the Educational Service could be satisfactory which was based on race, and not on the nature of the work done. The Indian and the Provincial Educational Services should be merged into one. The present arrangement only gave rise to heart-burning, whilst a great many officers smarted under a sense of positive injury. It was not consistent with a sense of self-respect that men equally educated, doing the same kind of work and of equal calibre, should be ranked in two different services. At present there was practically no difference between the kind of work done in a college by a Provincial and an

Imperial man. The Provincial Professor was doing precisely the same kind of work, was teaching the same classes and giving the same quality of an instruction to those classes as his senior Professor.

83,685. Recruitment should be made by the Local Government, and not by the India Office. The India Office would not give a fair chance to Indians. The posts should be advertised first in the local market, and if suitable men were not forthcoming and then alone the Local Government should send to England for a qualified man. If there was an eligible Indian in England, the Local Government ought to appoint him with the aid of a committee of experts in India. The Secretary of State should have nothing to do with the matter. The Local Government would be in a position to give better advice on the subject even although the Indian resided in England. As bearing out his contention, he mentioned that the Calcutta University had managed to bring out such men as Dr. Young, F. R. S., and Professor Jacobi without the help of the India Office at all.

83,686. Recruitment for the more responsible posts in the service should be both by direct appointment from the universities in India and by promotion. He preferred the method of direct recruitment, but certain posts should certainly be reserved for promotion from the lower ranks.

83,687. He set some store on the average Indian undergoing a European course. A man with this experience would often be a more efficient officer than one who had been appointed straight from an Indian university. He desired to point out, however, that there were very eminent men in India, *e. g.*, Sir A. T. Mukherji, Dr. Rash Behari Ghose and Mr. Gokhale, who had never any sort of education in Europe. There would be no hard-and-fast rule on the point.

83,688. With regard to salary, many of the witness' colleagues were in favour of two classes of pay, but he (the witness) deprected any such system. He would give all members of the service the same pay, but to those who had shown extraordinary merit he would add something in the shape of a compensation allowance.

83,689. The bare fact that a man was a European, and had been educated in a British University, did not mean that he was likely to turn out a successful teacher. It was too often assumed that, because a man had been brought out from England, he was therefore an expert and a specialist. This was quite inaccurate.

83,690. All the divisional inspectorships and practically all the principalships of the colleges had now been reserved for the Indian Educational Service. That had been done four or five years ago whilst Sir Archdale Earle was Director of Public Instruction. The few principalships in the Provincial Service, which had been promised at the time of the reorganisation scheme, had been snatched away. There was only one divisional inspector now left in the Provincial Educational Service, and there was no knowing when that post would also be taken away.

83,691. There was a sufficient staff in his college for the work to be done.

83,692. (Lord Ronaldshay). The education which an Indian received in India was ordinarily quite sufficient to enable him to carry out the duties which would be required of him when he joined the Educational Service. He did not think that any period of training in Europe in addition to an Indian education was essential, but it had its uses.

83, 693. The recommendation that a special allowance, not exceeding one-fourth of their ordinary pay, might be given to Europeans appointed in England, in view of their service in a distant country, expressed the view which the members of the service now generally held, but they thought it should be applied only to exceptional cases. The authority making the appointment would decide in each case whether the candidate had made a name for himself or not.

83,694. (Sir Theadore Morison.) The scale of salary for the proposed amalgamated service might run from Rs. 300 to Rs. 1,500; but in exceptional cases, such as the head of a department, higher pay should be granted. The proposal that there should be five grades beyond the time-scale was the view of his colleagues, and not of himself.

83,695. The amount of the monthly increments should depend on whether the officer was an average man or was of exceptional ability, and had made a name for himself by his researches. For an average man a suitable arrangement would be to begin at Rs. 300 and rise to Rs. 700 or Rs. 800 by annual increments of Rs. 30. If among the officers recruited at Rs. 300 a month a man of unusual capacity was discovered, he should either be promoted over the heads of his seniors to the Rs. 500 grade, which would no doubt cause some heart-burning or be given a special personal allowance.

83,696. (Mr. Gokhale.) There were exceptional facilities for carrying on original research at the Presidency College, and there was as good material in the country as elsewhere for this purpose. Two of his own pupils, for instance, over and above their academic distinctions, which were of the highest, had contributed papers to all the leading scientific journals in England, Germany and America. Again, only last week he had received a letter from Sir Henry Roscoe, in which that gentleman congratulated him, not so much on account of his own researches, as of the brilliant work done by his pupils. If some of his pupils had the further advantage of visiting some of the laboratories in Europe and seeing the kind of work which was done there, and coming in contact with the great men in their subject, they could fill the chairs of chemistry in India with the greatest success and would do the work as well or better than any young man who could be brought out fresh from the European Universities, which is more or less of the nature of a dark horse.

83,697. (Mr. Fisher.) Recruitment should be in the hands of the Local Governments, and they should advertise appointments both in England and in India. In this way each Local Government would have three alternatives before it on the occurrence of each vacancy; it might either promote to the foot of the cadre a junior who was already in the service, or appoint a freshly graduated Indian of distinction over the heads of those who were already in the service or it might call in a man from Europe, either an Indian or an Englishman.

83,698. Promotion within the service should very largely be regulated by distinction in original research, but it would also be necessary at times to advance men who had done no research work but who had other important educational qualifications. He quite admitted that in an Indian College, as in an English College, a great deal of the educational work was on a very much lower plane than the plane on which he and Dr. Bose conducted their researches, and that it was primarily important to obtain men who were efficient teachers and guides of youth. Such men would very often not possess great scientific attainments, but yet might be a most valuable element on the teaching staff of the college. It followed from that that it was really in the interests of advanced college education in India that exclusive stress should not be laid upon power to conduct original research. That must always be the prerogative of the rather highly talented man.

83,699. (Mr. Macdonald.) The witness was aware that he might be charged with sacrificing teaching to original research, but he had found that in England a man who was appointed to professorial duties could only rise to that distinction by reason of the work which he had produced. When a chair fell vacant in England, the Board of Selection was guided more by a man's original contributions in the particular branch of study than anything else. Moreover, the best teachers were ordinarily those who were the best original workers and experimentalists.

83,700. (Mr. Madge.) He agreed that there was room for improvement in the present system of education in Indian universities, but the universities were now starting on a new phase and the present state of things would not continue for very much longer.

83, 701. (Mr. Abdur Rahim). An Indian who received a European education, did acquire thereby a certain advantage, in that his outlook on life was widened and his views broadened. He did not at all under-rate the value of European education, but he found the custom was for a man to take a Cook's holiday trip, spend six months or a year abroad, and then return with some indifferent degrees, and claim credit over his Indian colleagues.

83,702. With regard to the suggestion that a certain European element in the Educational Service was of great advantage in modelling the character of young men, the witness said that was a ver delicate subject. It entirely depended upon the personality of the teacher. The right man would produce a very wholesome influence and the wrong man just the opposite effect. His contention was that an Indian teacher could produce a much greater effect than the European, because the former lived and moved and had his being amongst Indians, whereas a European, however well disposed he might be, lived in a world apart. He quite admitted that there were certain exceptions to that rule and there was no denying the fact that Europeans had to a large extent built up the educational system of India.

83,703. (Sir Valentine Chirol.) It could be assumed that a graduate of an Indian university possessed the same educational equipment as a graduate of a British university of the same degree.

83,704. (Sir Murray Hammick.) Professor Young had come out for three or four years on a salary of Rs. 1,000 a month and house allowances. Dr. Oldenburgh was to be a university reader for a few months at a special fee and Professor Sylvain Levi was in the same position. Mr. Leslie had been appointed Assistant Professor of Political Economy. Dr. Strauss's salary was Rs. 600 a month. The latter appointment was for a certain number of years.

83,705. (Mr. Biss.) While there was only one Indian Divisional Inspector, it was true that there were two European Inspectors in Bengal.

83,706. The Presidency College had no monopoly of research work. At Dacca, Professor Watson was doing research, and some of his pupils were giving a good account of themselves. Professor Watson was doing excellent work, and the University of London had conferred the degree of Doctor on him during the present year.

83,707. It was the fact that the European Professors of the Presidency College had for a very long time been asking for quarters to enable them to come into closer contact with the students.

83,708. He could not conceive of any considerations which could be urged in favour of the employment of Englishmen as Englishmen.

83,709. (Mr. Gupta). Under his scheme for the amalgamation of the Provincial and the Indian Educational Services, the Laboratory assistants in the Department of Chemistry should come into the subordinate service; but if they showed exceptional merit, they should be promoted to the higher service.

83,710. Indian Professors on the Art side should be placed on the same footing as graduates of English Universities, and the same pay and privileges should be extended to them. One effect of the inauguration of the Provincial Educational Service, some years ago, had been to scare away the best intellects of the country from the Educational Department. The general interest of education in Bengal had suffered very much on that account.

RECRUITMENT OF THE EDUCATIONAL SERVICE

The following is the text of the Memorandum on the Recruitment of the Educational Service presented to the Islington Commission by P. C. Ray of the Bengal Provincial Educational Service:—

I have expressed my views in my corporate capacity on the undesirableness of ear-marking a branch of the Educational Service as 'Provincial.' In the present memorandum I shall confine myself to one or two points in connection with the method of recruitment of the service and the disadvantages under which its members have to labour.

In the Despatch of the Secretary of State for India on the "Reorganisation of the Educational Service of India" 1896, occurs the pronouncement: "In future natives of India who are desirous of entering the education department will usually be appointed in India and to the Provincial Service." This momentous and unfortunate decision has had the effect of virtually excluding Indians from the higher or the Imperial branch of the service. In reply to a question put in the Imperial Council last year the Hon'ble Mr. Butler replied that out of 211 appointments in the Imperial branch only 3 were held by natives of India.

The present system stifles the legitimate aspirations of our countrymen and keeps away the most meritorious amongst them from the fold of the education department. The hardships of the "Provincial Service" members can best be brought home to the Commission by referring to some concrete instances. Let us take the case of Dr. P. C. Ray, the senior man in the Bengal P. E. S. He studied science at the Presidency College for four years (1878—82) up to the B. A. standard under Sir John Eliot and Sir Alex. Pedler. In order to round off his education he proceeded to England in 1882 and studied at Edinburgh for 6 years (1882—1888) and sat at the feet of eminent Professors of Science. He took the degree of B. Sc. in 1886 and that of D. Sc. in 1887. It is scarcely necessary to point out that for the latter qualification aptitude for original investigation is a *sine qua non.* Even after taking his D. Sc. he stayed on for another year so that he might continue his original researches and specialise himself in chemistry. At the completion of his six years' studies he appeared before the India Office, backed by influential friends, and applied for a post in the education department; but his efforts were unsuccessful. He was advised to return to India and apply to the local government. The sequel to this narrative can be told in a few words. Dr. Ray entered the Education Department in 1889 on a pay of Rs. 250 per month and served on that remuneration for 7 years at the end of which period he was promoted to the Rs. 400 grade and after some 17 or 18 years' service he got to the top of the ladder and was entitled to the maximum pay of the Provincial branch, namely, Rs. 700 per month. Other members of the service with distinguished European qualifications, *e. g.*, Dr. D. N. Mallik, Dr. Ganesh Prasad, Messrs. J. N. Das Gupta and M. Ghosh have met with a similar fate.

I have given an unvarnished statement of my own case in order to present a vivid picture to the Commission of the differential treatment accorded to the two branches of the service.

In the "Indian" educational branch the initial pay is Rs. 500 with the *guaranteed* increment of Rs. 50 per annum, or in other words, in 10 years an officer gets Rs. 1,000 per month; then he is entitled to a further allowance of Rs. 100 per mensem and in special cases he gets a Principalship with a further allowance of Rs. 250 to Rs. 400 per month as also house allowance.

As far as I am personally concerned I may be allowed to state that the pursuit of science for its own sake has been a sufficient reward and stimulus to me; at the same time it is my duty to point out that the prospects held out even to the most deserving members of this service have failed to attract men of brilliant parts to the Educational Service; they have fought shy of seeking a career in this department. I shall relate a short story here. While I was serving on Rs. 250 for years, a gentleman holding a high position in society asked my advice as to the future career of two of his sons who were my pupils. As he was anxious to give his boys the benefit of an education in England, I naturally suggested that they should study some branches of science and enter the educational service. "What, another P. C. Ray!" he exclaimed. From his own point of view I think he was fully justified, for both his sons competed for and entered the Civil Service.

The present system also penalises the intellectual activity especially the pursuit of science amongst our countrymen. India is a backward country—her people compared to that of the western countries lack in public spirit and self-help and in the power of organisation. Here the State is often called upon to undertake duties which in England are taken up with alacrity by the people themselves. Scientific education is the crying want of India and one naturally looks up to the State for fostering and encouraging it. One of the ways in which the Government can do its duty in this matter is by providing employments to the scientifically trained Indians, but by a bitter irony of fate the Indian has been virtually excluded not only from the higher appointments in the educational service but also from the Geological Department, and rigidly denied admission in the Great Trigonometrical Survey, the Metereological Department, the Botanical Survey as also from the "Imperial" branch of the Pusa Agricultural Institute and the Forest and Telegraph departments, and so forth. The denial of a suitable career takes away all incentive for the specialised study of sciences either at home or abroad. An embargo has thus been placed upon the cultivation of science in this country.

The present method of selection by the Secretary of State is open to serious objection for more reasons than one. It is now a matter of common knowledge that only men of indifferent attainments care to come out to India and the filling up of the posts by them has seriously lowered the standard of scholarship in India. A raw graduate fresh from college, even if he can boast of First Class honours, is a dark horse. The committee of the Dacca University Scheme have fully realised this evil as they observe :

" In general, men of about 40 years of age will be best, as younger men will not have had the necessary experience. At this age, too, successful men will have acquired habits of study and research which should withstand the effects of climate and environment. Young Englishmen, however brilliant, who, having only just finished their examinations, and started original work, come out to India to find in many cases their enthusiasm weakened by the lack of an inspiring environment, and their difficulties exaggerated by the absence of the accustomed facilities and the help of older men. Under such circumstances a few men of exceptional calibre and strength of character will still manage to advance knowledge and earn a reputation, but the many, who might have been successful under more favourable conditions, will very soon drop original work altogether."—(p. 56.)

The method of recruitment in vogue has created serious discontent amongst the members of the Provincial Educational Service. The differentiation between the two services is based upon racial ground and not on merit, for it cannot be said that the higher service is filled with men of higher intellectual calibre. If sound scholarship, life-long devotion to the subject of choice and capacity for original researches be accepted as tests and criteria of an efficient teacher, I believe the "Provincial" men will on the whole score over the "Imperial." Pandit Hara Prasad Sastri, C. I. E., as an antiquarian, Professor Monomohun Ghose, poet and *literateur*, Dr. D. N. Mallik (wrangler) on whom the University of Dublin conferred the degree of D. Sc. on account of original researches in mathematical physics, Professor Jadunath Sarkar, who is rightly regarded as a high authority on "India under Aurangzib" have had few equals in the service.

Under the existing artificial and arbitrary mode of filling up vacancies in the Imperial branch, the best local men—natives of India—some of whom have earned a European reputation by their researches are excluded, while third rate men of Great Britain and Ireland find easy admission. It is a sad mistake also to take for granted that merely because a man has been educated in an Indian University he is necessarily of inferior calibre and attainments. The competition lies between the third rate men brought out from England and first rate Indians. In this connection I cannot do better than reproduce here the short speech which I delivered at the last "Congress of the Universities of the Empire" in my capacity as a delegate of the Calcutta University:

"I rise, my Lord, to associate myself with the weighty remarks made by my brother delegates from the Colonies, Prof. H. B. Allen (Melbourne) and Prof. Frank Allen (Manitoba).

"The Indian graduate also is placed under peculiar disadvantages when he undertakes to pursue his post-graduate studies in a British University. My Lord, I plead for a more generous recognition of the merits of an Indian graduate; he has, I am afraid, the badge of inferiority stamped upon him simply because he happens to be an India-made ware. I can speak with some degree of confidence about the particular subject which I have the honour to profess, namely Chemistry. Now, of late there have been some brilliant students engaged in post-graduate researches and as their communications find hospitable reception in the columns of the leading British Chemical Journals, I take it that they are considered as of a fair degree of merit and yet it is a strange anomaly that when the authors of these investigations come over here and aspire for a high British degree, they are made to go through the trodden path in the shape of having to pass the preliminary examinations and this has a depressing and deterrent effect upon the enthusiasm of our youths. I endorse the suggestion made by a previous speaker that such a scholar should only be made to pass through a probationary period under the guidance of a teacher whom he chooses and if he fully satisfies him the Colonial or Indian student should at once be allowed to go up for the highest degree on the strength of his thesis alone.

"Sir Joseph Thomson has spoken about the rich endowments and scholarships required to encourage a post-graduate scholar. The Calcutta University has already founded a good few post-graduate scholarships and expects to have more. But I beg, however, to remind the representatives of the British Universities present here that we in India have from time immemorial held aloft the high ideal of plain living and high thinking and that with even comparatively poor stipends and bursaries we hope to achieve much.

"My Lord, I do not for a moment claim that the teaching our Universities impart is of the same degree of efficiency as in the sister British Universities—in fact we have much to learn from you—but I beg leave to remind you that in spite of their many defects and drawbacks, our Universities have produced some of the brightest ornaments of our country. The foremost lawyer of Calcutta—a man renowned throughout India for his high forensic attainments—is a graduate of the Calcutta University. Three of the most eminent physicians and surgeons of Calcutta who have attained to phenomenal success in their professional career are, again, graduates of my own University and last but not least the present Vice-Chancellor of our University, who enjoys the unique distinction of being three times in succession elected to his onerous duties by the Chancellor of the University, who is no other than the Viceroy himself,—I say, Sir A. T. Mookerjee is also a product of the same University.

" My Lord, before I resume my seat I once more plead for a more generous recognition of the teaching imparted in our Colleges."

In the sphere of original researches in science, especially in Chemistry, some of our graduates at the Presidency College are showing remarkable capacity —their investigations are being published in the leading scientific journals in England, Germany and America and yet whenever any vacancies occur in the department, their claims are cooly ignored and the sad spectacle is witnessed of the posts being filled up by raw graduates from England, who are admittedly their inferiors and who have got no original work to their credit.

The Indian graduates suffer a grievous injustice and the obvious way to remedy it would be to throw the gates of admission wide open to merit alone, irrespective of racial considerations. Recruitment should be in the first place local and the power of selection should also be entrusted to a thoroughly representative Board of Literary and Scientific Experts in India. In case of a vacancy, the Board should be empowered to advertise in the local papers and to receive applications. It is only in the contingency of a suitable candidate not being available on the spot, a requisition should be made to the Secretary of State.

In the next place there should be one Educational Service in the country and the system of two compartments of the service, one called the Indian Educational Service and the other Provincial Educational Service, should be done away with. The proposed service would have one cadre of appointments with equal pay and prospect and the consideration of fitness and merit should be the only criteria for promotion to the highest posts of the service. In the case of Europeans appointed in England a special allowance not exceeding one-fourth of their ordinary pay may be given to them in view of their service in a distant country. In other respects the rights and privileges of the Europeans and the Indians in the service should be absolutely similar.

There is another strong reason in favour of employing Indian agency. A European naturally looks to India as a land of exile and his thoughts are always turned homeward. As soon as he joins his appointment, he begins to look forward to his furlough and even during summer holidays he often runs home. Socially speaking, the European lives quite apart and it is only in rare cases that he is found to mix on equal terms with his pupils. The result is that that he fails to create anything like an intellectual atmosphere. Moreover, the European when he retires from the service leaves India for good and all the experience which he gathered during his tenure of office are clean lost to the country. But the mature experiences of an Indian after retirement are always at the disposal of his countrymen; he is in fact a valuable national asset.

REFLECTIONS ON THE CENTENARY OF PRESIDENCY COLLEGE*

The following is the reprint of an article contributed By Dr. P. C. Ray to the "Calcutta Presidency College Magazine," Jan. 1917 :—

A mighty river if traced to its origin is often found lost amidst tiny rills and rivulets. The early history of the old Hindu College, of which our Presidency College is the direct lineal descendant, scarcely gives an idea of the part it was destined to play in the future. The 14th of May, 1814, was a memorable day ; on that day on the requisition of Sir Edward Hyde East, Chief Justice of the Supreme Court, David Hare, Baidyanath Mukerjee and others, a meeting of the citizens of Calcutta was convened with a view to take steps for the opening of a school on an improved basis for teaching English literature and science.

Perhaps a slight digression is necessary in order to enable one to comprehend the full significance of the expression "a school on an improved basis for

* For the materials made use of in this article I have borrowed freely from Pearychand Mitter's Biographical Sketch of David Hare and Rajnarayan Bose's short account of the Hindu and Presidency College in Bengal, and also my little book on "India" (Edinburgh, E. & S. Livingstone, 1886).

teaching English literature and science," used above. To the average student of to-day Warren Hastings is chiefly known as the hero of Burke's impeachment and the despoiler of the Begum of Oudh and so forth. It is however clean forgotten that "the first educational institution on a European model established in Bengal" is the Madrassa, founded in 1780, by the first Governor-General. The object of its institution was to impart an Arabic education to the Mahomedan youth. Warren Hastings provided for it a building at his own expense and assigned a jagheer yielding an annual revenue of Rs. 29,000 for its maintenance.* Warren Hastings was also the first to bring the sublime and transcendent truths of the Gita before the European world as we gather from his preface to Wilkins' translation. He also took a leading part in the foundation of the Asiatic Society of Bengal.

"In Persian and Arabic literature he was deeply skilled. With Sanskrit he was not himself acquainted; but those who first brought that language to the knowledge of European students owed much to his encouragement. It was under his protection that the Asiatic Society commenced its honourable career. That distinguished body selected him to be its first president; but, with excellent taste and feeling, he declined the honour in favour of Sir William Jones."†

Although the home authorities, in their infinite wisdom, had established a Crown Court in Calcutta,

* Kissory Chandra Mitra.

† Macaulay.

to "administer English law on the model of the courts in Westminster," it was found impossible to obey their commands in their entirety. The rulers on the spot found it absolutely necessary to inquire into the customs of the people, as sanctioned in their religions, their laws of inheritance, and so forth. This could not be done without a knowledge of the Shastras and the Koran. Thus it was that the maulavie and the pundit became the referees of the English judge, who, before he had set foot on the soil of India, had probably in all simplicity and innocence concluded that the Orientals had stolen the principles of their jurisprudence from Justin and Alfred. The appointment of Sir W. Jones, a Puisne Judge of the Supreme Court, brought about the advent of a new era. The occult lore of the Brahmins, the hidden treasures of the East, were now to be unlocked and poured forth into the West. Warren Hastings, who himself was a Persian scholar, could not fail to appreciate the researches of the great linguist.

A Madrassa (Mahomedan College) was established by the State at Calcutta A.D. 1780, as we have seen above, and this was followed twelve years later by a Sanskrit College at the great seat of Brahminical learning.

It is not easy to perceive what led to the creation of the aforesaid institutions; it is probable that underneath this lay some deep political significance—popularity-hunting. The foreign rulers thus posed before the Oriental eyes as patrons of learning. The Benares Sanskrit College could not have even higher pretensions than the numerous Brahminical seminaries scattered throughout the same place, where alone the higher studies of the Shastras and the Vedas are cultivated. After all, the two Government colleges could not have cost more than £2,000 annually. Here closes the first chapter of education in India under British rule, to be followed by one written in far brighter characters.

The fact is, in those days nothing was farther from the aims of the East India Company than the enlightenment of the people of India. So late as 1811, a worthy of the name of Sir John Austruther who had been once Chief Justice of the Calcutta Supreme Court, and who, on his return home, had secured a seat in Parliament, inquired with surprise and horror "whether it was really meant to illumine the people of India, and whether it was really desirable to do so." The prevailing idea was that diffusion of Western sentiments was incompatible with the preservation of the Empire.

The year 1813 is a memorable one. Partly stung with the reproach that, while they had wasted millions of Indian gold in aggressive wars, they had not spent anything worth the name for ameliorating the condition of the millions committed to their charge, but chiefly under pressure from Parliament, the Honourable East India Company had at length consented to set apart a lakh of rupees, (*i.e.*, deduct the same from the dividend on the stock) "for the revival and promotion of literature, and the encouragement of the learned natives of India, and for the introduction and promotion of a knowledge of the sciences among the inhabitants of the British territories." An ambitious scheme, indeed, for a sum of £10,000! The above *regulation* practically remained a dead letter till the year 1823, when Lord Amherst took the matter up, and appointed a committee to draw up a report as to how the Parliamentary grant might be spent. The Burmese War, however, diverted the attention of the Governor-General from this useful measure.

We said the grant of the State for education was only £10,000; but insignificant as the sum was, it has an historic importance, for over it was fought a battle the issue of which has been far-reaching. This was the time when Lord William Bentinck was the Governor-General, with Macaulay as his right hand. The Committee of Public Instruction had hitherto spent the money made over to its charge in the encouragement of Oriental learning; but now a difference of opinion arose as to how the decree of Parliament would be best given effect to. The impetus given to the study of Arabic and especially of Sanskrit among the servants of the Company had produced a number of Oriental scholars who had become strongly "Brahminised" or "Hinduised." Horace Hayman Wilson, as an Oriental scholar second to none, made himself the spokesman of one party. The blind advocates of the study of Oriental languages, putting a far-fetched construction upon the Charter of 1813, maintained that the assignment was expressly meant to be devoted to the encouragement of Oriental learning, and that it would be a "downright spoliation" to divert the funds to the teaching of Western sciences through the vehicle of English. Macaulay, who was President of the committee, led the opposite party. In a masterly Minute, the eminent essayist, in the clear, forcible, and convincing style which is his own, smashed the arguments of his opponents item by item, and concluded with a threat (which was quite unnecessary) that he would rather retire from the chairmanship than be lending his countenance to what he firmly believed to be a mere delusion. Macaulay's was the victory. The Governor-General in Council was of opinion that the "great object of the British Government ought to be the promotion of European literature and science amongst the natives of India, and that all the funds appropriated for the purposes of education would be best employed on English education alone."

The leaders of the Hindu Society had however by this time come to realize that the "education" as imparted in the tolls and muktabs will not bring about the regeneration of India, and thus we find the greatest among them protesting against the "perpetuation of ignorance" by the establishment of a Sanskrit College at Calcutta, and praying for the foundation of an institution in which European gentlemen of talents and education would instruct the natives of India in Mathematics, Natural Philosophy, Chemistry, Anatomy and other useful sciences. Rammohan Ray's masterly letter to Lord Amherst in 1823 reveals the longing and thirst among the elite of the Hindu community for Western literature and science.

Trifling events often lead to momentous issues. Baidyanath Mukerji, grandfather of the late Justice Anukulchandra Mukerji, in the course of his daily round of constitutional walk, used to call on Sir Edward Hyde and discuss with him the need of opening an institution for the purpose noted above. David Hare and Rammohan Ray warmly seconded the proposal. Rammohan, although the life and soul of the movement, took care to keep himself in the background, as the leaders of the orthodox Hindu community who were scandalised at the illustrious reformer's social and religious propaganda, refused to join it unless he withdrew from the committee.

The 20th January, 1817, must be regarded as a red-letter day in the annals of the educational progress in this country—the day which witnessed the opening of the Hindu Mahavidyalaya or the Hindu College of Calcutta. It is only necessary to recall the prophetic utterance of Baidyanath Mukerji on the solemn occasion of the opening ceremony. He compared the infant institution to a tiny little seedling of Bar-tree (Ficus religiosus). "Who knows," he exclaimed, "that in course of time it may not grow into a gigantic tree with outstretching branches covering acres of land?" The prophecy has been fulfilled to the letter. The Presidency College of to-day with its new extensions occupies several acres of land and under the sacred shades of this hallowed academy generations of Hindus have been nurtured and have received their intellectual *pabulum*.

We can scarcely give expression to our feelings to-day. Let us revere the memory of David Hare, the warm philanthrophist and faithful friend, who devoted his life to one generous end—

> "To bless the Hindoo mind with British lore
> And truth's and nature's faded lights restore!"

of Sir Edward Hyde East, Rammohun Ray, Baidyanath Mukerji, as also of the foundation donors headed by Maharaja Tejchander Bahadur and Babu Gopimohan Tagore and others.

In the brief notice at our disposal it is scarcely possible to attempt a connected narrative of the Hindu College or to follow it through its checkered career and the vicissitudes it has encountered. Head-master D'Anseleme presided over it from 1817 to 1833, and associated with him as teachers were Tytler, Ross, Theodore Dickens and John Peter Grant, father of the Lieut.-Governor of the same name. In my "Forty Years of Chemistry at the Presidency College" published in the College magazine just two years ago I forgot to mention that the first lecturer on Chemistry was Ross; but his knowledge of the subject seems to have been very poor—at any rate his pupils were not at all favourably impressed by his lectures. The only thing he was conversant with was Soda, and he was never tired of dilating on its properties. No wonder one of them, Krishnamohan Bandopadhyay, (afterwards famous as Rev. K. M. Banerji) contributed to the papers a sarcastic article entitled "Soda and his Pupils." But the man who really won the hearts of all the students, who exercised the greatest moral influence over them was the fourth teacher H. L. V. Derozio, the Eurasian poet. Every one of his pupils looked upon him as his friend, philosopher and guide, in fact whoever came in contact with him was a changed man. Even during the short interval of the tiffin time, they forgot the pinch of the stomach and crowded round their beloved teacher and idol to hear him talk on subjects, social, moral and religious. The flower of the Hindu College, who constituted the "Young Bengal" of the day, owed their inspiration to him and regularly visited him at his house, so that they might drink deep at the fountain-head. The makers of modern Bengal—Rasikkrishna Mullick, Dakshinaranjan Mukerji, Ramgopal Ghosh, Ramtanu Lahiri, Radhanath Sikdar, Madhabchandra Mullick, Govindachandra Basak and others—each and all worshipped Derozio.

After the Derozio *regime* Mr. Speed presided over the Hindu College; he evidently believed in "spare the rod and spoil the child" doctrine and put it to a practical test. He used to go round the classes from the lowest to the highest unsparingly using the cane. Bengal however owes him a debt in quite a different line. Speed's hobby was horticulture. He wrote a book entitled "Indian Gardener" and introduced the cultivation of arrowroot in this country. Next to Derozio, the teacher who mostly influenced his students was Captain D. L. Richardson—himself a poet and Shakespearean scholar; he inspired them with a love of English literature, and Macaulay wrote to him after his return home: "I can forget everything of India, but I can never forget your reading of Shakespeare."

Richardson was promoted to the Principalship of the Hindu College in 1841, and in 1846 he was appointed Principal of the Krishnagar College, where my father who was then a student in the Junior Scholarship Department came in contact with him. A copy of Richardson's 'Lives of British Poets' which is still with me I regard as a precious legacy from my father. It is needless to say that the beautiful poem inscribed on the mural tablet in Hare School is from Richardson's pen.

From 1849 to 1854 Lodge was the Principal of the College, and in the latter year on the initiative of Lord Dalhousie, the Presidency College was established with the two Senior classes of the old Hindu College as the starting point. As I have said at the outset, the blood of the latter College thus runs geneologically through the veins of our own College. Mr. Sutcliffe was, I think, its first Principal and I well remember his genial and affable countenance in the early seventies of the last century when I was a student of the Hare School. Mr. Sutcliffe used regularly to visit every class of the Hare School on Saturdays. I need not proceed farther. Suffice it to say that the alumni of the Hindu College and latterly of the Presidency College have played an important part in the intellectual renaissance of modern Bengal. When it is further remembered that the Bengalees have been the pioneers of Western education in the United Provinces and the Punjab the *role* played by our institution in the making of *New India* will be well realized. Sir Frederick Halliday who had been Lieutenant-Governor of Bengal during and after the Mutiny observed in his capacity as member of the Secretary of State's Council:—

"Every educated man has proved a missionary of education in his neighbourhood and among his dependants; and every considerable landholder vies with his neighbour in establishing and fostering village schools; until in 1869, one half of the whole State expenditure for vernacular education was met by private subscriptions and contributions from a people who, only a few years back, could by no means have been made to comprehend the value of education to themselves, still less the obligation of extending it to others."

It will thus be seen that each and every one of the alumni of the Hindu College became a focus of religious, social and political intelligence, which gradually permeated and filtered through among his less favoured countrymen. Indeed, a little leaven leaveneth the mass. I have had occasion to mention above the names of some of the distinguished sons of Bengal who received their education at the old Hindu College. It now remains to follow up the list with the names of some other famous alumni of the Hindu and Presidency Colleges—Pearychand Mitter, Digambar Mitter, Rajnarayan Bose, Debendranath Tagore, Ramaprasad Roy, Durgacharan Banerji (father of Mr. Surendranath Banerji), Kisorichand Mitter, Michael Madhusudan Dutt, Pearychurn Sircar, Prasannakumar Sarvadhikari, Bhudev Mukherji, Gourdas Bysack, Justice Dwarkanath Mitra, Keshav Chandra Sen, Dinabandu Mitter, Mahendralal Sarkar, Bankim Chandra Chatterji, Hemchandra Bandopadhyaya, Anandamohan Bose, and others. I purposely refrain from mentioning the well-known names of many who, I am happy to say, are still in our midst. It is enough to say that everybody who is anybody in Bengal owes a debt immense of endless gratitude to the Presidency College. The history of the Presidency College, in one word, is emphatically the history of the rise, development and progress of the intellectual activity in Bengal.* May it long continue to prosper in its career of usefulness. As one who has had the privilege of being connected with the Presidency College for the last 27 years I cannot conclude better than with

* The Provincial Government Colleges at Dacca, Krishnagar and Hughli and the missionary institutions—the Free Church's and the General Assembly's—have also played an important part in this respect and nobly seconded the aims of the Presidency College.

a message to the students in the words of the poet-professor and my early predecessor in the sacred vocation, Derozio—

> "Expanding, like the petals of young flowers,
> I watch the gentle opening of your minds
> And sweet loosening of the spell that binds
> Your intellectual energies and powers, that stretch
> (Like young birds in soft summer hour)
> Their wings to try their strength. O how the winds
> Of circumstance, and fresh April showers
> Of early knowledge, and unnumbered kinds
> Of new perceptions shed their influence,
> And how you worship Truth's Omnipotence;
> What joyance rains upon me, when I see
> Fame in the mirror of futurity
> Weaving the chaplets you are yet to gain,
> And, then, I feel I have not lived in vain."

THE BENGALI BRAIN AND ITS MISUSE

This paper originally appeared in the Vernacular Journal, the "Suprabhat." A free translation of it with much additional matter appeared in the "Bengalee" in successive issues. Although the article refers to the state of things in Bengal, it is equally applicable to other provinces. It was published in pamphlet form in 1910.

In the course of my presidential speech delivered at the last Literary Conference at Rajshahi I had occasion to observe in one place: "For nearly a thousand years the Hindu nation has been as good as dead. As the son of a rich man having wasted his paternal property has to live a life of penury, but is full of conceit and vanity because of the wealth once possessed by his ancestors, so is the Hindu of the present day. According to Lecky, the spirit of inquiry began to be noticeable in Europe after the torpor of the Dark Ages about the 12th century A.D. From about this time, India, however, became enveloped in intellectual darkness. Professor Weber very justly says that Bhaskara is the last star in the Indian firmament. True it is that we are wont to take pride in the acuteness of the Bengali intellect as evidenced in the subtleties of disputations based upon the modern school of Nyaya as also of Smriti (of Navadwipa); it should, however, be borne in mind that while the great promulgator of Smriti (Raghunandana) was ransacking the pages of Manu, Yájnavalkya, Parasara and others and laying down the rigid rules of fasting to be observed by a child-widow of nine years of age and in default thereof holding out the terrors of hell-fire for her ancestors on the paternal and maternal side; while Raghunadha, Gadadhara, Jagadisa and other mighty logicians were engaged in composing glossaries and commentaries on the classical works of logic and were thus adding to the consternation of the pupils of the *tols*; while our astronomers were calculating the omens and prognostications from the cawing of a crow at a particular moment in the south-west quarter; while our pandits were disturbing the peace of the assemblies by acrimonious dispute over the controversy: whether the sound raised by the falling of the palm-fruit accompanied it or was an after-effect—I say, while the intellectuals of Navadwipa were thus utilizing the precious gift of time, in Europe Galileo, Kepler, Newton and other philosophers were unravelling the mysteries of nature and ushering in a new epoch and thus glorifying the intellect of man."

Let us enter more deeply into the spirit of the remarks made above. The more so as Bankim Chandra says somewhere in reference to the above-named Bengalis and Kullukabhatta (the commentator of Manu) that even in her fallen state Bengal has given birth to mighty intellects. We should now pause and reflect whether in these days of keen struggle for existence we should take our admission in the *tols* of Navadwipa and study modern logic and 'Smriti' and consider the learning and wisdom of the civilized world as erroneous and whether the Bengali race is not already threatened with being wiped off the face of the earth for our failure in realising the situation and moving with the spirit of the times.

In order to estimate the greatness and exalted position of a nation it is first of all necessary to find out the materials contributing to these elements. To me it appears that those who base their estimate of past glories of the Bengali, nay of the Hindu nation, in the light of the writings of Bankim Chandra and Bhudeva are unconsciously led into cherishing mistaken ideas. If we hug the past and look upon the commentaries of Raghunandana and Kullukabhatta as our infallible guides and spurn with contempt the new ideas and aspirations which are vitalizing the other nations of the world, I am afraid the Bengali nation will cease to exist ere long. Rationalism is the very fountain of a nation's life; the downfall of the Bengali nation commenced from the time when this fountain began to dry up and with it originality and the spirit of inquiry disappeared. When a man ceases to think for himself he naturally places greater reliance upon the thoughts of others. What is the prerogative of being born a man? What is it that differentiates a man from the lower animals? I suppose it is the mind with its power of infinite expansion. The cultured Hindu proud of his intellectual attainments began to look down upon the lower classes, he surrendered his own judgment in favour of the injunctions of the *Shastras*. He chose to live cribbed, cabined and confined within his own narrow coterie and regarded those who lived outside his own charmed society as so many barbarians from whom he had nothing to learn and profit by.

The history of the past thousand years tells us that the Hindus have been living all these years in stupefaction like so many opium-eaters. The world's history, however, reveals the fact that when a nation is reduced to this state of intellectual stagnation, it loses the capacity to think for itself and places unshakeable faith in the past. It forgets that the world moves—that progress is the law of nature—that a nation, if it means to survive, must alter its manners and social customs according to the exigencies of times. When a nation is reduced to this abject and fallen state, it begins to look upon the scriptures as infallible and borrow light therefrom for its guidance in every-day life. This stage in the life of a nation may be characterised as its dark age. At this period two classes of men appear on the scene, following the law of demand and supply, namely the law-giver and his commentator.

When the spirit of inquiry dies out in a land, in vain do we look for the capacity for original investigation among its people. Naturally the sayings and injunctions of the holy fathers, Rishis and saints, are looked upon as the gospel. Hence arises the necessity for the commentators. A fresh disaster overtakes the society. In proportion as man loses faith in self-reliance and in the efficiency of his own individual efforts, he builds faith in miracles and in divine and superhuman interposition in his affairs. The priest has now a good time of it. He being inspired can alone read omens and interpret dreams. At this period no medicine is considered more efficacious than the holy water over which the inspired man has pronounced his benedictions. This was the state of things which obtained in Europe in the middle ages. Lecky in his *Rationalism in Europe* says :—

"There was scarcely a town that could not show some relic that had cured the sick * * * * men who were afflicted with apparently hopeless disease, started in a moment into perfect health when brought into contact with a relic of Christ or of the Virgin. The virtue of such relics radiated in blessings all around them . . . . . All this was going on habitually in every part of Europe without exciting the smallest astonishment or scepticism. Those who know how thoroughly the supernatural element pervades the old lives of the saints may form some notion of the multitude of miracles that were related and generally believed from the fact that M. Guizot has estimated the number of these lives, accumulated in the Bollandist Collection at about 25,000." The reader will not fail to detect a strange family relationship between the commentators of Europe and their Bengali *confreres*, namely Raghunandana and Kullukabhatta. The period in a nation's life when its best intellects are busy with writing commentaries and interpretations upon the sages of old is not a period to take glory in—it is a period of decadence.

Let us now turn our eyes to the really glorious period in India. She has not always been under the domination of the *Shastras.* Rationalism and the spirit of inquiry were the redeeming features of ancient India. The sage Kapila even goes the length of calling in question the very existence of God for it cannot be proved to demonstration. Kapila at any rate pays homage to the Vedas. The Upanishads and the six systems of Hindu philosophy also in a manner have admitted the infallibility and the revealed character of the Vedas and have thus disarmed the opposition of the orthodox classes. But the sage Charvaka has gone a step further. He boldly repudiates the divine origin of the Vedas and proclaims to the world:

"The Vedas with their descriptions of the heaven and hell are the creations of the fertile imagination of a few rogues and impostors, who have secured an easy means of earning their livelihood by working upon the fears and superstitions and the credulity of the princes and the people at large. As these wily priests themselves preside at the vedic rites and ceremonies (*yajna*), their offices have become indispensable and they thereby amass wealth and support their families in comfort. The Vedas again are full of contradictions. The authority of the *gnana kanda* is rejected by those who maintain that of the *karma kanda.* The three Vedas themselves in fact are the incoherent ravings of maniacs. These impostors have the hardihood to assert that the animals which are sacrificed in the *yajnas* are translated to the Heavens. If these rogues really have faith in their assertions why do they not decapitate their own parents and offer them as sacrifices? * * *"

The philosophy of Charvaka bears eloquent testimony to the spirit of inquiry in ancient India. The religion of Buddha later on preached the creed of universal love and brotherhood. The gates of learning were thrown wide open to every class of people and thus every class in its turn contributed its humble mite. To the Buddhists India is deeply indebted for the cultivation and improvement of the sciences of medicine and chemistry. It is enough to mention the name of Nagarjuna who recast the "Susruta tantra."* The treatise of *Susruta* bears distinct impress of Buddhistic tenets; it points out that the dissection of dead bodies is indispensable to the students of surgery and it lays particular stress on knowledge gained from experiment and observation. Vagbhata, the author of "Ashtangahridaya" was also a Buddhist and lest the orthodox Hindus should disregard his views he observes in one place not without a tinge of sarcasm: "If a work is to pass current as authoritative simply because it is the production of a sage of old, why are the treatises of Charaka and

---

* *History of Hindu Chemistry,* Introduction, Vol. 1 2nd Ed., XXIV.

Susruta alone studied and not those of Bhela, Jatukarna and others? It thus follows that a work is to be preferred not on account of its authorship but because of its intrinsic merit." In another place this great medical authority says "medicine is to be judged by its efficacy alone. It makes no difference whether it be administered by Brahma himself or by any one else." The great Nagarjuna rendered signal service to the science of chemistry. According to Chakrapani it was Nagarjuna who first introduced iron preparations in medicine; while according to Rasendrachintamani he is the inventor of the process of distillation.

In ancient India not only philosophy and literature reached a high level of perfection, but medicine, astronomy, mathematics and chemistry were zealously cultivated. The question now arises: why did all this intellectual progress come to a standstill and even stagnation?

According to some writers, it is due to the downfall of the Hindu princes with the advent of the Mussulman conquerors. But history belies this theory. The decadence of the Hindu intellect had commenced long before the followers of Islam had set foot on the Indian soil. Mussulman supremacy had never been permanently established in the Deccan and we might naturally have expected that Hindu learning and science would seek asylum in Southern India. It is again significant that the two great seats of learning in Bengal in the later period, namely

Navadwipa and Vikrampur, have flourished within easy reach, nay under the very glare of the eyes of the Nawabs of Murshidabad and Dacca. Roughly speaking, from the time of the Upanishads up till the period of the Mahayanist activity, *i.e.*, from about 600 B. C. to 700 A. D. has been named the " Rationalistic Age of India "—an age prolific of the best specimens of the Hindu brain-power. It was during this period that Panini composed his incomparable grammar and the *Rishis* their six systems of philosophy. Aryabhatta, Brahmagupta, Varahamihira and other mighty intellectual giants elaborated astronomy and the mathematical sciences. But the glory of India began to fade away.

Inscrutable are the laws which govern the rise and fall of nations. With the decline of Buddhism the Brahmins began to recover their lost ascendancy. But these latter-day Brahmins were the degenerate offsprings of those to whom we owe the rich treasures of the Upanishads and the six systems of philosophy. The religious books were now recast and remodelled and every care was taken to magnify the glories of the Brahmins and even to raise them to the position of deities. The spirit of inquiry now received a rude shock. Buddhism with its fundamental doctrine of universal brotherhood had thrown the gates of learning wide open to every class of people. The very essence of the rejuvenated Brahminism was exclusivism, if I may so use the expression. Guizot has pointed out the mischievous results of this kind of rule. This thoughtful writer has observed that in its very nature a priestly despotism restricts learning to its own classes and renders progress impossible, because while the mass of the people remains ignorant, its rulers have no incentive to improve or expand the learning which they possess. Hence in course of time learning loses its vitality and becomes a mere fossilized tradition useful only for the purpose of imposing on the ignorant and credulous. Religious speculation is of course strongly repressed and religion gradually degenerates into superstition combined with the mechanical observance of prescribed rites and ceremonies which are in themselves of no value. Unhappy India had now to pay a heavy penalty in the shape of intellectual stagnation. By the 5th century A.D. we find that the beginnings of a scientific astronomy had been laid. Varahamihira distinctly sets forth the doctrine of the diurnal revolution of the earth on its axis. Again Varahamihira, Aryabhatta, Srisena and Vishnuchandra offered the true explanation of the solar and lunar eclipses. But by and by, this scientific explanation came to be discarded. In compliance with the prejudices of the bigots an eighth planet, Rahu, was invented as the immediate cause of the eclipse. Astronomy thus slowly degenerated into astrology. Manu now laid down that the very touch of a corpse would defile the sacred person of a Brahmin and thus we find that shortly after the time of Vagbhat the handling of a lancent was discouraged and anatomy and surgery fell into disuse and became to all intents and purposes lost sciences to the Hindus.

In my "History of Hindu Chemistry" under the chapter devoted to the "Knowledge of Technical Arts and Decline of Scientific Spirit," I have thus summed up the pernicious consequences of the "Laws" of Manu. "It was considered equally undignified to sweat away at the forge like a Cyclops. Hence the cultivation of the Kalas by the more refined classes of the Society of which we get such vivid pictures in the ancient Sanskrit literature has survived only in traditions for a very long time past.

"The arts being thus relegated to the low castes and the professions made hereditary, a certain degree of fineness, delicacy and deftness in manipulation was no doubt secured, but this was done at a terrible cost. The intellectual portion of the community being thus withdrawn from active participation in the arts, the *how* and *why* of phenomena—the co-ordination of cause and effect—were lost sight of—the spirit of inquiry gradually died out among a nation naturally prone to speculation and metaphysical subtleties and India for once bade adieu to experimental and inductive sciences. Her soil was rendered morally unfit for the birth of a Boyle, a Descartes or a Newton and her very name was all but expunged from the map of the scientific world."

Had Manu and other law-givers rested contented with merely prohibiting dissection of dead bodies, we should have been grateful to them for their moderation. But they went farther. Sea-voyage was equally interdicted. We learn from the travels of the

Chinese pilgrim Fa-Hien that he sailed on his homeward journey from Tamralipti (Tamluk). to Ceylon and travelled in company with Brahmin merchants. It is well-known that the Hindus had colonized the islands of Java and Bali and vestiges of Hindu religions and temples are still to be found in these places. We also learn from Buddhistic literature that an extensive maritime trade was carried on between Varocha (modern Broach) and Alassandra (Alexandria). It is now believed that there was not only commercial, but also intellectual intercourse between India and Egypt and that the Neo-Platonists thus received the doctrines of the Upanishads. Commerce secures exchange of ideas, rounds off the angularities of nations and binds together mankind in the golden tie of brotherhood. The more we know a people by actual contact the more we begin to think charitably of it. It is because of this mutual contact with one another that the different nations of Europe have attained to the same degree of civilization and scientific eminence. Whenever new discoveries have been made in the realm of science or new doctrines have been preached by reformers, the entire European world has profited by them. When Martin Luther shook off the thraldom of the Pope and boldly placarded his protest in the Church-gate of Wurtemberg, the glad tidings reached from one corner of Europe to the other and stirred the inmost depths of society. Then again no sooner had Galileo, Copernicus, Kepler and Newton published the results of their observations in Astronomy and Physical Science than they became the common heritage of every European.

Our Shastras by proscribing sea-voyage aimed a death-blow at our future progress. Conservatism, it is true, has its uses, but there is a limit to it. Progress —social, political and intellectual—is the law of Nature. A nation which refuses to move with the altered condition of the times is doomed to stagnation and decay. Ruskin says somewhere that a man is in depth of degradation when he loses the power of appreciating the noble qualities of his fellow-beings. The Hindu began to regard himself as the quintessence of all that is good and noble in creation and to look down upon those who had the misfortune to live outside the pale of his society. The latter were contemptuously named *barbarians* from whom nothing was to be learned.* The Hindu now began to live in a world of isolation like the proverbial frog-in-the-well. I have so long been using the term " Hindu " in a wide sense. It should be noted here that by this term is not to be meant the mass of people who were simply allowed to live on sufferance under the pale of the society, but a handful of men who had managed to monopolise all the privileges of a dominant caste. Swami Vivekananda truly observes :—

" A religion which does not feel for the miseries

* But the Hindus of an earlier age were more liberal in this respect. Varahamihira enjoins that as the Mlechchha teachers (Greeks) are experts in Astronomy we should sit at their feet and venerate them like Rishis.

of the poor, which does not uplift man, forfeits the name of "religion." Our religion has degenerated into a creed of the "touchable" and "untouchable." O! my God, the country whose best intellects have for the last two thousand years busied themselves with such abstruse problems as the propriety of taking up the food with the right hand or the left, whose *mantras* begin with the mystic *kat et krang, kring, hihi*—that country only courts and richly deserves downfall."

When a country is reduced to this abject state thousand and one pernicious customs spring up and corrode and eat into the vitals of the social fabric. With the expulsion of Buddhism from Bengal and the re-assertion of Brahminical ascendancy, the "Kulinism" as instituted by King Ballala Sen reared its head. The down-trodden "low-caste" people whom the cruel tyranny of the hierarchy drove to the condition of the "untouchables"—the *Doms, Bagdis, Chandals, Handis*, etc.—writhing in agony and smarting under indignity, now sought relief by embracing Islamism, which not only preaches but practises the brotherhood of man. We may give credit to those who were responsible for the institution of *Kulinism* when they made it the reward for personal merit and intellectual and moral attainments. But when *Kulinism* became hereditary the Bengali sank deeper and deeper in the mire of degradation. The hour makes the man. Devivara Ghataka now appeared on the scene. Erudite works on the genealogy of the *Kulins* were composed.

The Bengali had already bound himself hand and foot by the injunctions of the *Shastras* as interpreted by the Pandits of Navadwipa. As if this were not enough he put on new fetters forged by Devivara and his worthy co-adjutors. When the Bengali thus voluntarily submitted himself to the operations of these artificial laws, Nature was not slow in wreaking her vengeance. *Kulinism* forbade matrimonial alliances with those in whose veins ran "impure" blood. The canker of polygamy thus entered into the social system.

The division of the Bengali society into numerous sects and sub-sects—the Varendra, Rari, Vangaj, etc.,—is the logical outcome of the ill-fated *Kulinism.* Standing on the threshold of the 20th century we can now take a survey of the multitude of evils wrought by this system. "I shall not marry your daughter"—"I shall not accept food of you"—"If I dine with you I shall be outcasted"—"If I tread upon your very shadow I shall become impure"—these and such-like inequalities have wrought havoc in our social economy. Man cannot live by bread alone. He longs for fellowship and sympathy. The "low-caste" people numbering millions who form the very backbone of the society thus began to cherish and harbour ill-feelings and even resentment against the higher classes. The Bengali people thus ceased to be a nation having community of interests, but was spilt up into a congeries of sects and classes. When Bengal was thus enveloped in darkness, a glimmering ray of light shone for a time in the person of the Prophet of Navadwipa.

The religion of love which Chaitanya preached did away with the inequalities and barriers of caste. The depressed classes rallied round his banner, nay, some of the best intellects of the day responded to his call. But the spirit of the time was not propitious. The enthusiasm kindled by the personal magnetism of Chaitanya soon died away. His religion shortly after his death ceased to be a living force and was encrusted over with dogmas. Still it is not too much to say that but for Vaishnavism 95 per cent. of the population of Bengal would have embraced Islamism.

Brahminism re-asserted its ascendancy. Little did Raghunandana and his holy *confreres* perceive to what depth of degradation unhappy Bengal would sink as the inevitable result of their stringent interpretation of the Shastric injunctions. When a man ceases to feel for brother man, he ceases to feel for his country. He cannot look beyond the horizon of his own immediate interests. He becomes a living personification of selfishness. The noblest gift of God—patriotism—had no meaning for the Bengalee.

Such was the state of the society in Bengal when the English appeared on the scene. The Bengalee leaders—Hindu and Mussalman—who figure in the eventful drama which ended with the downfall of Mir Kasim, were some of the sorriest specimens of humanity—dead to the dictates of conscience and humanity. Each and one was ready to sell his birthright for a mess of pottage. Mr. Kaliprasanna Banerji in his admirable "History of Bengal under the Nawabs"—a work which has made Bengali literature all the richer—thus sums up in a nut-shell the results of his studies :—"I have been compelled to criticise severely the deeds and characters of many persons; in doing so, I have not lost sight of the fact that the latter were only creatures of circumstances. Individuals are the products of the social evolution of the age; they can seldom rise superior to the spirit of the times. The downfall of the Mussulmans and the rise of the British power do not redound to the credit or glory of either party. But the infamy and the stigma of the nefarious deeds must for ever blacken the leading Hindus of this period. The English, inspite of their many defects, could act in a corporate capacity and with singleness of aim and it is these qualities which secured them the supremacy."

In the early days of the British power a grand opportunity presented itself. A handful of English traders had laid the foundation of a vast Empire. But the foreign rulers could not get on without the help and co-operation of the children of the soil, especially in the department of the collection of revenue. A good many Bengalees thus secured lucrative appointments on the Dewany (civil) side. But their infamous deeds have stamped indelible stain on the Bengalee character.

Another and still grander opportunity was lost upon the Bengalees. When the East India Company first set foot on the soil of Bengal they began with establishing factories in Cossimbazar, Govindpur, Sutanati and other places. Ignorant of the manners, customs and language of the people, the early English traders had to rely entirely on the help of the Bengalee. The founders of some of the families of Calcutta of to-day thus amassed fabulous wealth. Even up till the fifties and sixties of the last century the European merchants could not do without the Bengalee agent, broker and *banian*. Traditions of the millionaire "Mutshuddis" of the big "Houses" survive to the present day. But the Bengalee neglected this tide in the affairs of men. Commercial enterprise has always been foreign to his nature. The "Mutshuddis" and their wealthy descendants lived a life of ease and luxury and never cared to start business on their own account. In the meantime, the European merchant, ever on the alert, began to gain in local knowledge and conscious of his own strength, learned to manage without the Bengalee agents. The latter thus began to be ousted from the position of vantage. True it is that the Bengalee is equally indispensable to-day; but it is only as clerks and quill-drivers on a wretched pittance. It should be noted here that the gap created by the incapacity of the Bengalee was not entirely filled up by the Europeans. The enterprising people of Bombay, Gujarat, Bikanir and the United Provinces, who have got a hereditary instinct for business, began to flock to

Bengal and establish themselves in the chief emporiums of trade.

In the meantime a new danger threatened Bengal. The substitution of steam-power for hand labour had created a revolution in the industrial world. From the early days of the East India Company an extensive export trade in cotton goods had sprung up bringing wealth to the tune of several crores of rupees to the pockets of the weavers of Dacca, Santipore, Chandernagore, etc. In fact the "drain" of wealth from England to Bengal had begun to draw the attention of a school of English politicians. In 1815 the cotton goods exported from India were of the value of £1,300,000. But by 1840 Dacca, once the Manchester of India, had fallen off from a very flourishing town to a very small one and its population had dwindled down from 150,000 to 30,000 or 40,000.

During the last half-a-century fighting against tremendous odds, Bombay has been able to rear a magnificent industry in textile fabrics. Bombay was roused from the sleep of stupor and could take time by the fore lock. Unhappy Bengal which boasts of the keen intellect of her sons chose otherwise. With the spread of English education, the foundation of the Calcutta University and the substitution of English for Persian as the Court language, there arose a steady demand for English-knowing clerks, Munsiffs and Deputy-Magistrates. Moreover, Bengal, with its Permanent Settlement and the numerous nice discriminations in the land tenure, has been a happy hunting ground for lawyers. University education in Bengal has thus come to be looked upon as a mere passport for a professional or a clerical career. It is true some members of the bar have scored success which must be pronounced as phenomenal and which fires the young aspirant with emulation. But the learned professions are already over-crowded and we doubt very much if one in ten has now a chance of earning a decent livelihood.

Since the foundation of the British power the Bengalee has learned to look upon service under the Government or in the numerous European merchants' houses as the be-all and end-all of his existence. Whenever a new territory has been annexed, the Bengalee has followed the fortunes of the British Raj as affording fresh field and pastures new for the display of his clerical genius. From the Punjab to Burmah there has thus been an unending chain—a network of Bengalee *keranis.* His sole ambition in life has been to court the favour and sedulously cultivate the good graces of his official superior. Brought up for generations in the school of servility and sycophancy the Bengalee lost manliness and self-reliance and even self-respect and fast deteriorated in some of the noble qualities which go to the making of a nation.

There does not exist a more miserable being on earth than a Bengalee youth, fresh from the University and crowned with her laurels. He will die of starvation unless he is taken care of by some tender hand and at once provided with a situation. He ends his days in quill-driving and thus makes a grave-yard of his academic lore.

The Swadeshi movement has brought home to us the necessity of engaging in commercial pursuits and starting industries. But our national asset in this direction has been of a poor type. The Bengalee has never been taught to stand on his legs. He cuts a sorry figure when he encounters the rough-and-tumble of the life of a man of business. The fact is that the Bengalee of to-day is but the product of the social evolution of the by-gone ages. I have already pointed out that through sheer criminal folly and negligence we allowed the internal and external trade of the country to slip out of our hands. The exports and imports of India have now reached the colossal sum of 300 crores of rupees. Barely an infinitesimal fraction of this huge trade we participate in. While our eyes remained fixed on the Government service as on the pole-star, the enterprising up-country people and the Marwaris managed to capture our trade. We in our turn have taken a noble revenge by applying to them the not very complimentary epithets of "brainless" and "chatukhor" (flour-eater), as if the very perfection of brain-power lies in the routine-work of quill-driving! It is of no use blinking stern facts. The Marwaris are already in the possession of the field of commerce and some members of the community are amongst our few merchant princes. The Bengalee youth cannot do better than learn the first principles of business at the feet of these enterprising people. He must go through the period of probation and apprenticeship in their warehouses. He must study the conditions of the market and must know where to buy and when to sell. Much of the success in business depends upon being able to grasp the psychological moment. The man brought up in commercial pursuits becomes self-reliant; he learns to stand on his own legs and grows in resourcefulness. In short, some of the noblest qualities of man are thus called into play. But the Bengalee has become utterly demoralized. The Swadeshi movement has come upon us as a god-send. But how futile our efforts have been in this direction! We have to cast wistful eyes to the mill-owners of Bombay so that they may come to our rescue by supplying us with clothes. Then there is the great jute-industry, which is *par excellence* the industry of Bengal. There are some 60 mills plying on the banks of the Hughli—but not even a solitary one is owned by a Bengalee.

I hope I have made it abundantly clear that the Bengalee youth must turn a new leaf in his career. He must not create new difficulties and add to his embarrassments. He, the proud winner of academic distinctions, sells himself to the highest bidder in the matrimonial market and inexorable Nature exacts her full penalty. He is sorely handicapped in the struggle for existence. When about to enter the world he is burdened with the cares of a growing amily and has to content himself with anything that comes in his way—a clerkship fetching Rs. 30 to 40 per month. All the hopes and aspirations are crushed out of him. At an age when the English youth is full of cheerfulness and elasticity of spirits and when the world presents before him gorgeous vistas of prospects, his Bengalee *confrere* looks upon life as a spring of dismal episodes and grows prematurely old.

It has become customary with certain writers to decry and inveigh against western civilization and hold up the Europeans to scorn as being worshippers of Mammon. But they forget that the Hindu society, *as it is*, is thoroughly permeated with materialism. Those who go up for University education are taught to look upon it purely as a means to an end. A diploma is judged by its monetary equivalent—as something which can be turned into cash.

We are concerned only with the present and not with the past—with the society of to-day. If such a state of things is to be characterised as conducive to spiritualism, as opposed to materialism, I do not know what vandalism is. The Bengalee is as fond of money as any people on earth, nay, he is perhaps the most mercenary of all. He has prostituted one of the noblest gifts of God, namely, thirst for knowledge. England, Germany and America are growing enormously rich—the wealth gathered from the four corners of the earth are being poured forth into these countries. But we must bear in mind that modern Europe and America alone can boast of devoted worshippers at the shrine of learning, engaged in unravelling the mysteries of Nature. Galileo suffered the tortures of the Inquisition and Bruno was burned at the stake for their fearless vindication of the doctrine of Copernicus. Nor need we pause here to allude to the life-long devotion to the cause of science of a Newton, a Faraday, a Scheele, a Pasteur and a Berthelot. It is to Europe that we must now turn our eyes for the realisation of the ideal presented by our own *Rishis* —unflagging and concentrated devotion to the pursuit of knowledge for its own sake. If Europe has become the mistress of the world, it is because she could not help it since *knowledge is power.* The man of science in Europe braves the rigours of the Polar Expedition and the malarial fevers in the almost impenetrable regions of Africa and heroically courts death by inoculating himself with the germs of many a fell disease so that he might study their activities on the human system. But what a sorry spectacle is presented by our own youths ! They bid farewell to the Goddess of learning as soon as they have secured the hall-mark of the University—it is the " diploma " that they really care for. Our boys of course are not to blame for this morbid appetite. They have been brought up amidst surroundings which have taught them to set a fictitious value upon a University qualification and upon book-lore in general.

Sir Walter Scott while at school was pronounced a *blockhead* by one master and a *dunce* by another. An eminent teacher of Bengalee youths in the good old days of the Hindu College, one who was the idol of his pupils, thus wrote more than sixty years ago: "Schoolmasters are generally very bad judges of the intellectual character of their pupils. They are apt to measure a boy's natural powers by his industry or acquirements alone, not remembering how often the first boy in a school turns out a dull man in the world, while many a youth who has been impatient of

"The drilled, dull lesson, forced down word by word"

has astonished, delighted and improved his fellow-creatures with the splendour and fertility of his genius. Mere idleness is often mistaken for incapacity, and close application for original mental power. The exertions of the memory also are too highly rated. It requires extreme sagacity to discover the real character of a boy's mind, which is sometimes more clearly developed in a casual remark than in an ostentatious display of scholastic acquisition. But even an early quickness of intellect is not a surer indication of future eminence than extraordinary advance in school-learning, whether the result of dogged labour or a retentive memory; and we often find a certain sprightliness in boyhood followed by dullness and stupidity in mature life, while the sluggish youth becomes a brilliant man. The human mind is like an April day: the dawn is exceedingly deceitful. These considerations may console the friends of apparently slow and unsuccessful students, who should never be disheartened by the difficulty they feel in keeping pace with their school-fellows."

We make too much of the "brilliant" man of the University forgetting that in nine cases out of ten in the world's broad battle-field he turns out to be a failure, "he is as a bankrupt to whom brilliant opportunities offer in vain." Our "brilliant" University man is often one who can develop a taste for half a-dozen subjects simultaneously. But in God's creation as one man can scarcely have genuine taste except for one subject, it is the *flashy* youth with a retentive memory who scores. The Empire-builders and the Captains of Industry have not, as a rule, been "brilliant" 'Versity men—but men with a dogged purpose who have been allowed to develop in their own way. George Eliot embodies this view in a few lines when she thus speaks of her hero Tom: "I think he is not a youth of whom you would prophesy failure in anything he had thoroughly wished: the wagers are likely to be on his side, notwithstanding his small success in the classics. For Tom had never desired success in this field of enterprise; and for getting a fine flourishing growth of stupidity there is nothing like pouring on a mind a good amount of subjects in which it feels no interest." If you are a lawyer or a physician or an engineer pray do not force your boy to be a replica or a facsimile of yourself but leave him alone to indulge his taste. Emerson also feels the cramping effect of the 'Versity education on genius when he says: "It is curious how perverse and intermeddling we are, and what vast pains we incur to do the wrong. Whilst we all know in our experience and apply natural methods in our business,—in education our common sense fails us and we are continually trying costly machinery against nature, in patent schools and academies and in great colleges and Universities." In another place this profound thinker observes: "Universities are, of course, hostile to geniuses, which, seeing and using ways of their own, discredit routine." We have begun to look upon the University as a kind of fetish and without hesitation pronounce the verdict of "a failure"—'an incapable' upon a plucked candidate and shake our head over his future prospects. How many a promising career has been blasted by this mistaken attitude of our society!

I shall conclude my paper with a few more remarks. I am afraid I have wounded the susceptibilities of some of my countrymen. I have written more in sorrow than in anger. I am as proud of the glories of the Hindus of old as anybody and I have spent the best years of my life in rescuing from oblivion and bringing before the world the contributions of the Hindus to the great branch of the science which I have the honour to profess. What I want to point out is that by our unquestioned acquiescence in the wisdom of the sages of the past—by regulating our every-day life according to the inflexible rules of the *Smritis* our social fabric has been brought to stagnation and decay.

Kullukabhatta and Raghunandana may be given their dues. We may even admire their learning. But they have had their days. The Hindu put on the shackles of the *Shastras* and *Smritis* and the result was that from morn to noon and from noon to dewy eve his life was a dreary routine of rites and observances. He became an automaton—all his movements being controlled from outside. He had no time to think for himself. No wonder he ceased to produce any work betokening originality. A philosophical writer thus eloquently summarises the causes which led to the downfall of Spain: "The victory gained by the church increased both her power and reputation. During the rest of the seventeenth century, not only were the interests of the clergy deemed superior to the interests of the laymen, but the interests of laymen were scarcely thought of. The greatest men, with hardly an exception, became ecclesiastics and all temporal considerations, all views of earthly policy, were despised and set at nought. No one enquired, no one doubted; no one presumed to ask if all this was right. The minds of men succumbed and were prostrate. While every other country was advancing, Spain alone was receding. Every other country was making some addition to knowledge, creating some arts, or enlarging some sciences, Spain, numbed into a death-like torpor, spell-bound and entranced by the accursed superstition which preyed on her strength, presented to Europe a solitary instance of constant decay. For her no hope remained; and, before the close of the seventeenth century, the only question was by whose hands the blow should be struck, which should dismember that once mighty empire, whose shadow had covered the world and whose vast remains were imposing even in their ruin."

Later on the same writer continues: "A people who regard the past with too wistful an eye will never bestir themselves to help the onward progress; they will hardly believe that progress is possible. To them antiquity is synonymous with wisdom, and every improvement is a dangerous innovation. In this state, Europe lingered for many centuries; in this state Spain still lingers. Hence the Spaniards are remarkable for an inertness, a want of buoyancy, and an absence of hope, which in our busy and enterprising age isolate them from the rest of the civilized world. Believing that little can be done, they are in no hurry to do it. Believing that the knowledge they have inherited, is far greater than any they can obtain, they wish to preserve their intellectual possessions whole and unimpaired; inasmuch as the least alteration in them might lessen their value. Content with what has been already bequeathed, they are excluded from that great European movement, which first perceptible in the sixteenth century, has ever since been steadily advancing, unsettling odd opinions, destroying old follies, reforming and improving on every side, but leaving Spain unscathed. While the human intellect has been making the most prodigious and unheard-of strides, while discoveries in every quarter are simultaneously pressing upon us, and coming in such rapid and bewildering succession that the strongest sight, dazzled by the glare of their splendour, is unable to contemplate them as a whole; while other discoveries still more important and still more remote from ordinary experience are manifestly approaching and may be seen looming in the distance whence they are now obscurely working on the advanced thinkers who are nearest to them, filling their minds with those ill-defined, restless, and almost uneasy feelings which are the invariable harbingers of future triumph; while the veil is being rudely torn, and nature, violated at all points, is forced to disclose her secrets and reveal her structure, her economy, and her laws, to the indomitable energy of man; while Europe is ringing with the noise of intellectual achievements, with which even despotic Governments affect to sympathise, in order that they may divert them from their natural course, and use them as new instruments, whereby to oppress yet more the liberties of the people; while amidst this general din and excitement, the public mind swayed to and fro is tossed and agitated,—Spain sleeps on untroubled, unheeding, impassive, receiving no impressions from the rest of the world, and making no impressions upon it. There she lies at the further extremity of the Continent, a huge and torpid mass, the sole representative now remaining of the feelings and knowledge of the Middle Ages. And, what is the worst symptom of all, she is satisfied with her own condition. Though she is the most backward country in Europe, she believes herself to be the foremost; she is proud of every thing of which she should be ashamed."—Buckle.

The above characterization applies with still greater force to our country.

We appeal to the past but we forget that in the days of our glory the stringency of the caste-system was unknown. Vyasa, the great compiler of the Vedas, was born of a fishwoman. Ram Chandra was not ashamed to embrace the *Chandal*, Guhaka, as his most intimate friend. Srikrishna in his infancy was brought up by a cow-woman. Why were not these great men out-casted and spurned away as *untouchables*?

In the India of the future there should be a harmonious commingling of the new and the old, a fusion of the West and the East. There should be equal opportunity for the growth and development of the Hindu and the Mussalman; of the high and the low; of the Brahmin and the Pariah. I have tried to bring home to my countrymen the following points: The Bengalees are inferior to none as far as the brain-power is concerned, but unfortunately his intellectual gifts have been misapplied. Hence the Bengalee's contribution to the world's stock of knowledge has been very meagre. During the Mussulman period his subtle genius was wasted in scholastic disputations and in the nice discriminations of the Shastric regulations and injunctions. Under the existing *regime* a race of lawyers has sprung up, who are maintaining the traditions of old as the intellectual descendants of the products of the *tols* and displaying admirable forensic acumen. But the law at best can offer careers only to a limited few,—to an infinitesimal fraction of our educated youths. The Bengalees have practically degenerated into a race of quill-drivers. It is time we were roused from our torpor. Let the vast latest potentialities of the nation be roused to activity. Let the Bengalee distinguish himself in the field of researches and scientific investigations; let him organise industries. He will soon have his place in the comity of nations and thus fulfil the will of God.

SOCIAL REFORM IN INDIA

The following is Dr. Ray's presidential address to the Indian National Social Conference held at Calcutta in December, 1917:—

I make no apology for appearing before you on this platform though I feel that my faith and training make my position somewhat delicate. I am, however, encouraged by the thought that I am one of you in spite of the particular hall-mark I may happen to bear. I crave your indulgence and hope that my humble words will be taken in the spirit in which they are offered.

We stand to-day on the threshold of a new era in our history as a nation. New ideas, high aspirations are pulsating in our hearts. A wave of democratic movement is spreading all over the world. It cannot be expected that India alone will remain a mere passive and silent on-looker unaffected by the time-spirit.

A dispassionate observer watching the present state of things from a position of detachment cannot fail to notice the weak points in our body politic. While the echo of *Swaraj* or Home-Rule is reverberating from one end of the country to the other,—while ambitious schemes of political re-construction are being propounded by every section of the people—while gorgeous visions of a United India are capturing our imagination—loud protests of indignation are raised by classes and communities amongst us which we can no longer ignore. Why is there this note of discord where there should be only peace and harmony? Why this rift in the lute?

The answer lies in a nut-shell. It is our failure to recognise that the question which presses for solution at the present moment is as much a political as a sociological one. By the nature of things, it must be so. For, however much we may try to divide and isolate the various parts of the national problem, they cling to one another as fast as ever and mock our attempts at self-deception. We cannot, with impunity, give undue preference to one over others. The law of *Karma* or causation is inexorable, and our past neglect in the work of social reform is bearing its evil fruit at the present hour. It has begun to clog the wheels of political progress. Let me state the problem clearly and definitely, and, in doing so, I shall confine myself chiefly to my own province, though what I am going to say will apply *mutatis mutandis* to the other provinces as well.

Leaving our brethren of the Islamic faith out of account, though they form the majority of the population in Bengal, we find that out of 21 millions of Hindus, Brahmins contribute 12½ lakhs, Kayasthas 11 lakhs and Baidyas only 89 thousands. As you are all aware, these three castes constitute what is called the higher castes in the Bengali social hierarchy. Then come the *Navasakas i.e.*, the various castes and sub-castes which are allowed to carry water for the Brahmins and are thus placed under the category of the touchables; these include the Tantis, Tilis, Kaivartas, Sadgopas, Gandhabaniks, etc.

Next come the vast majority of the population most of which occupy the lowermost rungs in the social ladder and are more or less classed as *untouchables.* It is not my intention to take up your valuable time or tire out your patience by entering into any lengthy details regarding them. If I at all refer to these, it is only to point a moral and adorn a tale —in this case, I regret to say, a tale of woe and national disgrace. It should be remembered that what is called a bold peasantry and stalwart yeomanry are mainly contributed by these so-called *untouchables.*

Let us for a moment take a historical retrospect of the gradual formation of the social strata of Bengal. From the 7th to 11th century A.D., this province was more or less converted to the Buddhistic faith. A brass image has recently been unearthed in East Bengal, from the inscription attached to which we learn that Queen Pravabati of Samatata (Gangetic Delta), though herself belonging to a dynasty professing the creed of Buddha, was by no means inimical to the worship of the Goddess Sarvani (a form of Durga). From another copper-plate we also glean that the Queen of Madanapala of the Pala dynasty made a grant of land to certain Brahmins who recited to her episodes from the Mahabharata. We also gather from the Chinese traveller, Hiouen Chuang, that in the 7th century A.D., King Siladitya of Kanauj (Harsabardhan) was a Saivite with Buddhist proclivities. In fact, the whole of Northern India from Kanauj to the Gangetic Delta was under the sway of Buddhism. It is scarcely necessary to point out that, during this period, the Caste System, if it did not altogether disappear, was very much relaxed and there were frequent inter-marriages among the members of different castes and classes.

On the decline of Buddhism, when the Brahminical faith once more began to rear its head, a sort of reorganization of the existing castes and sub-castes took place. Hinduism with its graded system of castes received an authoritative stamp under King Ballala Sen, the reputed founder of *kulinism*. Those who were the earliest to recognise the signs of the times rallied round the king and supported his reconstituted hierarchy, and thus secured for themselves social precedence. There were many, however, who called in question the pretensions of this ruler and held aloof. They were mostly degraded to the lower ranks; the Suvarna-baniks and the Jogis suffered most, inasmuch as water offered by them is not drinkable by the members of the privileged classes.

Here we have in a nut-shell an insight into the social history of Bengal. A convenient legend has been given currency to in later times that as, during the Buddhist period of social disintegration, religious rites as enjoined in the Vedas were well-nigh forgotten in Bengal, five learned Brahmins were imported from

Kanauj by King Adisur to revive the *Sanatan Dharma* whatever it may mean.

Granting that there is some sub-stratum of fact in the above legend, it may be reasonably asked how many of the 13 lakhs of Brahmins in Bengal to-day can claim direct lineal descent from these five prolific ancestors, who, by the bye, were not accompanied by their consorts. As Mr. Ramprasad Chanda, a devoted worker of the Varendra Research Society, very tersely puts it:—"One other obstacle to the credibility of the stories of the origin of the Bengali Brahmans as given in the geneological works of Radhiyas and Varendras, is that it involves the assumption of the practical absence of Brahmans in Bengal 30 to 35 generations, or, say, eight to ten centuries before. According to the geneologists of Radhiyas there were seven hundred Brahman families in Bengal at the time of the coming of the five Brahmans from Kanauj. But now-a-days representatives of the seven hundred families are nowhere to be met with, whereas, the descendants of the five immigrants fill the whole country." Scratch a *Saptasati* Brahmin and you will find non-Aryan blood in him.

It is well known that when a handful of men, even of a superior race or culture migrates to a distant land and settles down in the midst of a backward race, the former is compelled by the laws of nature to choose their mates from among the latter. It is also believed that some of the sub-castes amongst Brahmans in other provinces are of foreign origin. I shall not name them for obvious reasons. A similar state of things is going on under our very eyes among the *Nambudri* Brahmins in Malabar. It is an historical as also a sociological fact that, barring a few isolated instances, the Brahmins of Bengal and other provinces are made up of a heterogeneous blend. Ethnology also tells the same tale, and anthropometric data and cephalometric measurements fail at any rate to detect much radical difference in the facial cantours of a Brahmin and a non-Brahmin. Mr. Chanda very pithily sums up the results of his own researches in the following lines:— "The head form of the Outlandic Brahman does not support his claim to be the pure-blooded descendant of the Midlandic Vedic Rishis but indicates his close physical relationship to his non-Brahman neighbours classed as Sudras and "antyajas," or outcastes. The wide difference in the head form of the Kanyakubjya Brahmans of the United Provinces and Maithila Brahmans of Bihar on the one hand, and the Nagar Brahmans of Guzarat and Radhiya, Varendra and Vaidika Brahmans of Bengal on the other, cannot be explained by the miscegeneration alone, but indicates that the Brahmans of the outer countries are at base Outlandic in stock and have not absorbed Midlandic elements in larger proportions than their non-Brahman clients (yajmana)." Sir Herbert Risley's ethnological conclusions may not be palatable to many of us, but Mr. Chanda's investigations at any rate go to establish the social identity of the various castes and sub-castes. So much for the Brahmins. As for the Kayasthas, there is a current Bengali saying 'whoever loses his caste takes shelter under the hospitable fold of the Kayasthas.' Apart from the Kulins and Mauliks, there are some 72 sub-classes among them. Any member of these, if he can graduate in the University or earn a fair competence, is sought after by our blue-blooded Kulins, who vie with one another in offering him his daughter in marriage; and thus promotion in pedigree from sub-class 72 to a *Maulik* is constantly going on. Again, according to no less an authority than M. M. Haraprasad Shastri, the Mauliks were mainly Buddhists.

It is unfortunate that chemical analysis cannot be applied to ascertain the degree of adulteration in the blood of Brahmans and Kayasthas as in the case of *ghee* (clarified butter). As far as one can see, the caste regulations in their present crystallized form dates from the time of Ballala Sen; and latterly, Raghunandan has done his bit, who was generous enough to concede that Kayasthas are after all Sudras—but of a higher order. Then again, the northern part of the Empire of the Palas was overrun by a horde of barbarians from Thibet and a kingdom was carved out by them which lasted for half a century till it was overthrown by Mahipala. These exotic settlers were finally absorbed in the main population as is attested by the numerous temples which they have left behind them. The kingdom of Kuch-Behar at one time also embraced considerable portions of Northern Bengal, and this lends support to the theory of an admixture of Mongolian blood amongst certain classes in the Varendra land. Tod's surmise that some of the clans of the Rajputs and Jats are of Hun and Scythian origin has been borne out by recent researches. This is not the time nor the place to enter into an elaborate discussion as to the infusion of non-Aryan blood into the high-caste Brahmins, but the following extract from Ranade's address on "Southern India a Hundred years ago" may throw a flood of light on this subject:

"The fact appears to be that the Brahmin settlers in Southern India and the warriors and traders who came with them were too few in number and too weak in power to make any lasting impression beyond their limited circle upon the vast multitudes who constituted the aboriginal races in the Southern Peninsula. In North India where their power was more distinctly felt they appear to have been, about the commencement of the Christian era, submerged by fresh hordes of Scythians or Sakas, of Huns and the Jats or Goths who subverted the Roman Empire. In Southern India, it was not foreign invasion, but the upheaval of the aboriginal Dravidian races which brought about pretty much the same result. There is a tone of despondency and panic in the Puranas written about this time which can only be explained by some such phenomena. However this may be, this is certain, that when Hinduism revived from the depression into which it had fallen in consequence of the rise of Buddhism, it did not revive in its old pristine purity, but in the more or less adulterated form as we now see it even at the present day. In their anxiety to destroy Buddhism and later on the Jain faith, the Brahmins allied themselves with the barbarians of the land, represented in the countless multitudes which they had till then contemptuously treated as Sudras and as out of the pale of their early institutions. From being sages and prophets, poets and philosophers they descended to the lower level of priests and purohits and thus sacrificed their independence for the advantage of power and profit. The gods and goddesses of the Dasyus or Rakshasas who held no place in the old pantheon were identified as being more or less pure forms of the old Brahminical Triad or rather of the two divisions of Shaiva and Vaishnava cults. The old elastic system of the three divisions of the Aryas and the fourth non-Aryan section became crystallised into local and professional castes of which the Brahmans became the priests; and these sub-divisions became strict and insurmountable barriers. Such a change as this could not be brought about without a surrender all along the line to the brute force of barbarian influences......................Brahmanism having failed to conquer from want of power allowed itself to be degraded and conquered by the multitudes whom it failed to civilise." Why then this boast of heraldry? Why this apotheosis of pedigree? Why then this insatiate craving for claiming descent from the Sun and the Moon and tracing geneology from the Vedic Rishis?

At present it is custom and traditions which have usurped the place of religion in the affairs of the Hindu people. It is noteworthy that Manu, and Parasara, and the Mahabharata were more liberal and catholic as regards marriage laws and caste regulations than the latter-day commentators and exegists like Raghunandan. I can only make time to read out to you one or two extracts from these:

"The Yaksha asked, 'By what, O King! birth, character, study or learning, doth a person become a Brahmana? Tell us with certitude.'

Yudhishthira answered—" Listen, O Yaksha! It is neither birth, nor study, nor learning that is the cause of Brahmanhood. Without doubt, it is character that constitutes it. One's character should always be well guarded, especially by a Brahmana. He who maintaineth character unimpaired, never impairs himself. He, however, whose character is lost, is lost himself."

(*Mahabharata, Vana Parva, Chap.* 312.

"Receive pure learning even from a man of lower caste, the highest law even from the lowest, and the gem of a wife even from a base family.

Wives, learning, (the knowledge of) the law, (the rules of) purity, good advice, and various arts may be acquired from any body."

(*Manusamhita, Chap. II*, st. 238, 240).

"The texts of Revelation contradict one another.

The traditions also contradict one another. There is not even one Rishi whose opinion can be accepted as infallible. The truth about religion and duty is hid in caves. Therefore, that alone is the path which is followed by great men."

(*Mahabharat, Vana Parva, Chap.* 312.)

"The maiden, though marriageable, should rather stop in (the father's) house until death, than that he should give her to a man destitute of good qualities."

(*Manusamhita, Chap.* 9—st. 87.)

"For the first marriage of twice born men (wives) of equal caste are recommended; but for those who through desire proceed (to marry again) the following females, (chosen) according to the (direct) order (of the castes), are most approved. It is declared a Sudra woman alone (can be) the wife of a Sudra, she and one of his own caste (the wives) of a Vaisya, those two and one of his own caste (the wives) of a Kshatriya, those three and one of his own caste (the wives) of a Brahmana."

(*Manusamhita, Chap. III*, 12-13.)

Eminent scholars like Bhandarkar are of opinion that on the revival of Brahmanism during the Gupta dynasty, the Scriptures and the *Puranas* were retouched and interpolations freely made to support the pretensions of the spiritual guides.

So much for the historical basis of the claims of the higher castes. I now appeal to you from a different standpoint. There is such a thing as expediency even in

Sociology. Is it fair, is it just, is it in the best interests of our country that a handful of privileged men should continue to monopolise all the advantages accruing to them through the accident of birth and drive the submerged teeming millions to hostile camps and compel them to live in a state of armed neutrality? A house divided against itself cannot stand. The backward classes are flesh of our flesh and bone of our bone, and it is the bounden duty of our men of light and leading to extend to them the right hand of fellowship and lift them up from the quagmire of degradation and despondency. We cannot afford any longer to have in our social frame-work a microscopic minority of Spartans lording it over the *helots*. The loss to the country from the intellectual stagnation of the overwhelming majority of her people is simply incalculable. We are loud in claiming political equality with our British fellow-subjects, but when it comes to yielding an inch of ground to our own countrymen we fight shy of it and cry help! murder!

We are never tired of citing the example of Japan when we want to prove that political progress can be achieved even in an Asiatic country. But it suits our convenience to forget all that the Land of the Rising Sun has done for her social regeneration. There, up till the seventies of the last century, the *Samurai* clans had monopolised to themselves all the privileges now arrogated by our Brahminical castes. The *eta* and the *hinin* (the *untouchables* of Japan) were regarded so impure and unclean that they were not even allowed to dwell in the ordinary villages but had locations assigned to them,—a state of thing now met with in some parts in the Southern Presidency. But on the memorable day of 12th October in 1871, the *Samurai*, with a spirit of chivalry no less of patriotism, voluntarily parted with their vested interests and abolished the artificial and invidious caste distinctions and thus laid the foundations of a compact and homogeneous nation.

What was possible in Japan in 1871 is found to be impossible in India even towards the close of the second decade of the 20th century. Even now we find that, as the saying goes, 12 Rajputs must have 13 cooking pots and 500 Congress delegates require as many kitchen arrangements. This at any rate is applicable to our friends of the Southern Presidency, who have worked out the problem to metaphysical nicety inasmuch as they have added a new category, namely, contamination by sight of the cooked food of a Brahmin when seen by a member of the Panchama class even from a distance, say by means of a telescope.

In Bengal, Behar and Orissa the situation is fortunately not so very acute and the pride due to racial superiority has been much softened. In fact, in Bengal, the Kayasthas and the Baidyas are quite the peers of the Brahmins in intellectual and in social position. Judged by the standard of literacy the Brahmins are found to occupy rather a subordinate position. Thus, in Bengal, the Baidyas *per mille* contribute 532,

Subarna Banik 451 and the Brahmins 399 and the Kayasthas 347; while in Behar and Orissa the Kayasthas top the list with 332 and the Brahmins 168: in other words, for every 2 Kayasthas who can read and write there is only one Brahmin who can do the same. Moreover, in Bengal, a sort of compromise was arrived at long ago by which the Kaibartyas, Napits, Sadgopas, and Tilis were made castes which may offer water to the Brahmins. But in Madras and Bombay the Brahmin literates are overwhelmingly superior in number to those of other castes and the gradation between a Brahmin and a non-Brahmin very abrupt.

This intervening of a wide gulf has been a fruitful parent of racial animosities. Out of a population of 41½ millions only a million and a half are Brahmins. The march of events is now very rapid. Hinduism has proved to be elastic and flexible in the past ages and we must make a vigorous effort to adapt ourselves to the altered circumstances. Toleration and charity should be our watchwords.

Some 7 or 8 years ago I spoke about the misuse of the Bengali intellect, which holds good for the rest of India also, and I cannot do better than quote what I then said,—"True it is that we are wont to take pride in the acuteness of the Bengali intellect as evidenced in the subtleties of disputations based upon the modern school of Nyaya as also of Smriti (of Navadwipa). It should however be borne in mind that while the great promulgator of Smriti (Raghunandan) was ransacking the pages of Manu, Yajnavalkya, Parasara and others, and laying down the rigid rules of fasting to be observed by a child-widow of nine years of age and in default thereof holding out the terrors of hell-fire for her ancestors on the paternal and maternal side; while Raghunadha, Gadadhara, Jagadisa and other mighty logicians were engaged in composing glossaries and commentaries on the classical works of logic and were thus adding to the consternation of the pupils of the *tols*; while our astronomers were calculating the omens and prognostications from the cawing of a crow at a particular moment in the south-west quarter; while our pandits were disturbing the peace of the assemblies by acrimonious dispute over the controversy 'whether the sound raised by the falling of the palm-fruit accompanied it or was an after-effect';—I say when the intellectuals of Nava-dwipa were thus utilizing the precious gift of time, in Europe, Galileo, Kepler, Newton and other philosophers were unravelling the mysteries of Nature and ushering in a new epoch and thus glorifying the intellect of man."

Swami Vivekananda truly observes,—"A religion which does not feel for the miseries of the poor, which does not uplift man, forfeits the name of "religion." Our religion has degenerated into a creed of the "touchable" and the "untouchable." O! my God, the country whose best intellects have for the last two thousand years busied themselves with such abstruse problems as the propriety of taking up the food, with the right hand or the left, that country only courts and richly deserves downfall."

See to what extent our intellect has been misused!

The problem of "touchableness" has assumed a scientific aspect in these days. If a pariah crosses your threshold you throw away your jar of drinking water as polluted, but ice and lemonade manufactured by the untouchables pass current! A distinction conferred on a member of our society becomes the occasion for giving a dinner in the Town-Hall catered by Peliti and the recognised leaders of the Hindu society take part in the function and their names are published in the morning papers, but when on the occasion of a marriage or *Sradh* you are guilty of sitting to a feast with a Christian or Moslem or even a Hindu of the lower castes you are threatened with excommunication. Reason, logic and common sense are thus scattered to the winds.

If you cannot see your way to abolish the castes, you can at any rate see that its bonds are loosened and its stringency relaxed. You render yourself incapable of cultivating the higher civic virtues if you allow your social structure to be honeycombed with inequalities and your mind to be distracted by petty squabbles over sectarian matters and the nice shades of distinction between tweedledum and tweedledee.

Listen to what the Apostle of the idea of National Unity says:

"When the Indians really believed that some of

them were born from the head, others from the arms' and others from the feet of Brahma, their Divinity, they organised their society by distributing mankind into castes; assigning to one caste an inheritance of intellectual labour, to another of military, and to others of servile duties; thus condemning themselves to an immobility that still endures, and that will endure so long as belief in that religious principle shall last."

Mazzini's words uttered some eighty years ago are still ringing in the ears of civilised mankind.

The future of India—her claim to call herself a nation—depends upon the solution of this burning question. Ancient India, however, was far more liberal and enlightened in this respect. The beautiful legend of Satyakama Jabala in the Chhandogya Upanishad exemplifies the fact that truth and learning opened out in those days a path to the highest honour and to the highest caste.

There is a prevailing belief that the submerged masses have all along been contented with the position assigned to them and have taken it lying down and that it is only of late that they have begun to raise a voice of protest in view of their awakened self-respect. A similar complaint is made by the Anglo-Indians about the present generation of Indians. Long before the advent of the Europeans and the spread of western democratic ideas, in fact, so long ago as the 12th century A.D., we find the bitter cry of the outcastes. In a poetical work of surpassing interest, recently unearthed by Pandit H. P. Sastri and published and which gives a vivid picture of the transitional period in Bengal when Buddhism was slowly merging into Hinduism occurs a remarkable passage of which I give the translation here:

"The Brahmins go about asking for gifts and if they fail to get them of any householder they threaten to reduce the world to ashes by their imprecations.

"Dhamma in Paradise was sorely aggrieved and produced darkness of illusion.

"Then Dhamma assumed the form of a Mussalman and put on a fez and took up in his hand a gun and a spear.

"The Gods of one mind put on pantaloons in delight: Brahma became Mahomet and Vishnu, a Paigambar and Siva, Adam; Ganesh assumed the form of Ghazi and Kartik of Kazi, Narada giving up his ascetic garb became a Sheikh... The sun and the moon and the other gods filled the ranks of infantry and began to beat drums and then laid under ruins the town of Jaspur." It is thus evident that even 6 or 7 centuries ago there existed bitter hatred against the Brahminical self-assertions.

Within the last three centuries, and from time to time there have arisen also in our midst saints and prophets like Guru Nanak and Kabir and Chaitanya to preach the Doctrine of the Brotherhood of Man and had it not been for their teachings a far larger proportion of the people of North India would have embraced Islamism.

The position of women in our society equally calls for radical reform. If ignorance is the curse of God, as the immortal poet has it, then it is ten fold so when applied to women. For, man, at any rate, comes in hourly contact with the external world, mixes freely with all sorts and conditions of people, and has all his angularities rounded off. But our women-folk, living in the seclusion of the zenana, cut off from contact with the outside world live, move and have their being like frogs in the well; she jealously cherishes all the absurd notions and superstitions which she imbibes with her mother's milk and takes every care to inoculate the child in her lap with the poison, and what is bred in the bone cannot go out of the flesh.

The tragedy of our home-life was depicted by our own Rabindranath some 30 years ago in a poem of singular pathos. The poet depicts a vivid picture of the expectant bridegroom on the first night of the honeymoon. He unbosoms to his partner for life his soul's aspirations and meets with a chilling response. The child-wife replies to his yearnings by only asking for plums, her favourite pussy, and finally wants to return to the lap of her grandmother.

Yes, it is the grandmother who plays the leading part in the moulding of the character of the child-wife. We have been talking a good deal about Home Rule the last few days but we forget that there is another Home Rule under the autocratic sway of the grandmother, who moulds the young wife according to her own ideals and pattern and thus takes good care to check any budding ideas of equality and comradeship with her enlightened husband. Thus our educated young man has to lead a two-fold existence in two distinct water-tight compartments. In the drawing room, our cultured youngman talks of Home Rule on Colonial basis. But as soon as he enters the zenana—the veritable Doll's House—he has to descend to the common places of an un-enlightened domestic environment.

Many of you with academic distinctions on your brow do not hesitate to sell yourselves to the highest bidder in the matrimonial market. It rends my heart to have to confess that some of you at any rate consciously or unconsciously have been or will be the instruments of self-immolation of many a Snehalata! Many a leading member of our society is found to prate on the platform on the evils of the dowery system, but when his own turn comes he gives the go-by to his preachings and is extortionate in his demands, and when he is taken to task he roundly lays the blame at the door of his mother and grandmother, or his wife, and washes his hands clean. I appeal to you, the rising hopes of our country, to take a solemn vow not to be a party to such bargaining.

Ancient India can boast of a Gargi, a Maitreyi; nor should it be forgotten that the authors of many Vedic hymns were women. In the palmy days of Buddhism also there were eloquent lady-preachers. We have evidently degenerated now.

It is no exaggeration to say that in some points our womenfolk even of the higher castes labour under all the disabilities and disadvantages of the "depressed" classes of the society. No doubt we feed them, we clothe them, we generally treat them well. But is that all? Are we not bound to educate them and bring them to the level of an educated man's culture and intelligence? For considerations alike of justice and expediency it is necessary to bring the light of education to them. A people, half of whom are immersed in darkness, can never expect to grow. Nation-building cannot proceed in this half-hearted fashion. Growth to be real must be harmonious. Those who think we are able to make any great headway in politics without a simultaneous advance in social and industrial matters, labour under a great mistake. Let us approach the national problem in a truly broad and catholic spirit and not grapple it by halves. I appeal to my countrymen with all the emphasis at my command to keep this ideal in view and I am sure as night follows day that their activities for the good of the country will be crowned with success.

Before concluding, I would desire a passing mention of the following points, but as the time at my disposal is short I leave these for other more competent speakers for discussion :—

(1) Advancing the age of marriage both of boys and girls in Hindu Society.

(2) Raising the 'age of consent' to 16.

(3) An Amendment, on Mr. B. N. Basu's lines, of the Act. III of 1872.

(4) Removal of social restrictions on sea-voyage.

In the great federation of the nations of the world, India at one time occupied the place of its brains and heart. Out of India, civilisation and culture spread to East and West, North and South. In that morning of ancient history, the world looked forward to India for light and guidance, for knowledge of the accurate sciences such as algebra and chemistry as shown in my *History of Hindu Chemistry*, for personal and social purity, for sacrifice and abstinence, for plain living and high thinking. Now, thanks to the cumulative effect of centuries of social inequalities and oppression, of the degradation of the condition of women and of large sections of the people, and the walls of differences raised between man and man by custom and tradition, India now lies at the feet of nations—powerless and helpless. The blood that flows from her heart and goes to her brain does no longer reach the lower limbs of the body-politic. As the consequence of this abnormal condition, India finds these parts of her organism practically paralysed and atrophied. So long as the blood does not begin to reflow and vitalise the limbs which now remain palsied, there is no chance for India to get back a place in the sun. I appeal to my fellow-countrymen, high and low, rich and poor, Brahmin and non-Brahmin, orthodox and heterodox, to forget the pride and vanity of place and birth, and begin ministering to the limbs the neglect of which now drags us down to a life of humiliation, and makes the name of our Motherland a bye-word of contempt and reproach in the civilised world. India must wake up, shake off her degradation, put life and heart into every class of her people, elevate her women and depressed classes and remove the galling restrictions of caste and all social inequalities. When this is done she will enter into a new era of her life and then, like Prometheus unbound, she will be recognised as a great power in the world and will have an unique place in the comity of nations. I appeal to you all, ladies and gentlemen, to direct your best efforts towards the consummation of that great ideal, the realisation of that aspiration. We owe it to our Motherland to rise equal to the occasion, face the situation and brave the difficulties, and, once we begin to help ourselves, I have no doubt Providence will begin to help us. *Bande Mataram.*

GOVERNMENT & INDIAN INDUSTRIES

Dr. Ray, as Director, Bengal Chemical and Pharmaceutical Works, was invited to give evidence before the Indian Industrial Commission in June, 1917, *during their enquiries in Calcutta. The following is the text of Dr. Ray's evidence both written and oral :—*

COTTAGE INDUSTRIES

In India special attention should be given to the development of cottage industries. There are cottage industries which will stand the competition of factories. In fact there are many such industries in which no competition exists at all; such as fine cotton and silk weaving, carpet weaving, pottery, carpentry and the artistic industries such as gold and silver work, ivory carving, metal inlaying, clay modelling, stone carving, lace making, lac work, etc.,—industries which still flourish in India. It is necessary, in the best interests of the country, to develop them by introducing labour-saving contrivances amongst the artisans and by offering them money at cheap rates of interest. For the latter purpose the spread of co-operative societies on the Raiffeisen model is needed. The village artisans will welcome any cheap machine or new process which will help their work. The only thing necessary is that the utility of the particular implement or machine should be demonstrated before them. The Commission should not neglect this important branch of industry, *viz.*, the cottage industry. The welfare of numberless people is bound up with the development of this branch of industry.

GOVERNMENT ASSISTANCE

The Government should help the development of industries by (*a*) the grant of financial and other aid to existing industries (*b*) by starting pioneer and demonstration industries.

The great object is to induce the people to become industrialists. The policy of abstention and aloofness of Government advocated by English economists will not do in India. The policy pursued in Japan ought to be followed.

The initiative of Government is justifiable when a particular tract is favourable to the starting of a new industry but the people from want of industrial skill and enterprise have not attempted it. The Government may also help an existing industry by suggesting new processes or new mechanical appliances of which the promotors of the industry are ignorant.

This policy was tried with success in Madras and the United Provinces. The aluminium industry in Madras and the sugar industry in the United Provinces are appropriate examples.

The silk, indigo, sugar and tea industries were all fostered by Government in British India.

It cannot be said that the policy of direct aid by Government is new. Some of the Native States have liberally helped private enterprises.

FINANCIAL AID

In giving financial aid the several methods suggested in question 5 should be kept in view. In several cases combination of two or three methods may be necessary. There cannot be one uniform method for all. Each particular industry will be helped according to its requirements.

The great principle in giving financial aid is that only the deserving industry should be helped. By deserving is meant an industry of which the promoters have studied the local conditions and shown considerable honesty and skill in the conduct of business and are in a position to make it successful by a timely aid. Aid to incompetent and ill-conceived ventures is to be discouraged. An industrial concern before it seeks for Government aid ought to show that it deserves it by its *bona fides* and good management. The initiative should, as a rule, come from within and not from without.

Sometimes the only aid which a particular industry will require will be expert advice or arrangement for the supply of raw materials. The Match Factory at Tollygunge has no supply of wood for match. But the Government plantations in Darjeeling have got the kind of wood. Yet the factory does not get them in spite of repeated representations to the authorities.

The ways in which the Government may help an industry are numerous and do not consist merely of financial aid. The finding of a market for locally manufactured goods is one of them or the supply of an essential ingredient on favourable conditions as supply of alcohol to a pharmaceutical factory. It is a notorious fact that the nascent industries are greatly handicapped for want of a suitable market. The local traders demand high rates of commission and throw other obstacles in the way. They push the foreign manufactures of which the supply is abundant and try to force most unreasonable conditions on the home products.

It goes without saying that Government should exercise some control over industries which it helps. The least objectionable way is by an independent audit by Government and by periodical inspection. The appointment of Government Directors may cause friction.

PIONEER FACTORIES

Whenever a pioneer industry has been established on a good basis and there is offer of purchase by an individual or a private or public company, the Government should part with it. Preference should be given to companies. But it is desirable that the Government should exercise some supervision for some years after purchase.

The purchase may be effected on the annuity system, the Government retaining some control till the last annuity is paid. This system will not impose undue burden on the purchaser.

The Government should pioneer the following industries: lac, tobacco, sugar and chemical industries for the manufacture of glass, bleaching powder, alum, bichromate of potash, permanganate of potash, soda, etc.

CO-OPERATIVE SOCIETIES

The industries which can best be developed by co-operative societies are handicrafts and small cottage industries and agriculture. The demonstration of the use of small machines or of processes in home industries may well be tried by the co-operative societies with the help and guidance of Government officers.

LIMITS OF GOVERNMENT ASSISTANCE

The Government may avoid the highly organised industries as a jute or cloth mill. But smaller industries and industries which are new to the place and will not compete with an existing industry ought to be taken in hand by the Government. This will not discourage private enterprise. For, the latter may wait and purchase the Government concern or have an industry in co-operation with the Government. The demand for a particular product may be great and there may be room for many concerns of a similar nature. Suppose glass factories are started both by Government and a private company. The latter may manufacture the cheap articles and the former only try articles of a superior finish.

The Government should not hesitate to aid or start a new enterprise even if it competes with an established external foreign trade. For, in that case no pioneer industry could be started in India, as there is a foreign trade in almost every article of ordinary use.

TECHNICAL AID

My province is at present in need of demonstration factories for the manufacture of glass, sugar, alcohol, tanning materials and leather and porcelain.

The Government should encourage the deputation of experts engaged in private enterprise to England and foreign countries to enable them to gain technical knowledge which they are in need of. It should be made a rule that in awarding scholarships for technical education preference should be given to those who are engaged in a particular industry or who have shown competence by possessing practical knowledge of the local industries.

INDUSTRIAL SCHOOLS

The industrial schools are greatly handicapped for want of facilities in practical training in factories. The Government should offer such facilities.

The industrial schools should be under the joint control of the Department of Industries and the Department of Public Instruction.

Our country is in need of night schools for the benefit of artisans.

There are private technical schools. The Government should properly recognise them and afford reasonable facilities wanted by them.

Industrial schools should be established all over the country. Besides, arrangements should be made for manual training in the existing secondary schools.

Students may be required to choose a career after some years of study. They should elect either to pursue their career in the ordinary secondary school or join an industrial school. It is no use having "B" standards in ordinary secondary schools.

The great defect of existing technical schools is the inadequacy of practical training. This can only be acquired in factories. Passed students of technical and industrial schools should be taken as apprentices in factories and workshops.

An Advisory Board of Industries is preferable.

OFFICIAL ORGANISATION

The Director of Industries, if one is appointed, should be a business man with general scientific and technical education. He need not be an expert in any particular industry. In no case should an executive officer having very little experience of business or industry be appointed to the post.

TECHNICAL AND SCIENTIFIC DEPARTMENTS

The scientific and technical departments of the Government should be organised on liberal lines by which Indians may be benefitted.

Qualified Indians find it difficult to enter these departments. Unless better facilities are offered for the admission of Indians who possess the necessary qualifications and are intimately acquainted with the needs and conditions of the country, the department will not be of much help to the growth of industries amongst the people of the land.

The Institute of Science (Bangalore) is located in a place quite out of touch with industries and beyond the pale of public opinion. There is no proper controlling authority. It is a matter of regret that vast sums of money have been lavishly and I would almost say recklessly spent, not commensurate with the real work taken in hand. But still it is premature to pass any opinion on its future. The technological researches on raw Indian products should always be carried out in laboratories established in Indian industrial centres as much time is lost in the transmission of raw products abroad and communication of results. Moreover, this would have the effect of giving opportunities to Indians being trained under proper expert European supervision. Research Institutions have their great value in highly developed industrial countries. But in a backward country like India what is more required is the direct encouragement of industrial habits and enterprise amongst the people by the starting of pioneer and demonstration factories than by establishing highly developed technological research institutions.

COMMERCIAL INTELLIGENCE

The Commercial Intelligence Department should publish monographs on industries and distribute them free of cost. The translation of these monographs in vernacular is desirable. It will be profitable to have a quarterly journal embodying these writings.

GENERAL

In order to give better facilities for the training

and employment of Indians the workshops in connection with railways should be thrown open to them and Indians should be engaged as apprentices in higher engineering work. Dockyards might also be established in such ports as Bombay and Calcutta for the building of steamers, *e.g.*, navy. This will give an opportunity to Indian engineers being trained in naval architecture. This was the scheme adopted by Japan in the early stages of her renaissance in the seventies of the last century.

I should also suggest that some of the river courses in lower Bengal might be reserved for Indians for gaining experience in steamer navigation, *i.e.*, protected from competition by powerful European companies.

ORAL EVIDENCE, 28TH NOVEMBER, 1916.

(*Mr. C. E. Low.*)—You are Director of the Bengal Chemical and Pharmaceutical Works? Yes.

Is it a limited company? Yes.

What is the capital? Five lakhs.

How much is actually paid up? Almost the whole amount is paid up.

Your works are in Calcutta? In the suburbs.

Have you been a Director of it since it was started? I have been connected with it from the beginning. It was started as a private enterprise and converted into a limited liability company some time in 1903. And as I am a Government servant I was not then in the directorate but of late I have been in it.

What are the particular articles which you

manufacture, speaking broadly ? Various kinds of medicines and acids and scientific instruments.

With reference to the first part of your evidence what do you consider should be the functions of the provincial Director of Industries in respect of cottage and organised industries respectively. Do you think that the Provincial Director of Industries should deal with both ? Our people are so very poor and we have got so few industries worth the name that utmost efforts should be made not only to revive but keep alive these existing cottage industries.

You point out the help which Co-operative Societies could give to cottage industries. Do you allude especially to credit or to purchase and distribution as well ? Both loans on favourable terms and also supply of raw materials.

Do you think that sufficient money would be forthcoming to finance these Co-operative Industrial Societies ? It depends on circumstances. If the products find a ready sale then of course money would be forthcoming. But if it is found that borrowers are unable to pay back their loans, then there will be difficulty as regards the flow of capital.

That would depend firstly on the industries being properly selected and secondly on the members being properly selected ? Quite so.

What should be the relations between the Director of Industries and the Registrar of Co-operative Societies ? That is very difficult to say off hand. I have thought about that a good deal. But I am afraid

I have not been able to come to a definite conclusion. I find there are departmental jealousies. One head of one department does not like the idea of his being interfered with by the head of another department. Harmonious working and smooth relations are not always easy to get at.

Would you consider it a suitable solution if the Registrar of the Co-operative Societies dealt with the business side and the Director of Industries with the technical side? I think that it would be a better solution and it would remove a good deal of friction.

You speak of the match factory at Tollygunge suffering for want of wood and you say that the Government plantations at Darjeeling have the kind of wood required. Do you know about this personally? I know a good deal about it.

Is the wood at Darjeeling accessible? I am afraid not. That is the difficulty.

It is not the difficulty of price. It is only the question of transport? It would be cheaper to get it from Australia than from these inaccessible hill regions.

Leaving aside the cottage industries, with regard to what I may call the small factory, do you consider that, if technical advice could be given on the part of Government, if Government experts could examine the thing thoroughly and place before the public the results of those experiments showing the possibility of running the industry at a profit would capital then be forthcoming to start such a concern? I think our countrymen are beginning to realise that capital is no longer shy even in Bengal.

Presumably capital would be more easily forthcoming locally in respect of small local factories? Yes.

I mean to say that the people of Rangpur would be more ready to subscribe to a tobacco factory in Rangpur than to some factory in Chittagong? Yes.

Do you think that fairly substantial amounts would be forthcoming? I think so.

When I say that Government experts would examine the thing, of course, Government would not take any responsibility. They will advise to the best of their information? Yes.

Would you explain exactly what is meant by the B standards of secondary schools? Sometimes these so-called technical schools are a misnomer. Sometimes a carpenter or a village smith is engaged and that is all the help that the boys are able to get.

What is its equivalent in the ordinary course? Side by side with the ordinary education we have the lower primary, the upper primary and then the secondary schools. The teaching is up to the matriculation examination.

Do you know whether any of the B standard boys go on to the University afterwards? Most of them go because they are not absorbed in any of the industries in this country.

Is it regarded as an easier path to matriculation than the ordinary literary course? I think that what is called the *bhardralog* or middle class feel a kind of repugnance to manual work but as competition is very keen, they are now taking kindly to such things.

Returning again to the B standard, I understand it gives an industrial bent to ordinary education? Yes.

But generally both officials and non-officials consider that it is inefficient and unsatisfactory and leads to no good results? If they are apprenticed to Railway workshops or such firms as Burn and Co., and Martin and Co., I think it may lead to good results.

Is there any difficulty in obtaining free entry into these firms for apprentices? My impression is that it is somewhat difficult. For instance, the Railway workshop at Jamalpur might give better facilities for the admission of students.

Do they confine their apprenticeship to the sons of people already in the works or in what way are they restricted? I think the average Bengali young man belonging to the higher classes has not the facilities that might be desired.

Have you heard instances of such men having applied and their being refused? I cannot tell that exactly. But that is the general impression.

Do you consider that technical schools are capable of creating industries? That is a very difficult question. In Bengal we are so very backward in commercial enterprises and business capacity that we cannot all on a sudden expect men from these technical schools to engineer big industries. They might be absorbed in industries which are already extant. But with only their help to start big industries would be a rather dangerous experiment.

Do you think that industries should precede technical training? They ought to.

You say an Advisory Board of Industries is preferable. Perferable to what? To a Director of Industries.

By Advisory Board you do not mean executive board? By Advisory Board I mean a board which has studied local conditions about the supply of raw materials and the demand for manufactured products and so on. They would start industries only after making the right kind of enquiries and experiments. For instance the match factory at Tollygunge. My view is that the experts should have taken ample care to see that the supply of timber was readily available on the spot. An Advisory Board would have helped in cases of this sort. They would have been able to warn the organisers that they were running a risk in starting the factory under the conditions. They would also advise as to the suitability of an industry to a particular locality.

Who would constitute the Board? Men concerned with the Commercial Intelligence Department who could get the necessary information.

People with expert knowledge you mean? Yes.

Experts in industries and in business? Yes.

Who would control these various experts? That is a difficult matter to pass an opinion upon.

After all that is an administrative question on which perhaps you are not in a position to give an opinion off hand. You say on page 2, "In a backward country like India what is more required is the direct encouragement of industrial habits and enterprise amongst the people by the starting of pioneer and demonstration factories than highly developed technological institutions." To what extent do you consider that factories were started without research? I mean glass factories for instance. There is also the aluminium works which was started in Madras under Mr. Chatterton's direction and advice. Such enterprises might be started.

You think there is a substantial amount of industrial work and opportunity which could be made use of by means of knowledge in the possession of certain persons already, to be obtained for the purpose? Yes.

Take for instance the glass expert. He comes here from some other country. He finds some differences in the quality of the sand which leads to results different from what he has been led to anticipate from experience with materials apparently similar in the country from which he comes. We have all seen instances of failures of industries owing to that cause. How do you propose that this difficulty should be got over? India is a vast country and the supply of raw materials can be secured from several provinces. The Geological Department and the Commercial Intelligence Department could give very valuable information. I believe that at Titagarh the company failed because of the want of experts. Experts were brought out from Germany. They suffered from malaria and then went away. In such cases Government might come forward with the help of a fresh supply of experts. I have often observed with regret that the so-called experts have been instrumental in leading people astray. They come back from Japan and the United States with a superficial knowledge of the subject and they do not collect the necessary local information. They start the work and find out the difficulties in the way when it is too late.

What is to be done to adapt the knowledge of experts who are not fully acquainted with local peculiarities, which means all the difference between success and failures. How is that small amount of very necessary knowledge to be obtained? You must have a certain amount of research facilities. Suppose a glass factory is started. First the experts should see that sand, soda and coal are available near at hand. Of course soda we have to import for the present. I have known cases where a glass factory has been started far from the supply of coal and the carriage of coal has proved prohibitive. They should have taken care that the glass factory was initially located in a place where the supply of coal was the first consideration. I find often that they realise their mistakes when it is too late.

In connection with the Bengal Chemical and

Pharmaceutical Works, you were not able to start it without a good deal of research undertaken by yourself. Don't you think that has made a good deal of difference in the matter of the success of the company? Work like this is based almost entirely on research, preliminary research work.

I suppose you are still going on with your research work and are constantly trying to open out new lines of business? We have a body of chemists of whom one or two are entirely detailed off for research work.

You generally direct the lines on which they should do research work with reference to what you consider commercially profitable business? Yes. We are very keen about securing the best scientific men available. We do not take any one who is not a M.Sc. of the Calcutta University or who has not got knowledge of that standard.

You are in a position to find out whether a particular man is suitable? It is left to me to decide. 99 per cent. of our graduates are theoretical, bookish men and one has to be very careful in selecting a proper person. He may score very high marks in the University examinations, he may get even a first class, but he may be a poor substitute in business. Whereas one who is a third class graduate may be very good as a business man.

And therefore you say that the existence of a man with a scientific training in high control of an industrial concern is often a very great advantage? Yes.

Have you ever had any experience of the working of the commercial museum? I know our firm is in frequent communication with it and often gets very valuable information.

Supposing these commercial museums were made provincial, that is to say, if similar museums were started in other provinces do you think it would be a useful advertising medium for Indian industries? I think so.

Do you think it would help you in the matter of sales? Yes.

(Honourable Pandit M. M. Malaviya.)—You say that it is necessary in the best interests of the country to develop these cottage industries by introducing labour saving contrivances among the artisans. Would you recommend the lending of machinery on the hire-purchase system? Yes. That would be a very desirable thing.

Then you say that demonstration factories would be of very great use. Would you have these demonstration factories only at the head-quarters of the districts or also in the sub-divisions? I would have them even in the remotest villages. For instance, take the extracting of juice from cane. The poor villagers have very crude ways of doing it. If a not very costly apparatus were brought to them and its use explained they would be the first to purchase it. Even they would go into shares and purchase it.

Do you think that there should be arrangement, made for making demonstrations from village to village or groups of villages all over the province ? Yes. It is a fact that the match factory applied for wood from Darjeeling but was not able to get it ? I think Mr. Mitter who has been cited as a witness will be able to give you better information about it than I can.

You recommend that students who have passed through the technical and industrial schools should be taken as apprentices in factories and workshops and you recommend that Government should make it a rule that workshops and factories which are patronised by Government should take in a certain number of apprentices ? That is what I suggested in a note which I submitted to Mr. Swan. I quoted very largely from a book published in Japan by the Principal of the late Engineering College in Tokyo (Mr. Dyer). He says that in the seventies they sent out the first batch of students who came out of the engineering college to Sir William Armstrong (New castle), and they made a conditional order to the firms who made their battleships that no order would be placed with the firms unless they took in a certain number of apprentices. The Secretary of State commands vast influence and patronage and he might well afford to dictate terms to the firms so that a certain number of apprentices may be taken.

You mean that the Government should arrange for it ? I feel very strongly on the subject. And my view is that Government has been rather backward in this respect. Government might very easily arrange for it. They might say to the firms that no orders would be placed with them unless they took in a certain number of apprentices. That would bring them to their senses.

You have seen the report of the Morrison Committee. They have made a recommendation to the effect that the Secretary of State should exercise his moral influence to secure the object? I should say not merely moral but direct influence. He can bring pressure to bear on the firms. He can afford to dictate terms. He need not go a-begging.

Do you mean that unless he made it a stipulation they would not take in apprentices? He commands huge influence and patronage. You know well how many millions worth of stores are bought through the India Office.

You say that qualified Indians find it difficult to enter the scientific and technical departments of Government, and recommend that better facilities should be offered them. One of your recommendations is that such a difference as exists in the Indian Educational Service should not find a place there? It should not. More of them should be taken in the scientific departments of Government like the Geological Survey and the Trigonometrical Survey. One reason why I say this is that other things being equal when an Englishman completes his 55th year, he retires, and all the technical and expert knowledge he gained in India is lost to India for good. Whereas if he were an Indian he would have resided in India and his expert knowledge would have been available to the Indians. Now I can illustrate this in my own case. I am about 55 and I am about to retire. If it pleases God to spare my life I would say that my advice would be absolutely at the disposal of my countrymen as long as I live. In the case of Europeans that knowledge is lost to the country.

You say then that in these scientific and technical departments, which you recommend should be developed, Indians should have fair play ? Yes.

You also say that Indians should be taken more and more as apprentices. Are not the students of the Sibpur Engineering College taken as apprentices in higher engineering ? Are they not put through a course of practical training ? I think they are, suppose a bridge is constructed they are put on there. Sir R. N. Mookerjee would be able to give better information on the point.

You say that research institutions have their great value in highly developed industrial countries. Did I understand you to say in answer to the President that you are not opposed to the higher kind of research ? I have spent the best years of my life in research and I should be the last man to decry it.

You think that knowledge that is available in the matter of industries should be more widely diffused and utilised in the country in the promotion of enterprise and that research should accompany the growth of enterprise ? Yes.

You have said that Bengal is industrially backward. Would you kindly let me know the reason for it? Bengal is not deficient in intelligence, and in every line of study that has been provided the Bengali has distinguished himself, in arts, law, engineering, medicine. Is not the industrial backwardness of Bengal due then to the fact that the system of education in vogue has been of an unindustrial kind so to say, that it is too literary and theoretical? There are also other reasons such as the permanent settlement and the fertility of the soil.

Do you think that if you had higher technological institutions and colleges of commerce to impart industrial and scientific education, there is no reason why the Bengali youth should not distinguish himself as well in these lines as in others? Mere technological institutes will be of very little use. The Bengali has very little forwardness at present in the matter of commercial enterprises. On the Bombay side we have mill-owners who have never been in any technical or commercial institute.

You recommend the establishment of industrial schools. Do you think that a general system of primary education should be the basis of industrial education? It should be.

Don't you think that the lack of general elementary education is a hindrance to industrial efficiency? It is.

(*Honourable Sir Fazulbhoy Currimbhoy.*)—Will you tell us why the chemical works of which you are a Director was exchanged from private ownership to a limited company? We could command very little capital. To tell you the full history would be to repeat a chapter in my own biography.

Was it not working profitably under private ownership ? It was working profitably. It was found that the proprietors could bring in very little capital.

Is it working profitably now ? I think so.

What dividends ? 8 per cent. The Directors want to give more but I am using my moral influence in restraining them.

If new industries are started they require big chemical works and capital just like America ? Yes.

Don't you think that they are first essential before we start many new industries ? Yes. Take for instance the Sunlight Soap Company of Messrs. Lever Brothers. It commands a capital of 14 millions.

You say you want grants from Government. In what way do you want grants ? Loans at favourable rates of interest.

Should Government guarantee interest on the capital ? Yes.

You say that some of the Native States have liberally helped private enterprises. Can you cite an example ? I know the Mysore Government have helped the starting of a spinning company. They have purchased a few lakhs worth of shares and gave suitable land and in course of time, these shares are sold to the public when the company was profitably working.

You say that an industrial concern before it seeks Government aid should show its *bona fides* by its good management. Suppose a new concern is being started, how can they show their *bona fides*? Take for example the great hydro-electric scheme. The bare name of the eminent directors would bring in any amount of capital.

Do you think that in the beginning also Government should help ? In special cases but one ought to be very careful.

Then about the match factory you say that the other man will be able to give information ? Yes.

Yo say that Government control over industries is best exercised by having an audit and periodical inspection. Suppose you had an auditor do you think that is a proper control of Government ? Don't you think that the Government should have their own directors ? It may lead to friction.

What friction can there be. He can only guard the interests of Government ? I agree with you there.

You say whenever a pioneer industry is started and there is offer of purchase by a private individual, Government should part with it, and you say that preference should be given to companies. What companies do you refer to ? Something like the Aluminium works in Madras.

You do not want private individuals ? It would be better if they were joint stock companies. An authorised syndicate should be formed. In the Bengal Chemical Company I have always been anxious to see that no man purchases a very large number of shares.

You say that industrial schools should be under the joint control of the Education Department and the Director of Industries? Do you think that would work smoothly? It would then be able to command knowledge of a two-fold character. Of course dual control is to be avoided. The spheres of the control of the two departments should be clearly defined.

You say that you are in favour of Government official journals and that they should be supplied gratis. Do you know what it will cost? I mean at a nominal cost.

You say that dockyards might be established. For building what? Battleships.

We want steel plates for it and we are not producing them at present? In the meantime we have to import. I read a good deal about it in the case of Japan. If we were to wait for ourselves making the steel plates we shall have to wait indefinitely. In the case of Japan it cost her very much to build her own battleships. Recent events have confirmed and justified the wisdom of Japan.

You say that if any industry is profitable, capital would be readily forthcoming. You know for example how successfully the jute mills are working. Why do not the Bengal capitalists put in their money? I think that they are now opening their eyes to the matter.

Do you think they will come out? I know there is a middle class who are anxious to invest their money in the Bengal Chemical Works. They are small capitalists.

Do you think that the permanent settlement is hampering industries? I alluded to that as one of the economic reasons, as affording a sure source of investment.

There is an association which is sending students to Japan and other countries. Do these men get employment on their return? I suppose Mr. Jogendra Chandra Ghosh might be able to give you better information. I heard that they are getting some employment or other.

(*Hon'ble Sir R. N. Mookerjee*).—In the last sentence of paragraph 5 you say ' It is desirable that Government should exercise some supervision for some years after purchase.' Do you think that it will encourage anybody to come and purchase? When I purchase why should Government continue to supervise? I meant until the money was all paid off.

You clearly say that Government should continue the control after purchase for some years? I meant only that it should be until the money has been paid off. After that nobody would like Government interference.

If your suggestion that the Secretary of State should force firms to take apprentices is adopted do you not think that indirectly we will have to pay for it ? When you order several millions of worth material the firm would readily oblige you.

Would they not increase their rate ? There is so much competition as regards the supply of goods that they would not dare to do that.

How many apprentices do you take in your own works ? We do not take any, we have many secrets in the chemical industry.

In the same way the other firms will have their own secrets also ? The chemists' secrets are somewhat different from the ordinary secrets; if, however, Government were to guarantee the placing in of large orders for a number of years, I would gladly advise the taking in of a limited number of apprentices.

You said that in your chemical industries you do not allow anybody to buy more than a few shares. Are the shares quoted in the market ? It has not been necessary to have them quoted in the market.

(Dr. E. Hopkinson).—You stated that the Japanese Government made it a condition that contracting firms should take Japanese apprentices. Do you think that the Japanese Government could make a similar condition to-day ? My point is that if you make large purchases from a firm they would always be ready to accommodate you.

I ask you with reference to the particular instance of Japan. Do you think they could make such a condition to-day ? Possibly not.

You think the Government of India would have no difficulty in making such a stipulation ? The

Japanese Government is a foreign Government and when they got such terms my point is that we should be able to get better terms.

Of what University are you a doctor? Edinburgh, Calcutta and Durham Universities.

For research work? Yes.

You have good opportunity of judging of the capacity of University students in connection with your chemical and pharmaceutical works? Yes.

You made a rather startling statement that 99 per cent. of the M. Sc. students of the Calcutta University were too bookish to be of any value for ordinary business avocations? They are good for research work but they are no good for business and commercial work.

What do you attribute that to? In Bengal there has been a kind of hereditary repugnance to taking to trade and commerce. We have always been notorious for choosing the clerical line, the law and the professions.

And then in the course of your evidence you press the point that there should be manual training in the secondary schools; no doubt if it became universal it would go a long way towards correcting tendency that you suggest. Would you not carry that manual training back to primary education? Yes. That would be the best possible way.

So that you would insist on manual training at the same time that the boy learns to read and write? I should very much like it.

Have you worked out a scheme? At first in the kindergarten system they would make gardens and learn the use of the spade. Then they will learn basket making, etc.

So you would devote some of the time now given to reading and writing to manual work? Yes.

And you think that it is quite feasible? Yes, especially in the villages in Bengal.

Then I suppose when they have advanced to secondary education manual training might take a somewhat higher form, *e. g.*, carpentry, directly in connection with some industry? Yes.

The two things might then go on together? Yes.

Can you tell us exactly what the B standard is? At present what is meant by technical schools in the places outside Calcutta means no more than securing the services of a carpenter and a blacksmith. That is the only help they get and they are spoken of as technical schools. That is not what is wanted. The B standard will give an industrial bent to education, I mean to general education.

If primary education is associated with manual training that could be carried to the secondary school and up to the time when a student goes to the University and this would more than anything else correct the present state of things which you deplore? Yes.

(*Mr. A. Chatterton.*)—Are the methods that you advocate in your written evidence those which you have pursued in so far as it was possible in developing a very successful chemical industry? Yes.

You did not apply for any Government assistance? Never.

You have had no financial aid of any kind from Government? We never asked for it.

You began on a small scale and gradually built up? We proceeded step by step.

Don't you think that other people also could do the same sort of things when they wish to start an industry? It has taken us nearly quarter of a century to make this progress. Now-a-days it is very necessary to start with a very big capital and secure the best possible experts if we are to compete with foreign markets.

How many chemists have you got in your employ? Four chemists in the higher department.

How many altogether? There are a number of people who make preparations like compounders and foremen. Four are M. Sc.'s of the Calcutta University. My services also are at their disposal.

Have you got any experience of students who have returned from Europe or America who were sent there by Government as technical scholars? Yes.

Do you think that it is a satisfactory system? I have suggested that those who have already been in business and have done some kind of work at home could be selected to go to Europe and learn the advanced methods. At present they are sending men indiscriminately.

Have you visited the Indian Institute of Science

in Bangalore? I have recently been to Bangalore. I am a visitor appointed by the Calcutta University.

You say there is no proper controlling authority. With reference to what? I have found that up till now 39 lakhs of rupees have been spent.

Is that accurate? That is what I saw in the papers and the central block cost 6 to 7 lakhs of rupees. Even the Director or the professoriate could not tell me what it is meant for. Seven lakhs for a block which is scarcely wanted and for which nobody would like to be held responsible! The money has been recklessly spent.

Whom did you get this information from? The Director and the professoriate. They could not give me any satisfactory information. There is a big clock-tower in the central building, which is meant to locate the library. There are some halls as big as those in the Buckingham Palace.

All this information that you have got is not strictly accurate. That is why I should like you to modify your statement to some extent? That was the universal complaint that I heard from the people of Madras and Bombay.

When you want to make a statement of this kind why did you not go to the Director and get the information? I have seen it published in the public papers. I got reports that up till now 39 lakhs of rupees have been spent in block and building and also in current expenses.

You are mixing up two very different things. It

is 21 lakhs. Would you not therefore withdraw that sentence. Whatever mistakes there may have been in the past things are on a better basis now and presumably there is some controlling authority at the present moment ? I am strongly of opinion that the constitution of the committee ought to be changed. Because the outside public have no voice in the matter. The professoriate and the Director are in overwhelming majority and they can carry on things in their own way and I believe even the donors have no hand in the matter.

You object to the location of the Institute of Science in Bangalore. Have you got any accurate knowledge of the amount of industrial work going on in the neighbourhood of Bangalore ? I have seen the harnessing of the Cauvery and the Kolar Gold fields. That represents a huge industrial enterprise. There are weaving, spinning and woollen mills.

Do you still adhere to your opinion that it is an unsatisfactory place in which to locate an industrial research institute ? I mean it is so far away.

It is of course a long way from Bengal but is it far away from the centres of industry in the South of India ? It is nearer Madras. I fully admit. Possibly it is of great advantage to the Government of Mysore.

Your complaint then is this that the Institute has not been of much use to Bengal. It may be of use to the South of India ? I do not know whether it has been of much use to Bombay which claims some of the biggest donors.

From this I understand that you would recommend the creation of a number of similar institutes in other parts of India, in the large industrial centres? It all depends, as I said. We are yet in the premature stages to pass any decided opinion. I have said nothing against the personnel of the Institute.

I am not now talking of the Indian Institute of Science and your opinion of it. I am asking you whether you are in favour of having similar institutes in Calcutta worked on proper lines? We have got centres of research in Calcutta and do not think a separate institute would be of much use. In the Presidency College and the University College of Science we have got researches going on.

Then you have got researches sufficiently developed? So far as chemistry is concerned we have got ample facilities.

Are these researches in Calcutta devoted to the prosecution of what I may call pure science or the application of science? It is for pure science.

Has any research work been done in connection with the application of science? Not at all.

Do you want any help provided for Calcutta? It would be useful for local institutions. If one wants to have some information connected with any industry in Bengal it would be inconvenient to go to Bangalore. Moreover, they would be overwhelmed with work from the various provinces of India, each province sending in its own peculiarities.

Would you be in favour of the development of

central research laboratories for the prosecution of these enquiries in India or do you want to have them locally? I should like to have local centres. Because it is the particular locality that would determine the conditions of work in that locality.

Do you want to have these scientific centres under provincial or imperial control? I should have provincial control.

(Mr. C. E. Low.)—Do you propose to have one in each of the provinces or in each of the major provinces? One for each of the provinces, one for Bengal, one for the United Provinces, one for the Madras and so on.

You do not propose to have one for Delhi? No. The smaller provinces could apply for help to the major provinces.

You would allow the smaller provinces to have access to the larger provinces? Yes.

Have you anything to add to the remarks you have made? We have been very unfortunate in the selection of our industries. And before any new industry is started it should be impressed upon the would-be organisers that they should take sufficient precautions to enquire as to the supply of raw materials and the scope of the sale of the articles and so on. In this connection the pencil making, to which I have referred, the organisers might as well have enquired where they were likely to get their wood. Many industries have been taken up. For instance soap-making. I find that the very important thing necessary, namely soda, has to be imported and then there is the glycerine which is a bye-product. In European countries it is the glycerine which keeps up the soap industry. We throw it away. Unless we start on a big scale we cannot recover the glycerine. It requires a big plant. At present to throw away the glycerine and to make the soap would be an impossible undertaking. The few industries that are surviving are able to keep on because patriotism pays a kind of bounty as it were.

ANANDA MOHAN BOSE

A MAKER OF MODERN BENGAL

The following appreciation of Mr. Ananda Mohan Bose was contributed by Dr. P. C. Ray to the "Indian World" in January 1907 :

In order to be able fully to understand the part played by the late Ananda Mohan Bose in the development of the extraordinary progress of Bengal it is necessary to recall for a moment the state of affairs in these provinces in the early seventies of the last century and the forces which were already at work when he appeared on the scene. Ram Mohan Roy may justly be regarded as the maker of Modern India. He was the first to give a rude shock to the canker which had for a thousand years been insidiously eating into the vitals of the great Hindu nation. He was the first to free this unhappy land from the intellectual paralysis and stagnation which had set in in India since the sixth century A. D. and which sounded the death-knell of what is sometimes called the rationalistic age. When Ram Mohan Roy was born, India was enveloped in cimmerian darkness. The laws of evolution can scarcely explain the rise of such a man at such a period unless it be on the theory that the potential activity of a great people, like the seed-grains entombed in the pyramids, may lie dormant for ages and burst forth into vigorous life even under comparatively untoward environments. The contact with the West had borne its first fruit. Ram Mohan had a colossal intellect and he foresaw that if this ancient land were once more to occupy her place of glory she must make progress all around. It is not therefore difficult to realise that the greatest Bengalee of modern times, himself an eminent linguist and a great admirer of Upanishads, the study of which had well nigh been forgotten in the *Tols* of Navadwipa and Vikrampore, should have rebuked Lord Amherst in a letter—regarded as a masterpiece in English literature—for his giving sanction to the establishment of the Sanskrit College, ignoring thereby the claims of modern anatomy, chemistry and physical science. Ram Mohan Roy gave the impetus to all the forces which go to the making of a great nation. His reforms embraced every field of activity. He had sown his seeds broadcast, some had been chocked up, but others had fallen on congenial soil and began to germinate. D'Rozio and his pupils of the old Hindu College had also taken their share in the great upheaval which took place now. Ramgopal Ghosh, Radhanath Sikder, Tarachand Chakravarty and Krishna Mohan Banerjee were like so many fire-brands; and they, by their example, exhortations and denunciations also paved the way for future workers.

Everybody knows that James Thomson was, in a way, the father of political agitation in Bengal, but it should not be forgotten that his followers had their noviciate and training in the school of Ram Mohan and Dwarkanath Tagore. The British Indian Association was the outcome of this activity, but its very existence was rendered possible by the lessons taught by Ram Mohan. In the early fifties, again, the great Iswar Chandra Vidyasagar had appeared in the field with his programme of widow re-marriage. His treatise on the subject, based as it was on the injunctions of the Shastras, with its pathetic and eloquent appeal, which could only emanate from the father of modern Bengalee literature, and the heroic personal sacrifice he made for the cause had stirred the inmost depths of the orthodox society. While our countrymen had scarcely time to recover from the shock imparted from the widow re-marriage reformer, another mighty figure appeared on the stage in the early sixties. Vidyasagar fought with his pen but Keshub Chandra Sen wielded his tongue no less efficiently and his appeal to young Bengal exerted the most marvellous influence. Those who hold that Keshub was only a Brahmo leader take a very narrow view of the situation. It is only a truism to say that for every young man who was actually drawn within the fold of the Brahmo Samaj, there were at least ten who were influenced by him for good within the pale of the orthodox society. Ananda Mohan Bose was himself brought under the personal magnetism of Keshub Chandra Sen and his career took its colour and shape in no small degree from that Brahmo apostle.

The writer well remembers the time when Ananda Mohan Bose returned to his native land after his brilliant academic career at Cambridge in 1874. It at once appeared that he had already shaped out the path which he was to follow in future. Within the brief period of a year or two Ananda Mohan Bose came to the fore-front both as a legal practitioner as well as a political leader. The Student's Association of which he stood a sponsor along with his co-adjutor, Mr. Surendranath Banerjee, caused a new awakening. Hitherto the student community was left very much to itself. To be able to get on and be prosperous in life in the restricted sphere open to an Indian was considered the be-all and end-all of a university degree. That the students of to-day make the nation of to-morrow—that it should be a part and parcel of their education to be trained to take up and discharge the duties of citizenship—that there is such a thing after all as one's own motherland—all these had then been but dimly realised. It was from this moral slough that the late Mr. Ananda Mohan Bose and Mr. Surendranath Banerjee rescued the rising generation; it was they who for the first time held up before young Bengal the ideal of a national life as well as patriotic citizenship. I need not proceed further on this head; suffice it to say that but for these two prominent figures—the makers of Modern Bengal—the new awakening to which the philosophical Secretary of State for India recently bore eloquent testimony would have yet taken a long time in coming.

Ananda Mohan achieved another great end, here again, it would be simply invidious to single him out for special notice. It may give scope for much futile speculation to the future historian as to whom is entitled the credit for first conceiving the formation of a political body like the Indian Association. The foundation of this institution was an epoch-making event in the history of Modern Bengal. To posterity—the names of Ananda Mohan Bose and Mr. Surendra nath Banerjee will be linked together as the joint founders of this historic organisation. The British Indian Association had outlived its short period of utility. Indeed, although an aristocratic body in itself, even in its palmy days, it drew its best blood from the rank and file of the middle class. Harischandra Mukherjee, Kristo Das Pal, Digambar Mitra and Rajendra Lall Mitra—none of these were born with silver spoons in their mouths. Ananda Mohan and his political comrades had the foresight to realise that if political agitation were to count as a factor in the uplifting of India, it must be broad-based upon a national basis—in other words it must gather its nourishment and strength from the great middle and lower classes—the commonality which in Bengal as everywhere else formed the real backbone of society. I believe it was at one time feared by some that this wrench and cleavage in the social strata would lead to disastrous consequences. Subsequent events have fully justified the wisdom of Ananda Mohan Bose in standing up for the ryot's cause, the people's rights and for the democratic spirit. England, the cradle of freedom and free institutions, has, as a rule, been fortunate in her aristocracy; it is to a blue-blooded Norman—Simon DeMontfort—that she is mainly indebted for her first Parliament; but at several critical periods in her history, when she turned to the nobility for help she was sadly disappointed, and Carlyle has made some scathing observations on the "High Essexes and Manchesters of limited notions and large estates."

The outline I have sketched above, however, go to cover only a phase of Ananda Mohan's many-sided activity. His spirit soared high above the aspirations of an ordinary man. Mr. Bose was a pillar to the cause of the Brahmo Samaj and as fire trieth the gold, so was he put to a severe ordeal. The great schism which took place in 1878 over the marriage of Keshub Chandra Sen's first daughter with the present Maharajah of Cooch Behar and which eventually led to the foundation of the Sadharan Brahmo Samaj called forth all his best energies. Here again he was to the fore-front. Under his counsel and guidance the vessel steered clear of the rocks ahead and the shoals beneath. His personality was deeply impressed upon all the earlier efforts of this Church and all the auxiliary institutions established in connection with it. In moulding the lineaments of a generation of Brahmo youths, in infusing in the young and old the craving for intellectual culture and the necessity of personal piety and devotion, Ananda Mohan had no equal in his days. The phenomenal success of the Sadharan Brahmo Samaj as a teacher of lofty principles and an example of moral austerity is not to an inconsiderable extent due to the personal purity and the courage of convictions of the late Mr. Bose.

As an educationalist also Ananda Mohan did signal service to his country. Lord Ripon, who had the knack of choosing the right man for the right place, appreciated his abilities in this field and appointed him a member of the Education Commission; as one of the founders of the City College, perhaps the only non-proprietory College in Bengal started under purely indegenous efforts, he will be entitled to the lasting gratitude of thousands of youths who have had the benefit of a liberal education under its auspices. It was Ananda Mohan Bose, again, who as a member of the Syndicate and Fellow of the Calcutta University raised his voice more than ten years ago against the purely examining function of that University and tried his best to amend the Act of Incorporation with a view to inaugurate the foundation of Chairs and Fellowships within the scope of that body. He was also very prominent in encouraging original study, research and investigations and in minimising the evil of cramming, in the system of education in vogue under the University. Mr. Bose was also a staunch advocate of high education among women. In co-operation with his friend, the late Mr. Durga Mohan Das, he founded the Banga Mohila Vidyalaya and both of them opened their purse freely for its maintenance. This was ultimately amalgamated with the Bithune College and formed the nucleus of the higher classes of this Girton of Bengal.

Ananda Mohan's eloquence and persuasiveness were simply marvellous. Competent judges have been heard to declare that had his lot been cast in England his talents would have found due scope, and he would have commanded the applause of senators at St. Stephen and in due course might have even risen to the rank of a cabinet minister. Ananda Mohan's speech on the Chowkidary Tax in the Bengal Council and that on the reform of the Calcutta University—delivered in the Senate House—will rank among the classics on these subjects. No one had more constantly and sincerely at heart the cause of high education. He believed that it had received a rude shock, nay, a severe blow, by what is now known as "Reorganisation of the Education Service." To this veteran educationist was entrusted the task of seconding a Resolution on the subject at the Calcutta Congress of 1896. Ananda Mohan had only some four hours' time for preparation and yet it was universally acknowledged that his speech was the speech of the session. The writer vividly remembers the effect it produced on the vast audience, which was simply kept enthralled and spell-bound during its delivery. One or two passages may be quoted here as illustrating the oratorical power of the late Mr. Bose:

"At the present time an Indian Professor in the Presidency College, and I know some most distinguished ones there, can become in course of time and by virtue of seniority the Principal of that college. There is absolutely nothing to prevent it. But under the new scheme we are excluded, we are debarred, from looking forward to that state of things. In Bombay and Madras every one of the Principalships is reserved for members of the higher branch, and not one left for the Provincial Service, or in other words, for the natives of the country. In the place of the old idea of an Open Service—open to all, whether European or Indian—we have now brought in by the new scheme the unhappy and harmful idea of certain appointments being reserved for the European members of the Service. Is this right ? Are we going onwards or backwards ? Is that gentlemen, to be the fruit of the awakening of the great social, moral and intellectual forces that are now dominating the face of this continent ? Is that indeed to be the result of the onward march of the vaunted progress and enlightenment of the country ? Is a new preserve to be created for the European members of the higher Service ? Is the area of exclusion for the people of the soil to be further extended ? From equality in the earlier years to inequality in 1880, and now in the closing years of the century to still further and grosser inequality, is that to be the order of things, the destined course of progress under the enlightened administration of

England for this great and ancient land? At any rate, by our voice and effort, we shall do, I trust all we can, to prevent that state of things and to bring home to the minds and consciences of our rulers and of the justice loving people of England the injustice that has been done."

Then again:

"I cannot venture to detain the meeting any further. I have already passed my allotted limit of time. I will therefore conclude with only one more remark. There is no cause which can be dearer to the members of the Congress than the cause of education. You, gentlemen, are the fruits of that education, of that great awakening of the national mind to which I have referred. And can it possibly be that you will for a moment neglect to do all that you can, all that lies in your power—with the help of our friends in England and in India, with the help of all those, wherever they may be, who look forward to human progress as a thing to be wished for, as a thing to be fought for—to see that your children are not ostracized from those higher branches of the Service with their higher opportunities of educational work and educational progress, to which, up to now, they have been appointed. There are no considerations such as those which are sometimes supposed, be it rightly or be it wrongly, to apply to appointments in the Indian Civil Service, which can have any application to those in the educational Service of the country. What possible shadow of a shade of justification can there then be for this enlarged and expanded edition of the policy of exclusion? Gentlemen, I believe in the intellect of India. I believe the fire that burned so bright centuries ago has not wholly died out yet. I believe there are sparks, aye, more than sparks, that still exist, and only require the gentle breeze of sympathetic help, of judicious organisation and kindly care, to burst forth once again into that glorious fire which in the past illumined not only this great continent but shed its lustre over other lands—into that intellectual life which achieved wonders in the field of literature and arts, in the field of mathematics and philosophy, which produced works which are even now the admiration and the wonder of the world. Fight with redoubled vigour in that cause, and then we may depend upon it that—in the Providence of God—righteousness and justice shall triumph, and this attempt to fix on the brows of the people of this ancient land a new stigma and a new disability shall fail as it deserves to fail."

But the best speech that he ever delivered or that has ever been delivered in India was his concluding address to the Congress of 1898 as its President. As he drew before his audience a picture of our distressed motherland and the numerous calls of duty which patriotic Indians have to answer, the whole house was literally filled with tears—'Love and Service'—was the text of this speech and 'Love and Service' he enjoined upon all his educated countrymen as the first article of their political creed—a shibboleth which he himself subscribed and acted up to since the beginning of his political career in the seventies of the last century.

Ananda Mohan was a man of culture to use the terms in its widest application. His mind was well balanced and he was pre-eminently endowed with a sense of proportion. He fully realised like Ram Mohan Roy that Society is an organic growth and that progress meant the harmonious development of all its limbs. As in the human body so in the social fabric the laws of physiology could not be violated with impunity. At the present moment in Bengal we are threatened with a grave danger. It is being constantly dinned into our ears that the one thing necessary for our march onwards in the path of progress is political agitation. It is clean forgotten that for the upbuilding of a nation, social, moral, industrial and intellectual factors do not play a subordinate part. Early or rather infant marriage, enforced widowhood of child wives, the abject and degraded ignorance in which our womanhood is brought up, and the rigid and hide-bound system of caste—these and other concomitant evils loudly call for redress. Alas! most of us turn a deaf ear to the call. We demand equality in the eye of the law, we denounce in unmeasured terms the invidious treatment meted out to the Indians in Natal and Cape Colony, but we conveniently ignore or cooly forget that we ourselves are guilty of worse enormities. In Madras the low-caste people—the Pariahs

—are treated as worse than cats and dogs. The touch of some of my fellow countrymen—though belonging to the same creed—contaminates my person and my food. With such engrained ideas permeating every stratum of our social fabric it is a little bit absurd to talk loud of patriotism, which practically means love of one's own fellowmen. Thus it was that Ananda Mohan threw himself heart and soul into every movement which had for its object the amelioration of the condition of the depressed classes of our people. Politics with him was not a thing apart, but a part and parcel of his very religion. With him to take recourse to make-shifts, to subserve temporary ends was tantamount to a crime and he would make no compromise with the eternal principles of justice and righteousness.

Ananda Mohan could never work in a half hearted way. Whatever cause he once espoused found in him a fervid champion for ever. I have often seen him return from the lengthy deliberations of a meeting of the Senate or the Syndicate of the Calcutta University and plunge afresh into the discussions of important matters before the Executive Committee of the Sadharan Brahmo Samaj. He was as much at home in addressing an audience on the temperance question as on the re-organisation of the Education Service at the Congress.

Everyone who had ever any occasion to approach Ananda Mohan felt the magnetism of his personality. His moral fervour, his piety, his suavity of temper, his sweet reasonableness, combined with his decision of character, lent additional charm to what he said and did.

It has often appeared to me as an anomaly that the first Indian to get through the Mathematical Tripos at Cambridge should have abandoned his own subject. Had he stuck to Mathematics probably his genius would have been rewarded by original contributions of a high order. There is, however, danger in the vocation of a specialist. He is apt to grow narrow-minded and bigoted and to disparage the value of things beyond his limited vision. As the poet has it :—

> " The man of science is fond of glory and vain ;
> An eye well-practised in nature, a spirit bounded and poor."

Ananda Mohan Bose's genius was versatile and his activity many-sided. Providence had destined him for the higher and nobler task of contributing to the making of a nation. It was but meet that such a soul refused to be cribbed, cabined and confined within the narrow sphere of a specialist.

DADABHAI NAOROJI

[*Dr. P. C. Ray, in unveiling the portrait of Dadabhai Naoroji at the Pachaiyappa's College, Madras, on the 3rd February* 1918, *said* :—]

He would draw certain lessons from the life of Dadabhai Naoroji for the guidance of the youngmen present there. The first thing that struck him, as it struck everyone else, was that they were making considerable progress towards nation-building. In Madras they had the Gokhale Hall, and now the portrait of Dadabhai Naoroji was being unveiled. This showed that forgetting to what nationality or creed one or the other belonged they only took into consideration the one thing that both of them were great sons of India. Dadabhai Naoroji had an abiding faith in the ultimate and innate sense of justice of the British people. He knew that Indians had to labour under many disadvantages which were due to the circumstance that nobody represented India in England. The English people only came to know of Indians through the distorted medium of Anglo-Indian misrepresentation. It was because of this that he thought England ought to be the place from which he should try to educate the English people. He (the lecturer) just now spoke rather disparagingly of Anglo-Indians—but then there were Anglo-Indians and Anglo-Indians; there were Anglo-Indians of the type of Hume, Cotton and Wedderburn, names which were enshrined in the hearts of the Indians. When Dadabhai Naoroji began his career in England, that great friend of India, the illustrious John Bright, was at the height of his glory and was fighting the battle of India just when the Queen's Proclamation was issued. Later on he was nobly seconded in his efforts by another great friend of India, the late Henry Fawcett. So, he had every hope that, securing the friendship of such eminent men, he would be able to get justice done to his countrymen. The one thing which Dadabhai more than any other person, tried to bring home not only to Englishmen but also to his own countrymen was the appalling poverty of India. From the time of Milton onwards the wealth of Ind had attracted many adventurers. "Now it is a myth," that was what he tried to prove. To the average Englishman India was an El Dorado—the land which overflowed with gold. They would forget that there were in India millions of people who toiled from morning to evening and yet could not get sufficient money to keep their body and soul together. At the beginning of the eighties the late Sir William Hunter was invited by the Philosophical Institute at Edinburgh to deliver a lecture on India. In his lecture he declared that one-fifth of the population of India did not know what were the pleasures of a full stomach. It was a most astounding revelation to many of them that this was a poor country, so ill-capable of bearing this costly administration which had been thrust upon her since the days of Lord Cornwallis. Dadabhai Naoroji tried to prove these two things, and he was eminently capable of such a task. There were many of our countrymen who took part in politics, but he was sorry to say that very few of them studied facts and figures.

Dadabhai Naoroji started on his career as a mathematician and his mathematical training stood him in good stead. By his careful analysis and calculation of the wealth of the country and of the produce thereof, he brought out the astounding fact that the average income of the Indian was a little over Rs. 15 per annum. Lord Curzon recalculated the income, but he was also compelled to say that it would be between only Rs. 25 and Rs. 30 per annum. The other day he (the speaker) met some of the European members of the University Commission at the Cosmopolitan Club. He told them "Here you see all that is best in Madras. From the point of view of Madras you find assembled, on one spot, a good many of the High Court Judges, lawyers and business men. You find beautiful buildings and a rich dinner awaiting your palate. You come to the conclusion that everyone is like this in India." But they confessed that within a stone's throw of that building there was appalling misery and heartrending distress. It was to bring home to the British people this state of things that Dadabhai Naoroji spent the best portion of his life in England.

For the first time Dadabhai Naoroji trained a body of men who were determined to devote themselves exclusively to political matters. Hitherto in India politics was rather a kind of recreation. They would find men, especially in Bengal, who after a day's work, run from their desks, get up a platform and deliver a political harangue in the midst of the applause of youngmen, and on their returning home, think that they had done their duty to their country. Dadabhai Naoroji was not a man of this type. He knew that politics was a thing to which one should devote his whole life. He not only showed the way but also prepared the ground for others to follow. The late Mr. Gokhale told the speaker that Ranade was in a way a disciple of Dadabhai Naoroji, and that he himself was greatly indebted to Mr. Ranade. Thus Mr. Gokhale was in a way the intellectual grandson of Dadabhai. Mr. Gokhale often pointed to the speaker that Mr. Srinivasa Sastry would be his successor. And now Mr. Srinivasa Sastry was in a way the great grand-child of Dadabhai Naoroji. They would thus see how the inspiring influence of one would travel to another. Many events of a far reaching character were now going to take place, and as the Prime Minister said the other day, people were marching through the track of centuries in the course of a few months. They should, therefore, prepare themselves fully by studying the questions relating to their country. He had often found members of the legislative councils interpellating the

Government without taking sufficient care to study the questions before-hand. The result was that they were immediately silenced by the official members. They should remember that the days for impassioned rhetoric were being numbered. Politics was no longer a field for amateurs. Nowadays, if people wanted to be heard by the public or in the council chamber they ought to be able to marshal facts and figures in order to carry conviction into the minds of of their hearers.

As an illustration, the speaker said how a few years ago Mr. N. Subba Rao was able in the Imperial Legislative Council to carry conviction to the Government with the aid of statistics. The result was the appointment of the Public Services Commission. Again, the notable minority report of Mr. Abdur Rahim was also the outcome of the Public Services Commission. They would thus see how from humble beginnings great events took place. They should study political economy thoroughly and the history of their own country, as well as that of European countries and compare them with their own country.

Another notable thing in connection with the life of Dadabhai Naoroji was that for more than half a century he made the grievances of India his sole study, and towards that end sacrificed his own personal good. At one time, when his countrymen presented him with Rs. 1 lakh, without spending anything out of it he arranged that the interest accruing from it might be spent on political propagandist work. This showed how utterly selfless and what a true lover of the country he was. By honouring such a man they would honour themselves. There were very few exemplars to be presented to youngmen, and they could not do better than always have portraits of the illustrious dead of the type of Naoroji. The speaker then dealt upon the parliamentary career of Dadabhai Naoroji and showed how by his untiring efforts he was able to win a unique distinction. The appointment of the Welby Commission on the recommendation of Sir Henry Fowler, the then Secretary of State, was due to Mr. Dadabhai's efforts.

At no distant date they would get some form of Swaraj whether it be on the colonial basis or any other basis, and they would get enlarged powers. So, in order to fit themselves up for the task they should study history and political economy. It was for this reason that Mr. Gokhale in his Servants of India Society at Poona collected a very good library for the use of political students. The other day when he asked some cultured youngmen what the import trade from Manchester was, they began to scratch their heads. If he would for a moment play the role of a schoolmaster, perhaps very few of those present in the hall would get off unscathed. The fact was scarcely known to them that they were importing fifty crores of rupees worth of piece-goods. They should study all these in order to know how much profit they could make out of this amount by opening mills in India. Statistics should be the breath of the nostrils to a politician. And it was, therefore, in the fitness of things that the Historical Association of the Pachaiyappa's College should have taken into its head to get the portrait of Dadabhai Naoroji unveiled. Dadabhai Naoroji's place in the national Valhalla was simply unique, and he hoped that young men in future would continue to draw their inspiration by looking at the portrait.

He concluded his lecture by repeating the lines of Longfellow:—

Lives of great men all remind us
That we can make our lives sublime,
And, departing, leave behind us,
Foot-prints on the sands of Time.

SIR WILLIAM WEDDERBURN

[Presiding over a public meeting at the Calcutta Town Hall on March 4, 1918, *to record the deep sense of loss India has sustained by the death of Sir William Wedderburn, Dr. P. C. Ray spoke as follows :—]*

We are assembled here this afternoon to perform a solemn and pious duty—to mourn the loss of one, who for a period of half a century and more, was indefatigable in his exertions on behalf of India. The death of Sir William Wedderburn has left a void which I am afraid it will be difficult to fill up. It is true, he has died full of years and honours, but at this critical and momentous juncture in the history of our political existence we can ill-afford to lose the services of such a sincere friend of our country.

Allan Octavian Hume, Henry Cotton and William Wedderburn form an illustrious triumvirate —they are the last of a race of Anglo-Indian administrators, which, alas ! bids fair to become as extinct as the Dodo. As a student of science I may be permitted for a moment to trace some of the potent causes which have operated to bring about this lamentable state of things. In the good old days of John Company when the voyage to and from India often occupied six months, when it was necessary to double the Cape in sailing ships, when salted beef with scurvy into the bargain was the dainty delicacy offered to the palate—the Civilian seldom turned his thoughts west-ward; he looked upon India as his home; he entered into the feelings and sympathised with the aspirations of the people, shared their joys and griefs. Just fancy Sir Charles Metcalfe returning to England in 1838 after an absence of 38 years! With the opening of the Suez Canal, and the running of the accelerated mail service, however, the old state of things was upset. To the average European, India became the land of exile and of regrets. The official began to regard himself as a stranger and sojourner in the land and to count the days from the time of joining till the beginning of the much coveted furlough—just as the pious Hindu counts his beads,—when he would be able to spend a couple of years at his "home, sweet home." Then again the moffusil stations have been brought within easy reach of the Presidency towns,—thanks to the railway and steamer communications. Life in the luxurious clubs has become attractive. The executive head of the district often makes over his charge to the senior Deputy Magistrate and spends the week-end in these resorts of recreation and amusement. The European officer or even the merchant thus lives in a world apart in a state of glorious isolation. No doubt in his daily transactions he mixes with people of all sorts and conditions but that is in a purely business capacity. An Indian is now to an European a sealed book—a thick impenetrable veil—I had almost said a sort of Chinese wall—has begun to partition off the one from the other.

Both Wedderburn and Cotton were competition-wallahs; but both had hereditary connection with India extending over a century and had thus imbibed the traditions of the Hailebury days—they formed a kind of connecting link between the *ancien regime* and the new. We are often told that the Government of India aims at efficiency but this kind of efficiency is being purchased at a bitter cost. The machinery with its elaborate paraphernalia has become top heavy. The table of the Secretariat now groans under the load of basketfuls of files. Desk and routine work and red tape-ism have become the necessary adjuncts of the system. It makes havoc of genius and originality and turns out hum-drum mediocres. Just half-a-century ago Sir John Kaye thus compared the old order with the new:—

"At that time the Civil Service was recruited with boys fresh from school. A stripling from the fifth form at Eton was suddenly converted in his teens into an Indian administrator, and launched at once into a sea of temptation, at an Indian presidency to sink or to swim, according to the degree of his own strength or of the power of the waves. How he managed "to fit himself for the public service" it was hard to say. His education was generally slender, and in its slenderness not of a kind to qualify him for the work of Indian administration. That good or bad angel of Examination had not at that time flapped his wings over the land. And yet, somehow or other, very good public servants had been, as the Court of Directors acknowledged, reared out of these adverse circumstances. Warren Hastings and John Shore, Jonathan Duncan and George Barlow—the Halheds, the Colebrookes, Neill Edmonstone, and St. George Tucker, had ripened under that system; and Mountstuart Elphinstone was growing rapidly." I may also add the names of Munro, Malcolm and Metcalfe.

A race of giants has been succeeded by a breed of pygmies who are incapable of taking a wide outlook of things and events. If I have gone a little out of the way in discussing briefly some of the causes which are responsible for the deterioration of the Services it is only to point a moral and adorn a tale. In the early days of his career Wedderburn was inclined to believe in the Indian Civil Service as the ordained instrument of India's regeneration, but the dream of youthful enthusiasm was soon dissipated. The disillusionment was not long in coming. His mature life-long experiences of the Indian bureaucracy are thus summed up in the following lines quoted from his Presidential Address to the Fifth National Congress, 1889:

"In certain important particulars the professional interests of our official administrators in India are in antagonism with the interests of the Indian tax-payer whose affairs they administer.

"The main interests of the Indian tax-payer are peace, economy and reform. But all those are necessarily distasteful to the civil and military classes. A spirited and well-equipped army naturally desires, not peace, but active service. And who can reasonably expect officials to love economy, which means reduction of their own salaries; or reform, which means restriction of their authority? It cannot be expected that as a class our official administrators in India will work for peace, economy and reform."

Love for India and her people was the dominant passion of Wedderburn. To quote his own words:—"I have passed a quarter of a century among you, and during that period of time I have not known what it was to suffer an unkindness from a native of India. During that period I have been in the service of the people of India, and have eaten their salt. And I hope to devote to their service what still remains to me of active life."

If ever out of the abundance of the heart the mouth spake it was on this occasion. On his retirement he did not seek repose at Bath or Cheltenham but entered Parliament so that he might plead the cause of India. He retired from the House of Commons in 1900 after sitting for 7 years because, as he himself confessed, he was overtaxed both as to physical endurance and financial resources. Perhaps it is not known to many of you that he spent over a lakh of rupees from his own pocket with the sole and exclusive object of advancing the moral and material well-being of the Indian people.

After the death of Hume, Wedderburn was the life and soul of the British Congress Committee. He was also a large instrument of the Minto-Morley reforms. He lived what would be called a *dedicated* life. As Mr. S. N. Banerjea said in his inimitable language at the Allahabad Congress of 1910 of which Sir William was the President: "In the muster-roll of distinguished Englishmen, who have loved India with an abounding love and have served her with passionate devotion, Sir William Wedderburn will be one of the most distinguished. How many of us, children of the soil, whose bones will rest here, whose interests, sympathies and reminiscences are centred in this ancient land, can claim to have exhibited in the record of their life-work, the selfless devotion, the unflinching self-sacrifice and the supreme love for India and her peoples, which have always been the dominating features in the public career of Sir William Wedderburn?"

The lives of men like Hume and Wedderburn should teach us the great lesson of the need and urgency of the development of a composite patriotism where the Englishman and the Indian may find enough scope to march shoulder to shoulder and work out the destinies of their own mother land.

There was a grand simplicity combined with nobility in the life that Sir William Wedderburn chose to live; something of the Puritan's moral earnestness and strength of character blended in him with the suavity of culture and the spirit of *noblesse oblige*. He was a British baronet by inheritance; as a Civil Servant he rose to be Secretary to the Bombay Government and Judge of the High Court. But there was no aristocratic aloofness in him no sense of repulsion from India and the Indians. He did not identify our nation with the hardened criminals, servile office-seekers and title-hunting snobs whom it was his lot to meet with in his official capacity, but always sought out and co-operated with the best and most patriotic representatives of our countrymen and was thus brought into intimate contact with men like S. S. Bengalee, Nourozjee Firdonjee, Dadabhai Naoroji, Bhau Daji, Mangaldas Nathubhai, Viswanath Narayan Mandalik, Ganes Vasudeo Joshi, Ranade, Mehta, Telang and Tyabji and latterly Gokhale, Messrs. Surendranath Bannerji, Bhupendranath Basu and others.

He sacrificed the evening of his life, long years of well-earned ease, the friendship of old comrades of his youth and manhood,—and what was probably least in his eyes, I mean his private income,—in furthering the political progress of the Indians. In words whose noble and hearty ring take us back to the golden days of antique Rome, he used to say: "India has given bread and the means of distinction to me and my forbears. It is only by serving her sons that I can repay my debt to her!"

There was enough in our people to discourage

him, enough to make him at times sick of his work. People, who labour to regenerate a fallen nation, often get an inside view of unspeakable sordidness, weakness and misery, which are hidden from casual observers. They have to work in an atmosphere almost stifling. But Wedderburn's stout heart never quailed. He had chosen the right path and he went straight ahead, unmoved by the failings of our countrymen, undeterred by the sneers of the Tory press and the Anglo-Indian clubs and an unsympathetic Secretary of State like Lord George Hamilton, ever ready to administer him sharp rebukes for his magnanimous advocacy of the cause of the dumb millions of India. He had caught a beatific vision of the day of India's liberation, and toward that promised land he marched through the valley of the shadow of death, knowing well that he would not live to see it with the eyes of flesh, but no less strenuously, no less hopefully than the youngest recruit in the army of India's political workers.

A generation before Sir William Wedderburn, Macaulay with his prophetic vision had foreseen the day, when the teaching of Roman History, English History and Athenian Eloquence to Indian youth would bear its natural fruit; according to him it would be the proudest day for England when, under her fostering care, the subjects of centuries of oriental despotism, the brown natives of a tropical clime, would feel inspired to make their country what the seven-hilled city was to her sons, what the City of the Violet

Crown was to Pericles, what England was to Hampden and Locke, Pitt and Palmerston. For that day, however distant, Sir William set himself to prepare both the rulers and the ruled. His position and past services eminently fitted him for the task of being the interpreter, "the honest broker," between the two parties. If his counsels were not accepted, if his devotion was not utilised by one of the two parties, his was not the fault; his was not the loss.

Sir William Wedderburn, like all right-thinkers, like our own Ranade, Gokhale and Sir Rabindranath, regarded the British conquest of India as a divine dispensation, and he deliberately made himself the willing instrument of that divine purpose, to bring the realisation of that high aim appreciably nearer. As John Stuart Mill long ago pointed out, where the race governing a distant dependency are different from and more civilised than the people whom they govern, the rulers are responsible only to the country from which they come, *i.e.*, the *people* of one country are ultimately the rulers of the people of another country. This, in Mill's words, is despotism, but it can be mitigated if the foreign rulers pursue a high ideal of policy instead of seeking selfish or racial interests.

The ultimate moral justification of England's rule over India is not *Pax Britannica,* not even the economic prosperity of the country, but the preparation of the Indian people for self-government. If that end is lost sight of in the pursuit of any subsidiary advantage or improvement, British policy in India will miss its true goal; its history will be the record of a huge failure, a record of immense preparations without fruition.

Sir William knew it, and therefore he kept his gaze steadily fixed on the true end and aim of England's mission in India, however distant that end might appear to his contemporaries. And he was only one of the noble band of Englishmen who have devoted their lives to the same cause. He was the "*ain brither*" of Henry Lawrence and Evans Bell, Henry Cotton and Allan Hume.

Such lives may seem to the short-sighted materialist, to the all-wise "practical politician" and the experienced bureaucrat "on the spot," as futile. But only such lives can build a bridge between the East and the West, only such Englishmen can make India's inclusion in the British Empire possible.

When centuries have rolled away from now, when the Divine purpose has wrought itself in India and the final history of our land comes to be written, the names of Wedderburn and Hume will shine in that record as a silver thread shot through the crimson web of the British conquest of India.

THE INDIAN SCHOOL OF CHEMISTRY

[To realise fully the enormous amount of original scientific research work done by Dr. Ray and his many distinguished pupils, one has only to glance at the list of their contributions and the account of the Bengal Chemical and Pharmaceutical works given herein.]

1. P. C. RAY.

1, Conjugated Sulphates of the Copper Magnesium Group. P. C. Ray. Proc. Roy. Soc., Edin. 1888.

2. Chemical Examination of certain Indian Food-stuffs. Part I. The Fats and Oils. P. C. Ray. Jour. Asiatic Soc., Bengal, 1894.

3. On Mercurous Nitrite. P. C. Ray. Jour. Asiatic Soc., Bengal, 1895.

4. The Nitrites of Mercury and the Varying Conditions under which they are formed. P. C. Ray. Jour. Chem. Soc., 71, 337—344, 1897.

5. Mercury Hyponitrites. P. C. Ray. Jour. Chem. Soc., 71, 348—350, 1897.

6. On the action of Sodium Hyponitrite on Mercuric Solutions. P. C. Ray. Jour. Chem. Soc., 71, 1097—1104, 1897.

7. On a New Method of Preparing Mercuric Hyponitrite. P. C. Ray. Jour. Chem. Soc., 71, 1105-1106, 1897.

8. On the Interaction of Mercurous and Mercuric Nitrites with the Nitrites of Silver and Sodium. P. C. Ray. Proc. Chem. Soc., 103, 1899.

9. Mercurous Iodide. P. C. Ray. Proc. Chem. Soc., 239, 1899.

10. Interaction of Mercurous Nitrite and Ethyl Iodide. P. C. Ray. Proc. Chem. Soc., 239, 1899.

11. Mercurous Nitrite. P. C. Ray. Annalen der Chemie, 316, 250—256, 1901.

12. A New Series of Dimercuriammonium Salts. P. C. Ray. Proc. Chem. Soc., 1, 96, 1901.

13. Dimercuriammonium Nitrite and its Haloid Derivatives. P. C. Ray. Jour. Chem. Soc,, 81, 644-650, 1902.

14. Dimercuriammonium Nitrite. P. C. Ray, Zeit. Anorg. Chem., 33, 209-211, 1902.

15. Decomposition of Mercurous Nitrite by heat. P. C. Ray and J. N. Sen. Jour. Chem. Soc., 83, 491—494, 1903.

16. Mercuric Nitrite and its decomposition by heat. P. C. Ray. Jour. Chem. Soc., 85, 523-524, 1904.

17. The Sulphate and the Phosphate of the Dimercuriammonium Series. P. C. Ray. Jour. Chem. Soc., 87, 9-10, 1905.

18. Theory of the production of Mercurous Nitrite and of its Conversion into various Mercury Nitrates. P. C. Ray. Jour. Chem. Soc., 87, 171—177, 1905.

19. The Nitrites of the Alkali Metals and Metals of the Alkaline Earths and their Decomposition by heat. P. C. Ray. Jour. Chem. Soc, 87, 177—184, 1905.

20. The Constitution of Nitrites. Part I. Two varieties of Silver Nitrite. P. C. Ray. Proc. Chem. Soc., 278, 1905.

21. Fischer's Salt and its decomposition by heat. P. C. Ray. Jour. Chem. Soc., 89, 551—556, 1906.

22. The Interaction of Alkyl sulphates with the Nitrites of the Alkali Metals and Metals of the Alkaline Earths. P. C. Ray and P. Neogi. Jour. Chem. Soc., 89, 1900—1905, 1906.

23. The Decomposition of Mercurous and Silver Hyponitrites by heat. P. C. Ray and A. C. Ganguli. Jour. Chem. Soc., 91, 1399—1403, 1907.

24. Mercurous Hyponitrite. P. C. Ray. Jour. Chem. Soc., 91, 1404-1405, 1907.

25. Cupric Nitrite. P. C. Ray. Jour. Chem. Soc., 91, 1405—1407, 1907.

26. The Decomposition of Hyponitrous Acid in presence of Mineral Acids. P. C. Ray and A. C. Ganguli. Jour. Chem. Soc., 91, 1866—1870, 1907.

27. The Double Nitrites of Mercury and the Alkali metals. P. C. Ray. Jour. Chem. Soc., 91, 2031—2033, 1907.

28. Silver-mercuroso-mercuric Oxynitrates and the Isomorphous Replacement of Univalent Mercury by Silver. P. C. Ray. Jour. Chem. Soc., 91, 2033—2037, 1907.

29. Preparation of Aliphatic Nitro-Compounds by the interaction of the Alkyl-Iodides and Mercurious Nitrite. P. C. Ray and P. Neogi. Proc. Chem. Soc., 246, 1907.

30. Molecular Volumes of the Nitrites of Silver, Mercury and the Alkali Metals. P. C. Ray. Jour. Chem. Soc., 93, 997—1000, 1908.

31. Lithium Nitrite and its decomposition by heat. P. C. Ray. Proc. Chem. Soc., 75, 1908.

32. The Molecular Volumes of the Nitrites of Barium, Strontium and Calcium. P. C. Ray. Jour. Chem. Soc., 95, 66—69, 1909.

33. The Decomposition and Sublimation of Ammonium Nitrite. P. C. Ray. Jour. Chem. Soc., 95, 345—349, 1909.

34. Decomposition of Ammonium Platini Chloride and Ammonium Platini Bromide by heat. P. C. Ray and A. C. Ghosh. Zeitsch. Anorg. Chem. 64, 184-188, 1909.

35. Decomposition of Dimercurammonium Nitrite by heat. P. C. Ray and A. C. Ghosh. Jour. Chem. Soc., 97, 323-325, 1910.

36. The Double Nitrites of Mercury and the Metals of the Alkaline Earths. P. C. Ray. Jour. Chem. Soc., 97, 326-327, 1910.

37. The Double Nitrites of Mercury and the Bases of the Tetralkylammonium Series. P. C. Ray. Proc. Chem. Soc., 172, 1910.

38, Ionisation of the Nitrites as measured by the Cryoscopic method. P. C. Ray and S. C. Mukherjee. Proc. Chem. Soc., 173, 1910.

39. Influence of Minute Quantities of Ferric Salts and of Manganese Nitrate on the rate of solution of Mercury in Nitric Acid. P. C. Ray. Jour. Chem. Soc., 99, 1012-1016, 1911.

40. Methylammonium Nitrite. P. C. Ray and J. N. Rakshit. Jour. Chem. Soc., 99, 1016-1018, 1911.

41. Tetramethylammonium Hyponitrite and its decomposition by heat. P. C. Ray and H. K. Sen. Jour. Chem. Soc., 99, 1466-1470, 1911.

42. Nitrites of the Alkylammonium bases : Ethyl-ammonium Nitrite, Dimethyl-ammonium Nitrite, and Trimethyl-ammonium Nitrite. P. C. Ray and J. N. Rakshit. Jour. Chem. Soc., 99, 1470-1475, 1911.

43. Nitrites of the Benzylammonium Series. Benzyl-ammonium Nitrite and Dibenzylammonium Nitrite and their Subli mation and Decomposition by heat. P. C. Ray and R. L. Datta .Jour. Chem. Soc., 99, 1475-1477, 1911.

44. Trimercuride-ethyl-ammonium Nitrite. P. C. Ray and J. N. Rakshit. Jour. Chem. Soc., 99, 1972-1973, 1911.

45. Nitrites of the Alkylammonium Series. II. Propylammonium Nitrite and Butylammonium Nitrite and their Decomposition by Heat. P. C. Ray and J. N. Rakshit. Jour. Chem. Soc., 101, 141-3, 1912.

46. Nitrites of the Alkylammonium Series. III. Triethylammonium Nitrite and its Decomposition and Sublimation byHeat. P. C. Ray and J. N. Rakshit. Jour. Chem. Soc., 101, 216-9, 1912.

47. Nitrites of the Alkylammonium Series. IV. Isobutyl-, Diethyl-, Dipropyl-, and Tripropylammonium Nitrites. P. C. Ray and J. N. Rakshit. Jour. Chem. Soc., 101, 612-6, 1912.

48. Nitrites of the Mercurialkyl-and Mercurialkylaryl-ammonium Series. P. C. Ray, J. N. Rakshit and R. L. Datta. Jour. Chem. Soc., 101, 616-20, 1912.

49. Molecular Conductivities of Potassium Nitrite, Mercuric Nitrite and Potassium Mercurinitrite. P. C. Ray and N. Dhar. Jour. Chem. Soc., 101, 965-8, 1912.

50. The Vapor Density of Ammonium Nitrite. P. C. Ray, N. Dhar and T. De. Jour. Chem. Soc., 101, 1185-9, 1912.

51. Nitrites of the Mercurialkyl-and Mercurialkyl-aryl-ammonium Series. II. P.C. Ray, N. Dhar and T. De. Jour. Chem. Soc., 101, 1552-7, 1912.

52. Benzylmethyl-, Benzylethyl-, and Allylammonium Nitrites. P. C. Ray and R. L. Datta. Proc. Chem. Soc., 28, 258, 1912.

53. Isomeric Allylamines. P. C. Ray and R. L. Datta. Jour. Asiatic Soc., Bengal, 1912.

54. Decomposition of Allylammonium Nitrite and the Isolation of a New Compound. P. C. Ray and R. L. Datta. Calcutta Univ. Pub., 1912.

55. Nitrites of the alicyclic Ammonium Series. Nitrosopiperazinium Nitrite. P. C. Ray and J. N. Rakshit. Jour. Chem. Soc., 103, 1-3, 1913.

56. Chlorides of the Mercurialkyl and Mercurialkylarylammonium Series and their constitution as Based on Conductivity Measurements. P. C. Ray and N. Dhar. Jour. Chem. Soc., 103, 3-10, 1913.

57. Equivalent Conductance and Ionization of Nitrites. P. C. Ray and N. Dhar. Jour. Chem. Soc., 103, 10-8, 1913.

58. The Vapor Density of Ammonium Nitrate, Benzoate, and Acetate. P. C. Ray and S. C. Jana. Jour. Chem. Soc., 103, 1565-8, 1913.

59. Equivalent Conductivities of Sodium Hyponitrite, Calcium Hyponitrite and Hyponitrous Acid. P. C. Ray, R. De and N. Dhar. Jour. Chem. Soc., 103, 1562-4, 1913.

60. Guanidinium Nitrite and its Decomposition by Heat. P. C. Ray, M. L. Dey and S. C. Jana. Proc. Chem. Soc., 29, 283-4, 1913.

61. Action of Monochloroacetic Acid on Thiocarbamide and Monoalkylated Thiocarbamides. P. C. Ray and F. V. Fernandez. Jour. Chem. Soc., 105, 2159-61, 1914.

62. The place of mercury in the periodic system. P. C. Ray. Chem. News, 109, 85, 1914.

63. Additive and substitutive compounds of Mercuric Nitrite with organic Thio-derivatives, I. P. C. Ray. Proc. Chem. Soc., 30, 140, 1914.

64. Action of Nitrous acid on Dimethylpiperazine. P. C. Ray. Proc. Chem. Soc., 30, 143-5, 1914.

65. Action of Mercuric, Cupric and Platinic Chlorides on Organic Sulfur Compounds. P. C. Ray. Proc. Chem. Soc., 30, 304, 1914.

66. Interaction of Dimercurammonium Nitrite and the Alkyl iodides. P. C. Ray. Jour. Chem. Soc., 107, 1251-4, 1915.

67. Molecular volumes of the hyponitrites of the alkali metals and metals of the alkaline earths. P. C. Ray and R. De. Jour. Chem. Soc., 109, 122-31, 1916.

68. Nitromercaptides and their reaction with the alkyl iodides. Compounds of the disulfonium Series. P. C. Ray. Jour. Chem. Soc., 109, 131-8, 1916.

69. Mercury mercaptide nitrites and their reaction with the alkyl iodides, II. P. C. Ray. Jour. Chem. Soc., 109, 603-12, 1916.

70. Interaction of iodine and thioacetamide in aqueous and alcholic solutions. P. C. Ray and M. L. Dey. Jour. Chem. Soc., 109, 698-701, 1916.

71. Mercury mercaptide nitrites and their reaction with the alkyl halides, III. Chain compounds of sulfur. P. C Ray. Jour. Chem. Soc., 111, 101-9, 1917.

72. Cadmium and zinc nitrites. P. C. Ray. Jour. Chem. Soc., 111, 159-62, 1917.

73. Velocity of decomposition and the dissociation constant of nitrous acid. P. C. Ray, M. L. Dey and J. C. Ghosh. Jour. Chem. Soc., 111, 413-7, 1917.

74. Alkaloidal derivatives of mercuric nitrite. P. C. Ray. Jour. Chem. Soc., 111, 507-10, 1917.

75. Synthesis of L. B. thiocrotonic acid. P. C. Ray and M. L. Dey. Jour. Chem. Soc., 111, 510-12, 1917.

76, Mercury mercaptide nitrites and their reaction with the Alkyl iodides. Part IV Chain compounds of sulphur, P. C. Ray and P. C. Guha. Jour. Chem. Soc., 1918.

77. Mercuri Sulphory Chloride. Chain compounds of sulphur. Part V. P. C. Ray. Jour. Chem. Soc. 1918.

78. Mercury mercaptide nitrites and their reaction with the Alkyli iodides. Part VI Chain compounds of sulphur. P. C. Ray and P. C. Guha. Publications of the College of Science, Calcutta 1918.

79. Interaction of Mercuric, platinic and Cupric Chlorides respectively, with the mercaptains and potential mercaptans. P. C. Ray. Jour. Chem. Soc., 1918.

80. Interaction of the potassium salts of Phenyl dithiobiazoline sulphydrate and Thiobiazole disulphydrate with the halogenated organic compounds. P. C. Ray, P. C. Guha and R. K. Das. Jour. Chem. Soc., 1918.

2. R. L. DATTA

(In addition to those with P. C. Ray).

1. The Formation of Dichlorocarbamide and its behaviour towards Amines. R. L. Datta. Jour. Chem. Soc., 101, 166-166, 1912.

2. Preparation and Decomposition of Benzylmonochloro- and Benzyldichloro-amines. R. L. Datta. Jour. Amer. Chem. Soc., 34, 1613-1615, 1912.

3. The double Platinic and Cupric Iodides of Substituted Ammonium Bases. R. L. Datta. Jour. Chem. Soc., 103, 426-432, 1913.

4. Double Carbonates of Alkaline Earth metals and Lead with Potassium Carbonate. R. L. Datta and H. D. Mukherjee. Proc. Chem. Soc., 29, 185-187, 1913.

5. Zincoso-Zincic Chloride. R. L. Datta and H. D. Sen. Jour. Amer. Chem. Soc., 35, 779-780, 1913.

6. The Double Cadmium and Mercuric Iodides of Substituted Ammonium bases. R. L. Datta. Jour. Amer. Chem. Soc., 35, 949-955, 1913.

7. The Preparation of Benzoylchloroamide. R. L. Datta and T. P. Ghosh. Jour. Amer. Chem. Soc., 35, 1044-1045, 1913.

8. The Action of Dichlorocarbamide on Amines. The Synthesis of 2, 4-Dibenzyl-3-Phenyl-6-Keto-3-hydroxyhexahydro-1,2,4, 5-Tetrazine. R. L. Datta and S. Das Gupta. Jour. Amer Chem. Soc., 35, 1183-1185, 1913.

9. Iodoplatinates of Substituted Ammonium and Sulphonium Bases. R. L. Datta. Jour. Amer. Chem. Soc.,35, 1185-1188, 1913

10. The Sublimation and Decomposition of Acetylurea. R. L. Datta and S. Das Gupta. Jour. Amer. Chem. Soc., 35, 1893-1895, 1913.

11. The Action of Chlorine on Ethyl Carbamic Ester. The isolation of Ethylmonochlorocarbamic Ester and its behaviour towards Amines and Acid Amides, R. L. Datta and S. Das Gupta. Jour. Amer. Chem. Soc., 36, 386-390, 1914.

12. The preparation of Allyl Iodide. R. L. Datta. Jour. Amer. Chem. Soc., 36, 1005-1007, 1914.

13. Chlorination by means of Aqua Regia. The Chlorination of Benzene, Thiophene, Toluene and Mesitylene. R. L. Datta and F. V. Fernandes, Jour. Amer. Chem. Soc., 36, 1007-1011, 1914.

14. Simultaneous Chlorination and Oxidation by means of Aqua Regia. The preparation of Chloroanil from p-Phenylenediamine and Hydroquinone. R. L. Datta. Jour. Amer. Chem. Soc., 36, 1011-1013, 1914.

15. Methods of Estimation of Semicarbazide by its interaction with Halogens and Halogen Oxyacids. R. L. Datta. Jour. Amer. Chem. Soc., 36, 1014-1017, 1914.

16. Indirect formation of Double Salts, V. The Double Platinic, Cupric and Silver Iodides of Substituted Ammonium Bases. R. L. Datta and T. P. Ghosh. Jour. Amer. Chem. Soc., 36, 1017-1022, 1914.

17. The production of Chloropicrin by the action of Aqua Regia on Organic Compounds. R. L. Datta and N. R. Chatterjee. Jour. Amer. Chem. Soc., 37, 567-569, 1915.

18. Contributions to the knowledge of Halogenation, VII Substituted Nitrogen Chlorides. The action of chlorine on Carbamic Esters and Biurets and the preparation of Chloro-carbamic Esters and Chlorobiurets. R. L. Datta and S. Das Gupta. Jour. Amer. Chem. Soc., 37, 569-578, 1915.

19. Contributions to the Knowledge of Halogenation, VIII. New Series of Chlorohydroxy Compounds. The Hydrolytic Chlorination of Dimethyl-Pyrone. The isolation of 2, 6-Dichlorohydroxy 3, 5-Dichloro-4-Ketoheptane and its decomposition into 3, 5-Dichloro-2,4,6-Trioxyheptane. R. L. Datta and S. Das Gupta. Jour. Amer. Chem. Soc., 37, 578—582, 1915.

20. Halogenation, X. Chloric acid as a reagent in Organic Chemistry. R. L. Datta and J. K. Choudhuri. Jour. Amer. Chem. Soc., 38, 1079—1086, 1916.

21. Halogenation, XI. Chlorination with Aqua Regia. The Chlorination of Hydrocarbons. R. L. Datta and F. V. Fernandes. Jour. Amer. Chem. Soc., 38, 1809—1813, 1916.

22. Halogenation, XII. The formation of Chloropicrin and Tetrachloro-quinone by the action of Aqua Regia on Organic Substances. R. L. Datta and N. R. Chatterjee. Jour. Amer. Chem. Soc., 38, 1813—1821, 1916.

23. Halogenation, XIII. Methods of estimation of Semi-Carbazide, Semi-oxamazide and Oxalylhydrazide by their interactions with halogens and halogen oxyacids. R. L. Datta and J. K. Choudhuri. Jour. Amer. Chem. Soc., 38, 2736—2740, 1916.

24. Halogenation, XIV. Bromination of Hydrocarbons by meansof Bromine and Nitric Acid. R. L. Datta and N. R. Chatterjee. Jour. Amer. Chem. Soc., 38, 2545—2552, 1916,

25. Halogenation, XV. Direct Iodination of Hydro-carbons by means of Iodine and Nitric Acid. R. L. Datta and N. R. Chatterjee. Jour. Amer. Chem. Soc., 39, 435—441, 1917.

26. Halogenation, XVI. Iodination by means of Nitrogen Iodideor by means of Iodine in the presence of Ammonia. R. L, Datta and N. Prosad. Jour. Amer. Chem. Soc., 39, 441—456, 1917.

27. Neutral Potassium Persulphate as a reagent in Organic Chemistry. R. L. Datta and J. N. Sen. Jour. Amer. Chem. Soc., 39, 747—750, 1917.

28. Indirect Formation of Double Salts, VI. The Double Silver, Lead, Bismuth, Copper and Mercurous Halides of Substituted Ammonium Bases. R. L. Datta and J. N. Sen. Jour. Amer. Chem. Soc., 39, 750-759, 1917.

PATENTS.

1. Manufacture of Chlorine. R. L. Datta. Ind. Patent, 2523, 1916.

2. Process of Producing Iodine. R. L. Datta. Ind. Patent, 2693, 1916.

3. Process of Producing Chlorine. R. L. Datta. United States Patent, Application No. 115554, 1916.

4. Process of Producing Bromine. R. L. Datta. United States Patent, Application No. 115555, 1916.

5. Process of Producing Nitro-Compounds. R. L. Datta and P. S. Varma. United States Patent, Application No. 115557, 1916.

6. Process of Producing Iodine. R. L. Datta. Brit. Patent, 12873, 1916.

7. Process of Producing Nitrophenols from Amido Compounds by means of Nitrous Gases.R. L. Datta and P. S. Varma. Brit. Patent, 17778, 1916.

8. A New Process of Burning Sea-Weeds and the like for the extraction of Soluble Matter and Iodine. R. L. Datta. Ind. Patent, 2902, 1917.

9. Alkali Sulphates. R. L. Datta. Ind. Patent, 3441, 1917.

3. R. L. DE.

(In addition to those with P. C. Ray.)

1. Relationship between the physical properties of isomeric cobaltamines and the electrovalencies of their coordination complexes. R. L. De. Jour. Chem. Soc., 111, 51-56, 1917.

4. B. B. DEY.

(In addition to those with H. K. Sen.)

1. Action of Hydrazine Sulphate upon Nitrites, and a new method for determining Nitrogen in Nitrites. B. B. Dey and H. K. Sen. Zeit. Anorg. Chem., 71, 236-242, 1911.

2. Hydroximes of Benzil and Diacetyl. M. O. Forster and B. B. Dey. Jour. Chem. Soc., 101, 2234-2240 1912.

3, Condensation of Acetone dicarboxylic acid with phenols. B. B. Dey. Proc. Chem. Soc., 29, 154, 1913.

4. Hydroximes of Methyl and Phenyl glyoxals. B. B. Dey. Jour. Chem. Soc., 105, 1039-1046 1914.

5. Coumarin Condensations. B. B. Dey. Jour. Chem. Soc.' 109. 1916.

5. N. DHAR.

(In addition to those with P. C. Ray.)

1. Dissociation Constants of Monobasic acids. N. R. Dhar and A. K. Datta. Z. Electro-Chem. 19, 407-409, 1913.

2. Distribution of some Electrolytes between water and a second solvent. N. R. Dhar and A. K. Datta. Z. Electro-Chem., 19, 583-585, 1913.

3. Inaccuracy of a Copper Voltameter. N. R. Dhar. Z. Electro Chem. 19, 746-748, 1913.

4. Properties of the elements and periodic system. N. R. Dhar. Z. Electro- Chem., 19, 911-913, 1913.

5. The Electrolysis of Silver Nitrites and the transference number of the Nitrite ion. N. R. Dhar and D. N. Bhattacharyya. Zeit. Anorg. Chem. 82, 141-144, 1913.

6. Conductivity of dilute solutions of some sodium salts in Ethyl alcohol. N. R. Dhar and D. M. Bhattacharyya. Zeit. Anorg, Chem. 82, 357-369, 1913.

7. Combination of dissolved substances with the solvents. N. R. Dhar. Z. Electro-Chem., 20, 57-81, 1914.

8. Instability and inconstancy of Cobaltamines. N. R. Dhar. Zeit. Anorg. Chem., 84, 224-226, 1914.

9. Physico-chemical investigation of some cuprous salts. N. R. Dhar. Zeit. Anorg, Chem., 85, 44-48, 1914.

10. Hydrolysis of Salts. N. R. Dhar. Zeit. Anorg. Chem., 85 198-205, 1914.

11. Molecular State of substances in solution. N. R. Dhar. Zeit. Anorg. Chem., 85, 206-213, 1914.

12. Some Complex Boric Acids. N. R. Dhar. Zeit. Anorg. Chem. 86, 196-200, 1914.

13. New Method of finding the second dissociation constants of Dibasic acids N. R. Dhar and A. K. Datta. Jour. Chem. Soc, 107, 824—827, 1915.

14 Volume taken up by ions in solution. N. R. Dhar. Z. Electro Chem., 19, 819—821, 1915.

15. Properties of elements and the periodic system. N. R. Dhar. Proc. Akad. Wetenschappen, 18, 384—398, 1915.

16. Catalysis, I. N R. Dhar. Proc. Akad. Wetenschappen, 18,1084—1096, 1916.

17. Catalysis, II. N. R. Dhar. Proc. Akad. Wetenschappen, 18, 1097—1133, 1916.

18. Catalysis, III & IV. N R. Dhar. Jour. Chem. Soc., 111, 690—762, 1917.

6. J. C. GHOSH.

In addition to those with P. C. Ray.)

1. Alternating Current Electrolysis. J. C. Ghosh. Jour. Amer. Chem. Soc., 36, 2333-2346, 1914.

2. Influence of alternating current on electrolysis by a Direct Current. J. C. Ghosh. Jour. Amer. Chem. Soc., 37 733-75 1915.

3. Relative Affinity of Metals in non-aqueous solutions, and their Reactivity in Insulating Media. J. C. Ghosh. Jour. Phys. Chem., 19, 720-733, 1915.

4. The discharge potential of ions on heated electrodes. J. C. Ghosh. Jour. Phys. Chem., 21, 426-432, 1917.

5. Equilibrium between Copper salts and mercury in presence of chloridion and bromidion. J. C. Ghosh. Proc. Ind. Assoc.,3, 150-157, 1917.

6. The abnormality of strong electrolytes. Part I. Electrical conductivity of aqueous salt solutions. J. C. Ghosh. Jour. Chem. Soc., 113,449,1918.

7. Do, Part II. J. C. Ghosh. Jour. Chem, Soc,, 1918,

7. J. C. MUKERJEE.

1. Electric Synthesis of Colloids. J. N. Mukerjee. Jour. Amer. Chem. Soc., 37, 292-297, 1915.

2. Coagulation of Arsenious Sulphide solution by Electrolytes J. N. Mukherjee. Jour. Amer. Chem. Soc., 37, 2024-2031, 1915.

8. P. NEOGI.

In addition to those with P. C. Ray.

1. New Method of Preparing Mercurous Iodide. P. Neogi Jour. Asiatic Soc., Bengal, 3, 133-134, 1907.

2. Reduction of Fehling's solution to metallic copper. Deposition of Copper Mirrors on Glass. P. Neogi. Zeit. Anorg. Chem., 59, 213-215, 1908.

3. Reactions in the Presence of Nickel. (*a*) Inability of Nitrogen and Hydrogen to combine in Presence of Nickel. (*b*) Reduction of Oxides of Nitrogen, Sulphur and Phosphorus in Presence of Nickel. P. Neogi and B. B. Adhikary. Zeit. Anorg. Chem., 69, 209-214, 1910.

4. Preparation of Ammonium Nitrite by the Sublimation in a Vacuum of a Mixture of Ammonium Chloride and Alkali Nitrites. P. Neogi and B. B. Adhikary. Jour. Chem. Soc., 99, 116-118, 1911.

5. Orthophosphoric acid as a Dehydrating Catalytic agent. Part I. The Condensation of Acetone in presence of Phosphoric Acid. P. Neogi. Jour. Chem. Soc., 99, 1249-1252, 1911.

6. Trialkylammonium Nitrites and Nitrites of the Bases of the Pyridine and Quinoline Series. Part I. P. Neogi. Jour. Chem, Soc., 99, 1252-1254, 1911.

7. Preparation of Penylnitromethane (w-Nitrotoluene) by the action of Mercurous Nitrite on Benzyl Chloride. P. Neogi and B. B. Adhicary. Zeit. Anorg. Chem., 69, 270-272, 1911.

8. Nitrites of Primary, Secondary and Tertiary Bases. P. Neogi. Jour. Chem. Soc., 101, 1608-1611, 1912.

9. Preparation of the Nitrites of Primary, Secondary and Tertiary Amines. Part I. P. Neogi. Proc. Chem. Soc., 41, 1912.

10. Direct Combination of Nitrous Acid with Primary, Secondary and Tertiary Amines. P. Neogi. Jour. Chem. Soc., 105,1270—1275, 1914.

11. Interaction of alkali alkyl sulphates and alkali nitrites, theories of the formation of aliphatic nitro compounds. P. Neogi. Jour. Chem. Soc., 105, 2371—2376, 1914.

12. Action of Nitrous acid on the Amines. P. Neogi. Chem. News, 111, 255, 1915.

13. Conversion of aliphatic nitrites into Nitro-Compounds. P. Neogi and T. C. Choudhuri. Jour. Chem. Soc., 109, 701—707, 1916.

14. Reduction of aliphatic nitrites to amines. P. Neogi and T. C. Choudhury. Jour. Chem. Soc., 111, 899—902, 1917.

9. J. N. RAKSHIT.

(In addition to those with P. C. Ray.)

1. Preparation of Secondary and Tertiary acid amides from their metallic derivatives. J. N. Rakshit. Jour. Chem. Soc., 103, 1557-1562, 1913.

2. Maximum yield of Amines by the reduction of Alkyl Cyanides. J. N. Rakshit. Jour. Amer. Chem. Soc., 35, 444-446, 1913.

3. The preparation of Triethylamine. J. N. Rakshit. Jour Amer. Chem. Soc., 35, 1781-1783, 1913.

4. Action of Stannic Chloride on Phenyl Hydrazine. J. N. Rakshit. Jour. Asiatic Soc., Bengal, 9, 131-135, 1913.

5. Limits of the attachment of Amino groups to a single carbon atom; attempts to prepare tetra-aminomethane. J. N. Rakshit. Jour. Amer. Chem. Soc., 36, 1221-1222, 1914.

6. Estimation of Sucrose in the presence of lactose and in the milk preparations. J. N. Rakshit. Jour. Ind. Eng. Chem., 6, 307-308, 1914.

7. A table of Specific Gravities of spirits corresponding to indications of glass hydrometers for use with Bedford's Corrected Sikes' tables. J. N Rakshit and S. N. Sinha. Jour. Soc. Chem. Ind., 33, 288-289, 1914.

8. Preparation of Dichlorodinitrimethane by the simultaneous nitration and chlorination of Acetone. J. N. Rakshit. Jour. Chem. Soc., 107, 1115-1117, 1915.

9. Decomposition of Sodium Diacetamide and Potassium. Acetamide. J. N. Rakshit. Jour. Chem. Soc., 109, 180-184, 1961.

10. Estimation of Acetone in presence of Ethyl Alcohol. J. N. Rakshit. Analyst, 41, 245-246, 1916.

11. Ammonia in opium. J. N. Rakshit. Pharm. Jour., 98, 255, 1917.

12. Titration and Estimation of Morphine with Iodic Acid. J. N. Rakshit. J. Soc. Chem. Ind., 36, 989-90, 1917.

10. H. K. SEN.

(In addition to those with P. C. Ray and B. B. Dey.)

1. Qualitative Detection of Nitric Acid in Presence of an Excess of Nitrous acid. H. K. Sen Gupta and B. B. Dey. Zeit-Anorg. Chem., 74, 52-54, 1911.

2. Action of Hydrazine and Hydroxylamine on Ferricyanides and New Methods for the Determination of Hydrazine and Ferricyanides. H. K. Sen Gupta and P. R. Ray. Zeit. Anorg Chem., 76, 380-6, 1911.

3. Condensation of Camphorquinone with phenols. H. K. Sen Gupta and B. B. Dey. Proc. Chem. Soc., 29, 155, 1913.

4. Oxidation of anhydrides of 1, 1-dihydroxydinaphthyldialkyl-methanes. (Prel. Note). H. K. Sen Gupta. Proc. Chem. Soc., 29,382, 1913,

5. Formation of hetrocyclic compounds from hydroxymethylene ketones and cyano-acetamide. H. K. Sen Gupta Jour. Chem Soc., 107, 1347-1367, 1915.

11. P. B. SIRCAR.

1. Behaviour of Ammonium Phosphomolybdate with Ammonium Hydroxide. P. B. Sircar. Jour. Amer. Chem. Soc, 63, 2372-2374, 1914.

II

Bengal Chemical and Pharmaceutical Works.

AN ANGLO-INDIAN APPRECIATION.

"*Business,*" *an Anglo-Indian Journal writes* :—

"The Electric Company would not give us power. We required a fan, so we made that," was the reply I received to my question about the unusually pretty looking fan that was whirling above the head of the Manager. It is a small two-bladed fan, run by a pulley and a string and works most efficiently as the temperature of the room gives evidence.

That fan is a symbol of the works. Nothing daunts these manufacturers They know what they want and they get what they want—somehow. They seem to have a peculiar habit of riding roughshod over all obstacles and " getting there " as the American expresses it.

Situated picturesquely on the outskirts of Manicktolla suburbs, far from the harassing jurisdiction of the nearest sleepy municipality, the factory of the Bengal Chemical and Pharmaceutical Works stands as a monument to the ingenuity and resourcefulness of a few men who are determined to do the things that others have only dreamed or talked about. The Master Mind here, who "dreamed the dream and is making it come true" is Dr. P. C. Ray, D.Sc., Ph.D., F.C.S., and he is well assisted by the men whom he has trained. The first thing that strikes one are the compact neatly built quarters of the officers and the rows of clean looking buildings above which smoking chimneys tower, which tell of the activity within. Everything around is clean, in fact so spotlessly clean, that one fails to realise that work is going on ceaselessly, for one always associates factories and manufacturing with black grease and dirt and dirty looking men, with soiled clothes, soiled hands and soiled, blackened faces.

The factory is not like other factories. There is machinery here, plenty of it, but not the kind of machines that one sees anywhere else. Most of the special machinery has been thoughout, designed and made in the works itself, to suit the purposes and requirements of the company. For instance, the lead chamber. This was not bought or imported: it was thought out by the assistants and put up by them, although they are not engineers: and so successfully and efficiently they have done it, that to-day they are the largest manufacturers of sulphuric acid in India. The engineering problem was not the only difficulty, they had to obtain lead-coated iron sheets, which could not be bought in India. They could not import it on account of the war. They had to make it. They did not know how to make it, but that did not please them. They set about doing it, experiment after experiment was made, failure after failure faced them but these were not the men to "give up," ingenuity combined with observation and persistency conquered. They made the lead-coated sheets—and the sheets are good. Then came the trouble of putting these sheets together. They could not be soldered, the sulphuric acid corroded the solder. They had to sweat the sheets together, which required a special process that they had to discover. To-day they are experts in coating iron sheets with lead and joining them together without solder. This fact has enabled them to put on the market the Fire King, fire extinguishers, which they are turning out as fast as they can to supply the Government order for them. They are now thinking out ways and means to turn them out faster, so as to meet the growing public demand for them. Five hundred hand-fire extinguishers are going to Government every week.

The latest mechanical achievements are the packing and compressing machines for bandages and medicated absorbent cotton that the Bengal Chemical and Pharmaceutical Works are supplying for war purposes. They have invented and made no less than four special machines to do this work, and improved one machine that they succeeded in obtaining from England. Two anda half yards of gauze by 36 inches wide is compressed into a package 2⅝ inches by 1⅝ inches by 1⅜ inches and it is hard enough for the Red Cross to use in self-defence as a missile against the Hun. It is easy enough to make the bandages and impregnate the cotton with drugs, but the trouble was to compress and pack them. They were ready to buy machinery, but they could not get them. They did not have any idea about a packing machine. They had never seen one. They had to pack the goods properly, for they had a Government order and they also wished to do their "bit" for the war. So they just thought it all out, machine and all, even the method of packing, for field dressings cannot be packed in the ordinary way there is a peculiar way of doing it. Sounds easy, and it was told me in the most offhand and casual manner; but it is not all so easy to solidity imagination into steel of given or required shapes and convert abstract ideas into concrete, efficient, working steel systems or machines. They transformed an ordinary hacksaw into an automatic knife to cut rolls of bandages into required lengths; they turned ordinary oil drums into disinfecting chambers; they made compressing machines out of bits of steel bars and a screw. And so goes the tale. The factory is full of small and big machines that have been practically invented and wholly made in the works.

I do not attach much value to the fact that the works cover ten acres of land, or that they have so many hundred workmen, or that they have a machine shop, a foundry and pattern shop, a department for making their own packing cases and a press to do all their own printing; money can buy equipment and any company with enough capital can put up a modern, fully equipped, up-to-date factory; all these have their value as the concrete results of daring enterprise and continued effort but greater than all these is the undaunted spirit, the intelligence and the resourcefulness, that would not be made bankrupt, which is expressed in all these and pervades and permeates the whole establishment.

To-day the standard of civilisation is measured by the output of machinery in the country, and the standard of efficiency of a factory is to be measured by the quantity and quality of the output. By this standard alone the staff and the working force of the B. C. and P. W. is most efficient; but that would be nothing remarkable, did we not know that these young chemists, the raw and inexperienced—and inefficient—products of an unpractical University have trained themselves to a pitch of excellence that they cannot only compete but dominated in their special lines. It is worth ruminating on. I met a number of the managing staff, they were silent men. The Manager, Mr. Rajshekhar Bose, took me round. I was with him over three hours and it was most noticeable, that perfectly courteous hospitable and ready to show and inform me about everything, he did not speak a superfluous word. It was the same with, the Works Manager, Mr. Dass Gupta, and all the other officers whom I met. There was silence in the office, a thing that is not so common, and it was not a forced silence, for everyone was busily concentrated on the work in hand and they seemed interested in it.

Mr. Bose, the Manager, informed me that some of their staff were going to foreign countries after the war to learn how in those countries manufacturers had overcome the problems that faced them. It seems to me the better plan to go to study abroad after gaining some practical experience here and knowing exactly what requires the greatest attention, than to go before one knows what is to be demanded of their knowledge.

The Bengal Chemical and Pharmaceutical Works have shown what Indian intelligence and local training can do, and they should be considered the true pioneers of a new industrial era in which enterprise is not supported by the charity of the Government or of unpractical philanthropic enthusiasts, who have more money to spend than ideas about the development and growth of industry and commerce. Tata has shown us what enterprise plus capital can do; the Bengal Chemical and Pharmaceutical Works have shown India what enterprise plus resourcefulness can do. They are both wonderful examples to an eager nation clamouring for recognition, industrial growth and a greater participation in the affairs of the Great British Empire. Such are the true leaders of the people and the builders of nations.

H. M. KING GEORGE'S

SPEECHES IN INDIA

A COLLECTION OF ALL THE SPEECHES

DELIVERED IN INDIA

DURING HIS TOUR AS PRINCE OF WALES
AND IN CONNECTION WITH THE CORONATION DURBAR.

To make this handy collection of His Majesty's Indian Speeches doubly valuable, a useful Appendix has been added containing among others, the text of the announcement relating to the Coronation Durbar Boons; the Proclamations of H. M. King George, Queen Victoria and Edward the Seventh on their accession to the throne and the messages of Queen Victoria and King Edward to the Durbars of 1877 add of 1903. With 8 Portraits.

Price Re. One.

To subscribers of the "Indian Review" As. 12.

☞ *If you have not already seen "The Indian Review," send a four-anna postage stamp for a free specimen copy to G. A. Natesan & Co., Madras. Current issues will not be given as specimen copies*

G. A. Natesan & Co., Sunkurama Chetty Street, Madras

IF YOU HAVE NOT ALREADY SEEN

THE INDIAN REVIEW

THE BEST, THE CHEAPEST AND

THE MOST UP-TO-DATE INDIAN PERIODICAL

EDITED BY MR. G. A. NATESAN

☞ *Send your name and address with a Four-anna Postage stamp for a Specimen copy.* ☜

THE PARSI.—As fresh, typical, and informing as ever.

THE SIMLA NEWS.—It is a magazine every intelligent European should read. (Annual subscription, Rs. 5.)

COMMERCE.—One of the best of its kind in India.

BENGALEE.—It is ably edited by Mr. Natesan, that distinguished publicist of Southern India.

THE SANJVARTMAN, BOMBAY.—The "Indian Review" may well be called the "Review of Reviews" for India. Any one who wishes to be always in touch with the progress of political, social or religious thoughts of New India must have a copy of this excellent "Review" always by himself.* * * Is undoubtedly a gem of its kind, and no cultured Indian cares to be without it.

With such a magazine as the "Indian Review" it is impossible to question the serious interest of our fellow-subjects in the dependency in all matters which affect world progress. The striking feature of such magazines is the detached and impartial spirit which animates the writers of the articles and the ready reproof of any utterance which belittles the high ambition of the Indian nation to deserve the respect of all nations.—*The Review of Reviews.*

Annual Subscription, Rs. 5, (FIVE); Foreign 10/-

Current numbers of "The Indian Review" (sold at Re. One.) will not be given as specimen copies.

G. A. Natesan & Co., Publishers, Madras.

PART II.—REVIEWS OF BOOKS

ANCIENT INDIA.

The following review of Mr. Vincent Smith's "Early History of India" appeared from the pen of Dr. Ray in the pages of The Indian World for June 1905 :—

Nature very often delights in paradoxes. Where we once feared that nothing much could be known, there we find ourselves overwhelmed with materials to-day. Up till a little over a century ago, the mosaic cosmogony obtained currency in the European world but that cherished conviction received such a rude shock from the careful investigations of geology and palaeontology that it was exploded before the age of reason had firmly established itself. As in geology, so in history, the day of blind faith has gone by and Indian history is no longer the sport of credulity and hypothesis. Though a people like the Hindus, with whom the world is a mere illusion and life a dream and who "let the legions thunder past, and plunged in thought again," could not be expected to take much interest in the passing events of the day or their future bearings, yet out of the fragments left by them has it become possible to construct a sober and connected history of this country from the earliest times.

Eighty years ago we had very little data upon which to construct a history of India, excepting the fragments preserved in the writings of Arrian and Megasthenes. But the discovery of the Asoka inscriptions and their successful deciphering by Prinsep mark an important epoch in the making of a reliable History of India. The Asoka inscriptions have proved the foundation-stone for the magnificent superstructure of the story of this land. Thanks to the labours of successive generations of archæologists and antiquarians, we have now abundant materials for a complete account of the early periods of Indian history. Like remnants of fossils and strata opening up a vista of research to the geologist, the rock-cut inscriptions and the Græco-bactrian coins have opened up wonderful fields wherein one can dig for any amount of materials regarding the history of this country before and after the Christian era.

Another epoch-making event in this direction was the publication of Mr. Stanislas Julien's method for deciphering and transcribing Sanskrit names. This eminent student of Chinese literature took to the study of Sanskrit at an advanced age in order that he might follow with advantage the phonetic transmutations of Sanskrit names in the Chinese language. In the course of his Sanskrit studies he made the magnificent discovery that *Fo* in Chinese was no other than *Buddha* of India and that *po-le-mi-ti* stood for *paramita* and *o-che-li-ye* for *acharya.* Julien's monumental work on the Life and Travels of Huen-thsang

(1853—8) remains still a standard authority on the subject, Beal's later English version having failed to replace and supersede it. It is gratifying to find that a large number of French orientalists have followed in the footsteps of Julien and widened our vision of ancient Indian history by several brilliant contributions.

Apart from the graphic account in the itineraries of Fa-Hien, Huen-thsang, I-t-Sing and U-Kong, we are now in possession of ample chronological data from such sources as Pali and Chinese accounts and from the Buddhist *tripitaka*, some 1700 of which are mentioned in the valuable catalogue of the great Japanese scholar, Bunyiu Nanjio,—all of which go to elucidate many dark chapters and episodes in the history of India.

Although we have no regular indigenous histories or accounts of India as a whole, we have undoubtedly some very valuable local accounts. Kalhana's *Rajatarangini*, an excellent edition of which has been published by Dr. Stein, the history of Guzerat under the name of *Rasmala*, the Ceylonese Chronicles in Pali—notably the *Dipavamsa* and the *Mahavamsa*—all stand as oases in the dreary desert of indigenous account of the country.

The *Jatakas* or "birth-stories" also throw considerable light on the social and political condition of India of the 5th and the 6th centuries B.C. These have been turned into excellent account by Prof. Rhys Davids in his recent work on *Buddhist India*.

Mr. Vincent Smith's *History of Ancient India* may be taken as a valuable supplement to Prof. Rhys David's *Buddhist India.* Mr. Vincent Smith has already earned a well-deserved reputation for his numerous contributions to the numismatic literature of India. His monograph on *Asoka,* in Sir William Hunter's *Rulers of India* series, showed that he had studied the pre-Christian era of Indian History with considerable devotion and diligence. The present work, which he calls the *Early History of India from 600 B.C. to the Mahomedan Conquest including the invasion of Alexander the Great,* is a monument of masterly investigation and research on the subject. Mr. Vincent Smith has written this book with a view to present a "narrative of the leading events in Indian political history for 18 centuries," based upon the most authentic evidence available, and everyone must admit that he has done it remarkably well. Why our author did not begin his work from an earlier period and include in it the times of the Vedas, the Ramayana and the Mahabharata, it is difficult to see. It is also a pity that Mr. Smith does not go into the details of the life and times of Buddha, or of the supersession of the Brahmanic age by the Rationalistic one. A disproportionately large space of the book is devoted to the marches, battles and armies of Alexander which is justified on account of "the exceptional interest of the subject" and also because they have "not been adequately treated in any modern book."

The intellectual world has undergone considerable changes since the days of Mommsen, Grote and Freeman in its conception of historical writings, and nobody, excepting professional military students, would care to sit down in these days to read weary accounts of how Alexander crossed the Indus, arranged his cavalry and infantry on the Karri plain on the banks of the Hydaspes and gave battle to Porus, and at what time of the day was the battle ended and how many were killed on both sides in that memorable engagement. The world will get none the wiser to-day by acquainting itself with the dreary details of a military raid of over 22 centuries ago, and, even if it did, it would find in Mr. McCrindle's exhaustive translations of all Greek accounts of that event more than enough materials for it, with various interesting informations relating to the people and the country besides. There is very little matter in Mr. Vincent Smith's *History* which one will not find in Mr. Mc. Crindle's series of translations, either in the texts or in the notes, and I wish that this event which bulks so largely in the pages of Mr. Vincent Smith had been compressed into half a dozen of pages instead. It is gratifying, however, to find the author of the book under review going into the details of the administrative organisation of the great Mauryas, including Asoka, the great Buddhist Emperor of India, of the rule of the Kushan or Indo-Scythian dynasty, among which figured the great Kanishka and of the story of the Gupta Empire and the white huns. The story of the reign of

Harsha forms an independent and a most interesting chapter in the work and, thanks to Huen-thsang's *Travels* and of Cowell and Thomas' translation of *Harsacharita*, we have a tolerably complete account of this period of Indian history. The last three chapters of the book deal with the mediæval kingdoms of the north, from 648 to 1200 A.D., and of the kingdoms of the Deccan and the south. This portion of the book is very scrappy, and is attributable, as Mr. Vincent Smith himself says, to the "limited interest of merely local histories.' It is difficult not to join issue with an observation of this kind, seeing what materials have been supplied to us for a complete and comprehensive history of India by *merely local histories* and still less apparently negligible fragments of history, preserved in stone, copper-plates, and inscriptions.

It also passes our comprehension to find Mr. Smith calling Delhi 'a modern city' and voting down the traditional glories of the prehistoric Indraprastha as hypothetical. Equally objectionable is his description of the Temple of Kailasa at Ellora as an 'architectural freak.' Of sumptuous rock-cut caves and shrines, there is no end in India; and at one time that sort of temple-building was much in vogue all over the country. It does not therefore stand to truth to describe the Kailasa at Ellora as 'an architectural freak,' while indeed it records only the high-water mark of a phase of Indian architectural development. Nor any close student of Indian art, literature and philosophy would endorse Mr. Smith's opinion that the Dravidian nations of the south were 'not inferior in culture to their Aryan rivals in the north,' a statement which the staunchest champion of Dravidian culture would not dare to advance in the light of known history. As to the *Ramayana* and the *Mahabharata*, it may not be possible to dignify them as sober histories, but at the same time to ignore them contemptuously as mere 'bardic tales' do not indicate any very intimate knowledge of their contents.

I make the following extracts from Mr. Vincent Smith's description of Chandragupta's administration:--

> The administration of the capital city, Pataliputra, was regarded as a matter of the highest importance, and was provided for by the formation of a Municipal Commission consisting of thirty members, divided, like the War Office Commission of equal numbers, into six boards or committees of five members each. These boards may be regarded as an official development of the ordinary non-official *panchyet* or committee of five members, by which every caste and trade in India has been accustomed to regulate its internal affairs from time immemorial.

> The first Municipal Board, which was entrusted with the superintendence of everything relating to the industrial arts, was doubtless responsible for fixing the rates of wages, and must have been prepared to enforce the use of pure and sound materials, as well as the performance of a fair day's work for fair wages, as determined by the authorities. Artisans were regarded as being in a special manner devoted to the royal service, and capital punishment was inflicted on any person who impaired the efficiency of a craftsman by causing the loss of a hand or an eye.

> The second Board devoted its energies to the cause of foreign residents which in modern Europe are entrusted to the consuls representing foreign powers. All foreigners were closely watched by officials and were provided with suitable lodgings, escorts, and, in case of need, medical attendance. Deceased strangers were decently buried, and their estates were administered by the Commissioners, who forwarded the

assets to the persons entitled. The existence of these elaborate regulations is conclusive proof that the *Maurya* Empire, in the third century B.C., was in constant intercourse with foreign states, and that large numbers of strangers visited the capital on business.

The third Board was responsible for the systematic registration of births and deaths, and we are expressly informed that the system of registration was enforced for the information of the Government, as well as for facility in levying the taxes. The taxation referred to was probably a poll-tax, at the rate of so much a head annually. Nothing in the legislation of Chandragupta is more astonishing to the observer, familiar with the lax methods of ordinary oriental Governments, than this registration of births and deaths. The spontaneous adoption of such a measure by an Indian native state in modern times is unheard of, and it is impossible to imagine an old-fashioned Raja feeling anxious that births and deaths among both high and low might not be concealed. Even the Anglo-Indian administration with its complex organization and European notions of the value of statistical information, did not attempt the collection of vital statistics until very recent times, and has always experienced great difficulty in securing reasonable accuracy in the figures.

The important domain of trade and commerce was the province of the fourth Board, which regulated sales, and enforced the use of duly stamped weights and measures. Merchants paid a license tax, and the trader who dealt in more than one class of commodity paid double.

The fifth Board was responsible for the supervision of manufactures on similar lines. A curious and not easily intelligible regulation prescribed the separation of new from old goods, and imposed a fine for violation of the rule.

Mr. Vincent Smith proceeds to place before his readers some further information on the duties of the Municipal Commissioners to keep in order "the markets, temples, harbours, and, all public works" and also on the maintenance by Chandragupta of an irrigation department "regulating the sluices" for distributing to every one his fair share of the water-supply of the town.

Had it not been for the fact that the narrative presented above is corroborated by the evidence of Megasthenes, Strabo, Arian, and other Greek writers, one would have taken it as a mere romance instead of sober history.

As might be expected of a great Indian numismatist, chronology is Mr. Vincent Smith's *forte.* In this respect, Mr. Vincent Smith's book is bound to prove a most valuable work of reference and should be regarded as a companion volume to Miss Duff's *Chronology of India.* He gives us a chronology (of course approximate) of the *Puranas*, of the *Saisunaga* and *Nanda* dynasties, of the *Mauryas* of Pataliputra from 326 B. C. to 184 B.C.; of the *Sunga, Kanva* and *Andhra* dynasties, of the *Kushans* and the *Guptas* and of the principal events of the seventh century A.D., besides a complete chronology of the Indian campaign of Alexander the Great.

Mr. Vincent Smith throws a flood of light on the age of the great *Kanishka*, which has for a long time been the despair of orientalists. The northern Buddhists as well as the author of *Rajatarangini* would place him some time between 57 B.C. and 78 A.D. Mr. Devadatta Ramkrishna Bhandarkar places him at 278 A.D., on the strength of a well-known *Kushana* stone-inscription. In this view of the matter Mr. Devadata has the strenous support of his father, Dr. Bhandarkar.* But the Bhandarkars seem however to be singular in maintaining this view. Mr. Vincent Smith accepts *circa* 125 A.D. as the date of the

* *Vide Journal*, Bombay Branch of the Royal Asiatic Society, 1900, pp. 269-302 and pages 356-408.

accession of *Kanishka*, which is a very important landmark in the chronology of ancient India. Mr. Vincent Smith displays no inconsiderable erudition and ingenuity in his attempt to fix upon the dates of Patanjali and Kalidasa, the former of whom he places about 150-140 B.C. and the latter about the close of the 4th century A.D. The age of Kalidasa has been a subject of endless controversy from the days of Weber and MaxMuller and sufficient materials have now been accumulated by the researches of Professor Macdonell and Mr. Manmohan Chakravarty to enable us to arrive at a finality on this point. If Mr. Chakravarty's date, the latter half of the 5th century A.D., be accepted as the correct one, a most knotty problem of Indian chronology will have been settled for good.

It is somewhat of a relief to find that Mr. Smith has, after all, been able to shake off to a large extent his bias of hellenic influence on the civilisation and architecture of ancient India. India has not been hellenised and has remained unaffected by the Maccedonian storm, says Mr. Smith in his present work, though so late as in 1892 he was found to observe that " Indian medicine also appears not to have been uninfluenced by Greek." * As I have discussed this subject at length in my *History of Hindu Chemistry* and proved, at least to my satisfaction, that Hindu medicine or chemistry owed nothing to Greek influence, I shall not go over that ground again.

---

* *Vide Journal*, Asiatic Society of Bengal, LXI, Part I, 1892, p. 71.

Mr. Vincent Smith, however, still clings to th cherished belief that the Hindu Drama, at least, owes much of its inspiration to Greek influence. We have been under the impression that the question had been finally settled by M. Sylvain Levi in his *Theatre Indien* on the strength of his own researches and of those of M. Pischel.† M. Levi's view of the absence of any Greek influence on the Hindu drama is corroborated by Mr. Macdonell of Oxford in his *History of Sanskrit Literature* in the following words:—

> While the Indian drama shows some affinities with Greek comedy, it affords more striking points of resemblance to the productions of the Elizabethan play-wrights, and in particular of Shakespeare. The aim of the Indian dramatists is not to portray types of character, but individual persons; nor do they observe the rule of unity of time or place. . . . The character of the *Vidusaka*, too, is a close parallel to the fool in Shakespeare. Common to both are also several contrivances intended to further the action of the drama, such as the writing of letters, the introduction of a play within a play, the restoration of the dead to life, and the use of intoxicants on the stage as a humourous device. Such a series of coincidences, in a case where influence or borrowing is absolutely out of the question, is an instructive instance of how similar developments can arise independently.

> "M. Pischel, que ost peutetre, entre les orientalistes de l'Occident, le plus familier avec la rhetorique et la poesie dramatique de l'Inde, a juge brievement cette opinion. S'imaginer, dit-il, que le theatre grec ait exerce une certaine influence sur la formation du theatre indien, c'est temoigner une egale ignorance du theatre grec et du theatre indien." (*Theatre Indien*, pp. 343-344).

From the standpoint of Weber and Windisch one would be far more justified in drawing the inference

† "Est-ce-donc la Grece qui a donne a l'Indeson theatre? M. Weber, que s'est signale par son opiniatrete a rechercher les traces de l'influence grecque sur la civilisation brahmanique, a prose hardiment la question dans son admirable *Historic de la Literature Indienne.*"

that Shakespeare was considerably indebted to the Hindu drama, specially to Kalidas.

To the accepted Anglo-Indian creed of considering India as a congeries of countries and peoples, Mr. Vincent Smith apparently does not subscribe. For, says he, "India, encircled as she is by seas and mountains, is indisputably a geographical unit, and as such is rightly designated by one name. Her type of civilisation, too, has many features which differentiate it from that of all other regions of the world, while they are common to the whole country, or rather continent, in a degree sufficient to justify its treatment as a unit in the history of human, social and intellectual development."

Mr. Vincent Smith's book is embellished with some illustrations and maps, the most interesting of which are the one of India in the 5th, and the other of the Empire of Harsha in the 7th. century A.D. The map of the Empire of Asoka (250 B.C.) is not half so interesting or informing as that given in Harley's Asoka. A full and comprehensive index adds materially to the usefulness of this *History*.

In conclusion, one cannot help regretting that a very good book has been spoilt and a splendid opportunity thrown away by Mr. Vincent Smith's attempt to replace the real history of the Indian people or of the country itself by an 'accurate chronological presentation of dynastic facts' and a faithful account of a military progress. Dynastic facts or the brilliance of military exploits are no longer considered by any modern historian as the basis of history, and, in his anxiety to supply materials for the above, Mr. Vincent Smith has partially, we will not say totally, neglected to present to his readers a connected narrative of the development and growth of the Indian people as well as of the varied and interesting phases of Indian civilisation.

BRITISH INDIA

"Speak of me as I am, nothing extenuate,
Nor set down ought in malice."—Othello.

The following review of " The Expansion of British India " was contributed by Dr. Ray to the " Indian Review " Madras, for December, 1918 :—

Indian history labours under a serious disadvantage. The Hindus with philosophic indifference have not thought it worth while to concern themselves with mundane affairs. Victor Cousin has very aptly remarked that a nation which has produced a *Gita* cannot be expected to take an interest in history " which " to quote the words of the immortal historian of the Roman Empire—" is indeed little more than a register of crimes, follies, and misfortunes of mankind." From the time of Mahabharata downwards to the pre-Mohammadan era we have occasional glimpes of the invasion of India by the *Mlechchas*, Yavanas, and Sakas and Hunas, etc., but such references are so very casual and vague that it is hopeless to piece together anything like a connected narrative*

We have no doubt of the " History of India as told

* *Cf.* " The Yavana besieged [Arun at] Saketa "

" The Yavana besieged [arunat] Madhyamikas. The above extracts from Patanjali's commentary on Panini have been, adduced as proof of the invasion of India by the Greek king Menander about 155 B,C.—Indian Antiquary, 1872, p. 299.

by its own historians"; but the Mussulman conquerors with their fanatical zeal for the spread of Islamism and in their flush of success had only scorn and contempt for the "infidels" and what they write has to be taken with a grain of salt. Indeed, Sir H. Elliot who collected his materials from these chronicles admits that they are "for the most dull, prejudiced, ignorant and superficial."*

When we come upon the period of British Rule in India we are on safe grounds. But here a fresh difficulty arises. It is all along the picture of the lion painted by himself. What Herbert Spencer calls "the bias of patriotism" comes into play and often warps the judgments of the historians. "Our country right or wrong," is a sentiment which not unfrequently vitiates their conclusions, as will be shown in these pages. Of late there is noticeable unfortunately a lamentable tendency on the part of certain English writers of Indian history, an attempt at whitewashing every dark or questionable episode and the result is that the press is being flooded not with sober history properly so-called but rather with their travesties.

It is on these grounds that we welcome the

* One or two extracts may be given here to make this point clear. "So God granted the Sultan the Victory of Nardin such as added to the decoration of the mantle of Islam."—Elliot, ii, 39; again: "The Almighty desired to grant a support to the power of Islam and to the strength of the Muhammadan faith, to extend his glorious shadow over it, and to preserve Hindustan within the range of his favour and protection; *ibid*, 360.

volume nnder review.* The authors very pertinently observe in the preface that "the study of Indian history in Indian schools and universities has been degraded by the use or rather abuse of text-books"—because of the tendency, we fancy, to pass or gloss over debateable transactions. The period covered by the book, namely, 1818—1858 is perhaps the most eventful from the point of view of the "Expansion of British India," embracing as it does the era of annexation of Lord Dalhousie. The policy or rather the impolicy of annexation has been discussed threadbare, but in no other Indian question has partizanship been so important a factor. "Give a man of talents" says Emerson, "a story to tell and his partiality will presently appear. He has certain observations, opinions, topics, which have some accidental prominence, and, which he disposes all to exhibit. He crams this part and starves the other part, consulting not the fitness of the thing, but his fitness and strength." Our authors have with commendable impartiality of judgment placed the views of both the schools in juxtaposition, leaving the reader to draw his own conclusions. They have been singularly felicitous in the plan they have adopted. The *dramatis personæ* have been brought upon the stage and they are allowed to tell their own tales in the shape of minutes, despatches to the Court of Directors etc. We are thus sup-

* The Expansion of British India, 1818—1858 by G. Anderson, M.A., Professor of History, Elphinstone College, Bombay and M. Subedar, B.A., B.SC., F.R.S.S., Professor of Political Economy of the University of Calcutta.

plied with first-hand information at every stage—the authors simply confining themselves to the task of summing up the conclusions. The First Afghan war and its genesis should arrest our attention for a while. "The crisis occurred," say our authors, "when the caution and experience of Metcalfe were replaced in 1836 by the ignorance of Lord Auckland, the new Governor-General. At that time the Whig Government of Lord Melbourne was in power in England, and its foreign policy was dominated by Lord Palmerston who considered it necessary to counteract the progress of Russian influence in Central Asia. It is probable, therefore, that Lord Auckland arrived in India with a foreign policy already prepared by his political chief, who was alarmed somewhat naturally by the march of the Persians to Herat in 1837. Lord Ellenborough in his memorable proclamation, dated Simla, Oct. 1, 1842 reversed the policy of Lord Auckland and released from captivity Dost Muhammad Khan, "whom we had spent fifteen millions sterling of the revenues of India to dethrone without a cause."* History repeats itself. The last Afghan War was also of England's own seeking. On this occasion Lord Lytton played the part of Lord Auckland and Lord Salisbury of Lord Palmer-

* With regard to this question the spirited protest of Mr. Bright from his place in Parliament (1858) may not be out of place here. "Last year I referred to the expense of the Afghan War—about £15,000,000—*the whole of which ought to have been thrown on the taxation of the people of England*, it was a war commanded by the English Cabinet for objects supposed to be English."

ston. Sher Ali wanted to live in peace and amity with the British government and never dreamt of being an aggressor but he was supposed to be intriguing with Russia for this purpose. The War cost India somewhere near twenty millions sterling. The iniquity of saddling India with the burden of a war undertaken for imperial purposes was one of the chief planks in the Midlothian Campaign of Mr. Gladstone and when he returned to power he tried to redeem his pledge. The Cabinet of which he was the head could not, however, be prevailed upon to repay more than five millions sterling and even what it gave with one hand it practically took away with the other, for a large proportion of the expenses incurred for the Egyptian war was charged upon the revenues of India.*

The policy of annexation of Lord Dalhousie, which is largely responsible for a vast expansion of British India and also for the Indian Mutiny naturally occupies a prominent place in the present volume.

When a map of India was spread before Ranjit Singh with the British possessions marked red, he exclaimed: "*Sab lal ho yaega*" (every portion will become red). The fulfilment of this prophecy was not long in coming. It should be remembered that there were two schools of Anglo-Indian administrations, one of which represented by such men as Sir Henry Lawrence, Colonel Sleeman and Sir James Outram was strongly opposed ot the policy of Dalhousie. Sleeman

* In spite, we believe, of the protest of Lord Ripon.

sounded the note of warning in no uncertain voice. " I consider their [the annexationist'S] doctrines" exclaims he "to be prejudicial to the stability of our rule in India and to the welfare of the people, which depends upon it." As for Henry Lawrence it is enough to say that the devotion and persistency with which he espoused the cause of the doomed or fallen chiefs almost border upon chivalry. When Lord Dalhousie wrote to him suggesting that a proclamation be issued announcing the virtual absorption of the Punjab into the British possessions, he replied with his characteristic candour and boldness: " My own opinion......is against annexation. I did think it unjust, I now think it impolitic." Within the limited space at our disposal it is not possible to deal adequately with every individual state, *e.g.*,Nagpur, Satara, Jhansi, etc. We shall con fine our attention to the case of Oude. At the outset it is necessary to remember that the oppression and misgovernment which prevailed in some of the feudatory states and notably in Oude was the direct outcome of the system which had been imposed upon them by the British Government. James Mill in his evidence before the Select Committee of the House of Commons in 1832 observes:

" In the ordinary state of things in India the princes stood in awe of their subjects. Insurrection against oppression was the general practice of the country.

The princes knew that when misgovernment or oppression went to a certain extent there would be revolt, and that they would stand a chance of being tumbled from their thrones, and a successful leader of the insurgents put in their place. That check is, by our interference, totally taken away; for the people know that any attempt of theirs would be utterly unavailing against our irresistable power; accordingly no such thought occurs to them, and they submit to every degree of oppression that befalls them."

Lord Hardinge also in a despatch, dated December 21, 1846, expresses "his reluctance on general principles, to revert to the subsidiary system of using British troops to support a Native Government while we have no means of correcting the abuses of a civil administration of a country ostensibly under British protection. A British force, acting as the instrument of a corrupt native agency, is a system leading to mischievous consequences, and which ought, when it is possible, to be avoided."

It so happens that the present writer, while a student at Edinburgh, now one-third of a century ago, felt tempted to study some of the burning Indian questions with special reference to the annexation policy of Lord Dalhousie and it is curious to find that the materials he had at his disposal are almost exactly the same as made use of by our authors, and the conclusions also identical. No apology is, therefore, needed for reproducing here a few excerpts from chapter iv of the little book, entitled "Lord Dalhousie an Annexationist."*

THE ERA OF ANNEXATION.

"And I beseech you
Wrest once the law to your authority."—
SHAKESPEARE.

"The narrative of annexations will have seemed sometimes, doubtless, more like counting out the spoils of brigands in a wood, than detailing the acts of English statesmenship in the light of history."—EDWIN ARNOLD.

---

* *India before and after the Mutiny.* By an Indian Student: Edinburgh: E & S, Livingstone, 1886.

"What the Koh-i-noor is among diamonds, India is among nations. No Indian prince should exist."—SIR C. NAPIER ("Life," iv., 188).

"The two hundred and fifty kinglings must inevitably and speedily disappear."—THE "FRIEND OF INDIA."

"Musty old parchments."—IBID.

No question has given rise to so many controversies as that of Oude. Fortunately, the materials at our disposal are abundant. We have here the testimonies of independent and non-official authorities, who are entitled to our highest respect. We must apologise for treating this matter in rather disproportionate detail; but we shall, however, take this opportunity of incidentally making some observations on the nature of our past dealings with native princes in general.

"What is Truth, said jesting Pilate, and would not stay for an answer."

Those with whom rested the final decision of the fate of Oude do not seem to have been at particular pains to get at the bottom of the affair. Complaints about the misgovernment of Oude have been brought to the notice of the Supreme Government since the beginning of this century. Grave as are the charges, deductions must be made for official colouring. Every one who has read Bishop Heber's "Journals" must have noticed the keen discerning powers of the author, and the extreme care he took in collecting accurate information. This eminent divine had no particular cause or party to vindicate. He saw nothing through a distorting medium; his vision was unimpeded by class prejudices. He resembled the great Continental poet and philosopher to whom "all national jealousies and prejudices were quite foreign, and who saw in man the human being only." Hence Bishop Heber's observations on the condition of Oude must be regarded as valuable. "I was pleased, however, and surprised, *after all which I had heard of Oude*, to find the country so completely under the plough; since, were the oppression so great as is sometimes stated, I cannot think that we should witness so considerable a population, or so much industry."* Bishop Heber was expressly cautioned against the lawless and ferocious character of the people of Oude; but his own experiences were quite of the opposite kind, for he was struck with "their *invariable civility and good-nature*," and he did not believe that "they were inflamed by any peculiar animosity against the English."*

That there were gross irregularities in the government of Oude it would be idle to deny. But who were primarily responsible for this state of things? A "grand policy," initiated by Warren Hastings, and carried into perfection by Lord Wellesley, quartered a "subsidiary army" on the resources of the native princes. The consequence of this heavy drainage on their exchequer was to paralyse the machinery of their administration. With an ill-paid police, with revenue often in arrears, no wonder that extortion and rapine should follow in the train. As Bishop Heber

* Heber's "Journal" (1846), vol. i., p. 210.

Cf.—"In the number of cattle, horses, and goods which they possess, and in the appearance of their houses and clothes, the people (of Oude) are in no points worse (in many, better off) than our own subjects. The wealth of Lucknow—not merely of those in authority, but the prosperity of the bankers and shopkeepers—is far superior to that of any city (Calcutta perhaps excepted) in the British dominions. How can all this be the case, if the Government is notorious for tyranny and oppression?"—("Notes on Indian Affairs," vol. i., p. 156, by Hon. F. I. Shore.)

justly observes: "They (the King of Oude's statements) show strongly the perplexities and mischief arising from the subsidiary system, which for so many years seems to have been our favourite policy in India, and to which it must be owned a considerable part of our greatness is owing."*

It was, however, in more ways than one that we made the efficient administration of Oude an impossibility. Sadat Ali, King of Oude, had appointed a man of remarkable abilities and administrative genius as his prime minister. In an incredibly short space of time he introduced several reforms, and Oude began to assume an appearance of prosperity. Here we must say a word or two about a peculiar personage with whom it is the lot of the readers of Indian history to cultivate acquaintance—the "Resident" or "Political." Whenever we find anything has gone abnormally wrong in our dealings with the native princes, we may almost be sure the Resident is at the bottom of it. This was pointed out long ago by the Duke of Wellington.† It is true, Elphinstone, Malcolm and Metcalfe won their laurels as "Politicals," and have left honourable traditions behind. Unfortunately, these are not the only names in the

* Sir T. Munro, speaking in 1817 of the subsidiary system, observes that it must "destroy every government which it undertakes to protect."—("Life," vol. i., p. 464.)

† "In our treaties we recognised them—the native princes—as independent Sovereigns. Then we sent Residents to their courts. Instead of acting in the character of Ambassadors, they assumed the functions of dictators, interfered in all private concerns, countenanced refractory subjects against them, and made the most ostentatious exhibitions of their exercise of authority."

pantheon of Anglo-Indian Politicals. Dismissed ministers and disaffected subjects of the native princes have often found indirect encouragement from our Residents. A weak-minded ruler and a pliant and unscrupulous minister are what have been most agreeable to the jealous and haughty temper of these mischief-makers. It is a mere truism that an honest and conscientious man cannot serve at the same time two masters of entirely different temperaments. Thus it was that the able and virtuous minister of the King of Oude was now sacrificed. Marshman has, in his own inimitable style, given us a short but graphic account of Hakim Mehdi,* but he has drawn a veil over the most important part. Bishop Heber† and Prof. H. H. Wilson have, however, supplied the missing

---

* "This extraordinary man—Hakim Mehdi—was the son of a Persian gentleman of Shiraz, who emigrated to India in search of political employment, and entered the service of Oude, in which he rapidly rose to distinction. He was one of the ministers who, in 1801, vigorously, but ineffectually, opposed the cession of territory demanded by Lord Wellesley. He identified the prosperity of his adopted country with his own happiness, and devoted his splendid talents to the improvement of the administration. It was gracefully remarked of him, that the poorest man never entered his house without a welcome, or departed without relief. . . . Lord Wm. Bentinck pronounced him one of the ablest men in India, and as a revenue administrator unsurpassed by any officer, European or native."—"History," vol. iii. p. 26.

† "His—King of Oude's—minister at the time of his death was Hakim Mehdi. A man of very considerable talents . . . and to the full as honest and respectable in his public and private character as an Easter Viziern can usually be expected to be. The new sovereign was said not to be very fond of him, but there seemed to be not the least inclination of removing him till his power was undermined, most unfortunately for all parties, *by the British themselves*."—HEBER'S "Journals," vol. ii., p. 221.

information, and thus we get a connected narrative of the whole story.*

Our dealings with the rulers of Oude have been always characterised by that strange admixture of cunning, shrewdness and duplicity, which would ever form one of the darkest chapters in the history of India. When Warren Hastings wanted money he let out on hire the Company's battalions to conquer and exterminate the brave Rohillas, and have their land added to the province of Oude. When the Nepal war emptied the treasury at Calcutta, Lord Hastings was glad to obtain a loan of half-a-million from the Vizier of Oude, in consideration of which the territories torn from Nepaul were conferred upon the latter, as also the proud title of "King." This last act had also a political significance—that of lowering the prestige of the descendant of the Great Moghul. Thus, while we were under obligations to the rulers of Oude, all our sympathy for the down-trodden millions of Oude evaporated.†

* "The Resident (Mr. Maddock) opposed his (Hakim Medhi's) elevation under the impression that Hakim Medhi was decidedly inimical to British rule. But the Government, anticipating important benefits from his acknowledged abilities, concurred in his nomination. His restoration to power was followed by measures of a beneficial tendency." The Resident however, remained surly, and reported that the state of Oude "had reached so incurable a stage of decline, that nothing but the assumption of the administration for a time could preserve it from utter ruin."—WILSON'S continuation of Mill's History.

† Mr. Bright, reviewing the whole transactions of the British Government with the rulers of Oude since the days of Warren, Hastings, estimates that £31,500,000 had been extorted from them under various pretexts (1858).—"Speeches of John Bright." Edited by THOROLD ROGERS, vol. i., p. 70.

It was Colonel Sleeman who, in a formal manner, brought to the notice of Lord Dalhousie's Government the miserable condition of the Oude peasantry. Sleeman, like Low and Henry Lawrence, was always a chivalrous upholder of native dynasties; but in this case he was the "missionary of a foregone conclusion." But Sleeman never for a moment recommended the seizure of the revenues of Oude. He, in fact, held the views of Henry Lawrence, who said: "Let the administration of the country be, so far as possible, native. *Let not a rupee come into the Company's coffers.*" Mr. Herbert Merivale, after carefully going over what both sides have to say, arrives at an opinion which is substantially the same as that recorded by Heber nearly thirty years before the "mission" of Sleeman. "Common justice will, therefore, compel us, who have no special cause to defend with the energy with which sides are generally taken in Indian politics, to own that Oude, when we annexed it, was a wealthy, populous, commercial region, which might fairly hold a comparison in these respects with many portion of our adjacent empire. Misgoverned it had been, and disgracefully, but not to the extent which really comes home to the mass of the population and paralyses industry."* Upon the whole we are inclined to think that the annexation of Oude was the result of

* "Life of Sir Henry Lawrence," vol. ii., p. 288.

The condition of Oude appears now to be worse. "They (the masses) are often underfed, generally underclothed, and have not, as a rule, anything that they can call their own" (1880).—H. C. IRWIN; "The Garden of India," p. 307.

that insatiable "earth-hunger" with which we had then been seized,* veiled though it was under the specious pretext of conferring the "inestimable blessing" of British rule upon the wretched victims of tyranny.†

Even the French writer of this period seems to have been infected with the then prevalent craze Lanoye speaks of the annexation of Oude as one of the "crowning acts" of Dalhousie's administration, and observes that we were not bound to abide by treaty obligations with a people among whom there had been no Grotius or Puffendorf. The French writer evidently forgets or ignores that, long before Minos, Lycurgus and Solon, Justin and Grotius, had given laws to the European nations, Manu had laid down the fundamental principles of jurisprudence in no vague terms, which still hold the Hindu mind spell-bound. Indeed, our conscience had been so much steeled to wrong-doing as regards our dealings with the native princes that we did not see the frequent violations of plighted faith in their true light; and not until the terrible catastrophe overtook us did

* The above was written nearly three months before the annexation of Burmah.

† Mr. Edwin Arnold has approvingly quoted Lanoye in support of the annexation of Oude. But a countryman of Lanoye's who, throughout his work, expresses his admiration for British rule, thus records his candid opinion: "Il est peu de villes de l'Inde dont le premier aspect charme plus l'entrager que Lucknow, et l'on comprend avec quelle convirtise les Anglais ont du longtemps contempler cette perle des cites de l'Hindoustan, jusqu' au jous ou sur un futile pretexte ils reussirent a s'en emparer."—ROUSSELET: "L'Inde des Rajas," p 679.

Mr. Irwin also takes the above view.

"L'Inde Contemporaine."—Edition of 1858, p. 287.

we rid ourselves of the notion that the "down-trodden" peasant awaited with anxiety our happy advent. It was forgotten that, whenever we had annexed any territory, there was always at our back the glistening bayonet to enforce our monstrous pretentions; that the awe-struck and dumbfounded people made a virtue of necessity. Passive acquiescence was thus confounded with direct approval.* It is probable that a mutiny would have broken out in the Bengal Sepoy regiment even if there had been no annexations; but certain it is that it could have been *localised* (as in the case of the Vellore mutiny), and thus nipped in the bud. It was in some of the newly annexed provinces e.g., Oude and Jhansi, that the masses made common cause with the mutineers, or, in other words, the mutiny assumed the gigantic proportions of a *rebellion*.†

If is only necessary to supplement the account given above with a few more extracts from the Hon.

* The precious lesson contained in the following dialogue was lost upon us in the moment of infatuation: "Miserable as we are, of all miseries keep us from that (annexation)!" "Why so?" said Captain Lockitt, "are not our people far better governed?" "Yes; but the name of Oude and the honour of our nation would be at an end."—Heber's "Journal," vol. i., p. 225.

† *Cf.*—That the Sepoys believed that the greased cartridges were destined to deprive them of their caste, is, I think, not to be questioned. *But they believed that calumny because the action of the British with respect to their own province (i.e., Oude) had so shattered their faith in the professions of their ruling power, that they were ready to credit anything against it.* . . . In a greater degree, the annexation of Oude and the measures which followed that annexation: in a lesser degree, the actual employment of animal fat, . . . constituted ample grounds for the distrust evinced by the Sepoys."—Col. Malleson's continuation of Kaye's "Sepoy War," vol. i., pp. 351-2.

F. J. Shore's "Notes on Indian affairs" quoted by our authors. (pp. 94-96).

"The motives of the Court [of Directors] in issuing such orders [for annexation] are obvious enough—gain.........But in Oude, the people have one great resource, of which they have been deprived, in a great degree, in our territories. Not having been cursed with "first-rate collectors," who would ruin a district to procure a good name and promotion for themselves, or with ryotwari systems, by which almost all the middling and upper ranks of society have been reduced to poverty to increase the Government rent-roll, there is still in Oude a pretty numerous middle class of land holders to whom the people look up with hereditary respect, and who are of the greatest use in settling claims and disputes, so that but a small portion are re-referred to the amils in the towns also, the merchants are very much in the habit of resorting to arbitration." Again: "The English Government are mainly to blame for this state of things. How is it possible that native princes who are kept in a state of pupilage, and almost treated like school boys and should have any self-respect or proper independence of feeling? This has been the case with Oudh, for the last forty-years. Had the British Government turned their supremacy to good account, by insisting on the education of the native chiefs, so as to qualify them for the art of Government, this would have been a measure entitled to the highest praise; but so far from it, the interference of the residents has been almost always exerted for evil; indeed, so extremely difficult is it to discover the slightest benefit arising to any class of people from the establishment of residents at the native courts that there is even ground for supposition that the measure has been adopted and maintained for the express purpose of promoting mis-Government and confusion in the different principalities, so as to afford plausible excuses and opportunity for our taking possession of them."

The author of the annexation policy on the eve of his retiring from the stewardship of India takes credit of being instrumental by means of the several territorial acquisitions in adding to the annual income of the Indian Empire four millions sterling—the province of Oude alone contributing close upon one and a half million.* How a province which has been subject-

* It should be remembered that Henry Lawrence insisted "that not a rupee should come into the company's coffers."

ed to the perpetual annual drain of such a vast amount could afford to be prosperous is beyond our comprehension. Possibly our authors in the third volume of the series, namely, the "Economic Policy of the Company" will have to say something and we should not anticipate their verdict.

Before we conclude we may be permitted to point out to our authors that they would have much more readily helped to explain the problem of the expansion of British India, if they had put in some extracts from Professor Seeley's philosophic treatment of the subject in his admirable "Expansion of England." The following passages are highly illuminating.

"In the early battles of the company by which its power was decisively established, at the seige of Arcot, at Plassey, at Buxar, there seems almost ways to have been more sepoys than Europeans on the side of the Company, And let us observe further that we do not hear of the sepoys as fighting ill, or of the English as bearing the whole brunt of the conflict. No one who has remarked the childish eagerness with which historians indulge their national vanity will be surprised to find that our English writers in describing these battles seem unable to discern the sepoys. Read Macaulay's Essay on Clive; everywhere it is the 'imperial people,' 'the mighty children of the sea,' 'none could resist Clive and his Englishmen.' But if once it is admitted that the sepoys always out numbered the English, and that they kept pace with the English in efficiency as soldiers, the whole theory which attributes our success to an immeasurable natural superiority in valour falls to ground. In those battles in which our troops were to the enemy as one to ten, it will appear that if we may say that one Englishman showed himself equal to ten natives, we may also say that one sepoy did the same. It follows that, though no doubt there was a difference it was not so much a difference of race as a difference of discipline, of military science, and also no doubt in many cases a difference of leadership.

'Observe that Mill's summary explanation of the conquest of India says nothing of any natural superiority on the part of the English. 'The two important discoveries for conquering

India were; 1st the weakness of the native armies against European discipline, 2ndly, the facility of imparting that discipline to natives in the European service.' He adds: 'Both discoveries were made by the French.'

"And even if we should admit that the English fought better than the sepoys and took more than their share in these achievements which both performed in common, it remains entirely incorrect to speak of the English nation as having conquered the nations of India. The nations of India have been conquered by an army of which on the average about a fifth part was English. But we not only exaggerate our own share in the achievement; we at the same time entirely misconceive and misdescribe the achievement itself. For, from what race were the other four-fifths of the army drawn? From the natives of India themselves! India can hardly be said to have been conquered at all by foreigners, she has rather conquered herself...... ....

"The fundamental fact then is that India had no jealously of the foreigner, because India had no sense whatever of national units, because there *was* no India and therefore, properly speaking, no foreigner."